A DEVIL INCARNATE

Best Wishes

1948 - 1952

Webb AZ

Willia Radley

A DEVIL INCARNATE

From Altar Boy to Alcatraz

By

Willie Radkay
as told to Patty Terry

Disclaimer: The material in this book has been printed exactly as my uncle told it to me. He is now an old man, and the veracity or accuracy of his stories cannot be vouched for by either the author or publisher. You decide … and enjoy the journey into the life of Willie Radkay as he has chosen to recount it.   *P.T.*

Documents and photographs that appear on pages 116, 137, 147, 154, 158, 170, 179, 181, 193, 201, 202, 210, 226, 227, and 228 were provided by the National Archives – Pacific Region (San Francisco). Reprinted with permission.

ISBN: 1-58597-326-2

Library of Congress Control No. 2005924102

A division of Squire Publishers, Inc.
4500 College Blvd.
Leawood, KS 66211
1/888/888-7696
www.leatherspublishing.com

This book is dedicated to my loving uncle and godfather, who always seemed to be there when I needed him.

Unk and me — 2002.

CONTENTS

PREFACE

I AM NOT a writer and I never intended for this book to be a novel. There are no proper structures or grammatical corrections to the sentences or words. I just wrote this simple story exactly as my uncle told it to me using his own words. The story of his life may start out simple and somewhat boring, but the action he has lived through and just the fact that he lived is amazing.

As I grew up, I began to hear stories about my uncle and knew he was in prison for bank robbery. I was told as a young teenager he'd been to Alcatraz, but that went way over my head in comprehension. My uncle even sent me George Kelly's fountain pen and Webster's dictionary after he died. The fountain pen by Schaeffer is a green tortoise shell mother of pearl with black streaks and a tip and trim of bright 14-karat gold. The dictionary is a Webster's Collegiate Dictionary.

It wasn't until the late 1990s while visiting and checking on my aging uncle that he'd start telling me all these stories. I never knew or heard of the guy he was telling the stories about and became spell-bound that he was talking about himself. Not only was I in awe of the stories themselves, but the details and names that he remembered from so long ago. I felt the history in what he was telling me was significant and had to be written for posterity.

I told him that he should write a book, and he said that he always had intended to but never could find the time. He had many books on writing and even inquired about a writing course at a nearby college.

I told him I'd help him and asked if I could bring a tape recorder to record his stories. I'd bring the tape recorder, and when I turned it on he'd tell me, "Naw, I don't want to do that today, maybe tomorrow." As soon as the recorder was out of sight, he'd start talking and telling me a story. I started writing crib notes on the palms of my hands, then grabbed used envelopes or borders of newspapers to write these stories down.

Also, when he related these stories to me, nothing was in sequence. He'd skip from 1920 to 1950 in three sentences, so the major part of putting this book together was to get it in chronological order.

I have hundreds of pieces of paper with written stories he's told me that compile the contents of this book.

This true story is only possible because of Willie Radkay's great memory and my wife's patience.

What inspired her to work three years writing this story is beyond my understanding. Perhaps her inspiration will be revealed as you read her words.

If society consisted of mostly bad guys, Willie would've been close to the President. Now, though, after 35 years, his criminal career over, and time served, he's a friendly and caring person. **He is as good now in society as he was bad back then.**

— Wallace Terry

INTRODUCTION

I WAS A kid that never should have been born. I found out at an early age that I had larceny in me, and I learned to use it to cut my way through life surviving only as I knew how. Times were rough for everyone during the 1920s and only increased in the 1930s during the Great Depression. I saw all the sorrow of hopelessness on the people's faces. No one had the expectation of looking forward to any future outlook for prosperity, only survival. I didn't want to live like that, working for pennies, six days a week and 10 hours a day, so that's when I began my introduction into crime. The way of life I chose was in itself history-making, but at the time I lived through it, history had nothing to do with it.

Sister Bonaventure, Mother Superior at St. John the Baptist on Strawberry Hill, used to tell me in the beginning that I was such a good boy, so intelligent and well-mannered, that I should consider entering the seminary and study for the priesthood. Later she would say in her broken English, "Villiam, why do I have to read such bad things about you in the newspapers?" Then she began reading worse things about me and all the criminal things that I was doing against the law. Whenever she saw me, she would say: You are the "Incarnation of the Devil." I had no idea what that meant and thought she was paying me a compliment at the time. After that, I would enter the classroom every morning saying: "Mother Superior, your Devil Incarnate is here!" Little did she know how true her statement would turn out to be when as a twist of irony I received the prison number of 666 years later on arrival at Alcatraz.

Right now I am the "sole survivor" of the early years on Alcatraz when "The Cream of the Criminal Crop" was sent there. My time on Alcatraz (1945-1952), along with the other prisons I was incarcerated in, brought me alongside some of the most-publicized, notorious and well-known criminals of all time. A few of them ended up being my most remembered and close friends who left me with memories that will never die.

* * * * *

I will start in the beginning, 94 years ago, when I was born on September 24, 1911, to a Croatian couple, Elias Radkay (Elijah Ratkaj), age 30, and Veronica (Scrakocic), age 21, with the assistance of a mid-wife named Mary Casni, at 344 Ann Avenue in Kansas City, Kansas. My godmother used to tell me that early on that morning when I was born my father was so excited and happy he ran down the street yelling to everyone, "It's a boy! It's a boy!"

Our family was a loving family, with two older brothers, Joe and Jimmy, who watched, cared for and attended to me relentlessly as the baby I was at the time.

After a hard week's work, my parents, along with many others in the neighborhood, frequented saloons on Saturday nights at 3rd and James Street in the West Bottoms. They would drink and dance at these places that were "wide open" in those days to break the monotony of many hard hours of work all week. There were many bars along the street to choose from, and each of them had a loudspeaker out in front trying to call you into their bar. This one night in particular the place was active and alive with drinkers and dancers filling the large dance hall with many people. Somehow my father got into an argument with another man who caused a brawl that came to blows. The fight escalated to the extreme, and my father grabbed a wood rasp for protection and hit the man on the head. When the man hit the floor without getting back up, my father grabbed my mother and ran for home. He was so worried and concerned that there would be payback for him and his family or even lock-up with jail time for him because of this incident that he fled from Kansas City to Indiana, to his brother-in-law's. First they speared my dad to Leavenworth, Kansas, and he stayed hidden out there until a guy drove down from Indiana to pick him up and take him out of town.

Uncle Mike Stojkovic (married to my dad's sister) had a successful horse-and-buggy delivery business of ice in the summer and coal in the winter to the homes in the East Chicago area. After my father got settled, he sent for my mother and us three boys to join him. I can still bring to mind how my mother bundled us all up for the trip with such excitement that we were going to rejoin my father. At first when we got there, we lived in a second floor flat above this saloon; then later on we moved to an apartment on Alcott Avenue.

(Clockwise) Willie's Mom, Uncle Mike, Dad, Willie,
and brothers Jimmy and Joe.

I remember in the dead of winter when my dad and Uncle Mike would go to the shores of Lake Michigan and walk way out onto the frozen lake to cut huge chunks of ice to bring back and store for the summer. My memory of the ice was that it was so clear and bright green in color as they dragged it by on a sled into the straw-insulated icehouse to be cut up into a mixture of different sizes for deliveries later.

When I was four, my mother had another baby, who was the first girl for our growing family. It wasn't long until our little sister Agnes was born. During that winter in 1915 my father contracted pneumonia and died.

I remember vividly the very next day when the undertaker brought the black casket into the bedroom where my father's body lay, and he began the burial preparation by powdering my dad's dark face. I still distinctly remember how quiet everyone was during those days of grieving. I can also recall myself riding in the hearse to the cemetery in Hammond, Indiana, where my father was put to rest, and where all the people around the casket mourned his passing. On later visits to the cemetery with my mother, I remembered that the grave was near the front gate and the headstone was very much in view from the roadway.

My mother could have stayed in Indiana with my Uncle Mike, but found out how hard it was to get a job to support herself, even after putting us in an orphanage. She decided to go back to Kansas City, Kansas, where her family was, so she returned home a widow with four children. My mother moved in with her sister Barbara, her husband, Roy Clements, and their four children, Joe, Dorothy, Frank and Lawrence. The little house at Fourth and Armstrong had only three rooms, so eight children and three adults made for a jam-packed living condition. In those days not all of the homes had electricity because of the high price, and this little house was one of them. It had gas lights that came through little mantles in such a small glow that you couldn't even read by them because they were so dim.

We then moved to Third and Armstrong Avenue when my mother worked at Cudahay's Packinghouse. My brother Jimmy and I would sit on the back porch waiting for her to come home at night. Jimmy was teaching me to count, and we would look across the Kaw River toward the Kansas City, Missouri skyline and count all of the city lights, which at that time totaled up to nine. To save electricity, they turned off most of the lights at around 11 p.m.

My mother had to work, and she was away from us all day, so she made the decision to put us in an orphanage until she got back on her feet and got a place of our own. My memory of St. Vincent's Home, 15 miles south of Leavenworth, Kansas, was being separated from my sister because the girls were on one side and the boys were on the other, I never could talk to her or even see her as it wasn't allowed.

Those nuns were a little queer as far as I am concerned because they would make all the boy's strip naked to whip them, and I got a lot of whippin's.

My mom did find work in a boarding house as a cleaning lady which didn't pay much at all, so eventually she made the decision to put us kids up for adoption to try to get us out of the orphanage and into a home. When all of us were put in this adoption process, my father's relatives, a childless couple who were my godparents at the time of my baptism, came to adopt me. I was seven years old. My mother was elated about that adoption, thinking that I would be in a home with relatives and well taken care of. Little did she know that when Isaac and Mary Radki adopted me, they had other plans for me. I was in the orphanage in Hammond Indiana, St. Vincent's in Xavier, Kansas, and St. John's Children's Home in Kansas City, Kansas.

For this adoption my mother took me up to the courthouse at Seventh and Minnesota in front of Judge Sims for the legalization process. The courthouse was a square red brick building that had a tall steeple atop the roof and four doors, one on each side of the building for entering. The courthouse also had a red brick wall surrounding the property, and the building itself sat up on a big mound right in the middle. The old wood floors would squeak with every step you took walking into the building toward the judge's chamber. Everyone had to sign my adoption papers, and the judge made it legal, and I left with my new foster parents. My foster mother could sign her name, but my foster father had signed three X's for his name. Although we went to a Croatian School, they taught us English, and all of the kids in school would go home to help their parents learn some English.

1

Growing Up On Strawberry Hill

IT WAS SOON after I took residence with my foster parents in a little one-room house that I noticed a stable on the other side of the wall with horses in it.

It wasn't long after I was moved in that I found out my new foster parents took out a life insurance policy on my elderly grandfather. The policy made me beneficiary which they, as my legal guardians, would collect if anything would happen to my grandfather, since I was a minor. My grandfather's son, my Uncle Johnny, was killed when he was very young. He had climbed up on the top of the James Street bridge to catch pigeons and fell. It was then a streetcar came along and cut him in half.

Back then, all the funerals were in the home, and it was too much for my aging grandfather to see his only son dead in front of him, and he too died from a heart attack the day of Johnny's funeral. They ended up having both funerals together at the same time. The funeral director would take white powder and put it on the blue and purple faces, and what a weird combination seeing these purple faces with white powder all over them!

My Uncle Johnny would read the newspaper to us kids while we sat on the steps of his house on Sandusky Avenue. He would tell us all about the Kaiser and all about the war from 1914-1918. He would walk us down to the railroad yards to the Riverview Station close to Central Avenue, and we'd watch as they would load up the men into boxcars, taking them to Fort Leavenworth to join the Army to fight in the war.

The house that my foster parents moved into after they got the money from my grandfather's death was a big two-story house at 250

1

North Fifth street. It had two big fireplaces on the first floor that heated the entire house through open vents upstairs, downstairs and even in the basement. The stairway had a landing before you went on to the second floor, and there was a large circular stained glass window that let in a multitude of colors when hit by the sunlight.

Atop the roof of the house was a big cupola, and underneath were two small rooms that had to be entered by pulling a rope in the ceiling to bring down steps to climb up into the rooms. In later years I would hide a lot of the things up there that I stole that I wanted to keep hidden from my foster parents.

We even had an indoor toilet plus a hot water tank in that house, which was a luxury back then.

When my foster parents collected on the insurance policy from my grandfather, they were able to move from the one-room house where we were living to a big two-story home on Fifth and Sandusky. Before my foster parents got the $5,000 insurance money from my grandfather, they lived in rentals, and the last place was a one-room stable that was converted into a shack. Right next to it and on the other side was a stable with a horse in it. I used to walk the horse up to the water troughs that were at every major intersection in the city back in those days. You could ride those horses all day for 15 cents, and kids could ride all day for a nickel.

My mother was working in a boarding house as a cleaning lady and eventually met and married one of the boarders. His name was Steve Tomasegovich, and he was a great man to marry my widowed mom with four children. He would have gladly taken me to raise if only I hadn't been adopted into hell with my foster parents. I have nothing but great respect for such a wonderful man and often wondered how I would have turned out living in such a loving home with him, my mother, my brothers and sisters. None of my siblings have ever gotten into any trouble with the law, and I know if he was my stepfather and I would have been with my mother none of what had happened to me in my life probably would have taken place.

When my mother and Steve got married at Saint John the Baptist Church on February 7th, 1917, they had the reception down on James Street, which was called the West Bottoms and close to Armour's pack-

Wedding picture of Steve Tomasegovich and Veronica Scrakocic.

inghouse. There used to be an elevated streetcar that ran from Central Avenue to James Street in those days that even ran through a tunnel that was at least four blocks long. The wedding reception was up on the second floor of this building on East Ninth Street. I was permitted to go to the wedding by my foster parents, and I remember my brother Jimmy and I playing on the steps leading into the dance hall on the second floor most of the evening, just running up and down the steps playing. My mother and Steve had two children, which gave me another sister and brother Frank whom my foster parents said I could not associate with nor visit. I wasn't allowed to visit my brother "Bubba" Jimmy; he was one year older than I. My foster parents would beat me if they found out that I went to see him. They wouldn't just whip you; they would "beat you." Jimmy would read the cartoon in the Sunday paper to me called "Little Jimmy," and I would listen intensely. I loved him so much and would follow him around like a little puppy dog. I was beaten many times for trying to go to visit my brothers, Joe and Jimmy, at my mother's home with Steve. Then finally my foster parents started allowing Jimmy to come down to see me, but only to sit in the yard; we could never go anywhere, just sit in the yard.

Jimmy died during the flu epidemic of 1918 he was eight years old. I remember that they took me to see him when he was very sick.

3

Mom was living at 12th and Jefferson in a two-story house in Kansas City, Missouri at that time. I remember that there was no grass on the front terrace; it was all just mud. They had me all wrapped in this blanket because I got sick, too, and they had to carry me up to the house to see Jimmy. That was the last time I saw Jimmy alive; he died right after that, but I got well and came out okay. I went with them to see his casket at Stein's Funeral Parlor. Even today I can't find his grave up at Mount Calvary Cemetery. I remember it had a small angel or lamb on the top of a tall tombstone. I inquired several times over the years, and they just tell me it's in the old section that they have no records on. Also, they said a lot of the old section was removed for widening State Avenue in the city. I found the stone once back in the '60s, but haven't seen it since.

It was just a matter of weeks before I found out my foster mother was a nymphomaniac, and every time her boss would come over I would get 50 cents. One quarter was for a half-pint of whiskey, and the other quarter was for me to stay away for a while. This one time I laid a newspaper down on the couch, and when I came back home it was all crumpled up. Her boss would come down almost every day, and conveniently enough, when he took his vacation she took her vacation, which ended up giving her many promotions, and later even got me hired for a position there.

My foster mother would tell everybody that her husband had a "short stem," but hell, even he was screwing around with other women. Everyone would laugh, knowing he was screwing around with a big fat women, and they knew he had a short stem, and they laughed wondering how he did the job. The old man would say he had to go to the dentist on a Wednesday night at nine o'clock, and the old lady would say she had to go see this guy about buying a Victrola at nine o'clock at night. They would drag me along, but give me money to go in another direction by myself until they were finished and had to go back home again. What a house I grew up in! My foster parents were strict disciplinarians of control during my life, which was hell on earth at times. Little did I know the education of life I was about to learn living with the two of them was far from a normal one.

My foster parents had plenty of boarders in the house, and my foster mother would screw all of them. She was also screwing all three of my uncles. People would tell me that my foster parents were good to me. Hell, they ruined me; they just had me there to do things for them. She was a nympho and she was screwing everybody. My Uncle Charlie had to disappear and leave town because of her wanting to pounce on him all the time and not leaving him alone.

I fondly remember my Uncle Charlie taking me to the dedication for the building of the Liberty Memorial right across the street from the Union Station. They used to call the area "ugly old vinegar hill," and it contained old shanty clad and dirty derelict elements that often hung around at the Union Station. It was on November 1, 1921, and there were thousands of people present to see the dignitaries that were to be there. My Uncle Charlie put me on his shoulder and walked close to the front toward the podium that was set up for the ceremony. I remember him telling me how important this was with the people present that day and to pay close attention to what was going on. I saw General Marshall Foch of France, along with the admiral from Britain, generals from Belgium and Italy. The most empowering appearance and speech there that day, though, came from our own General John J. Pershing of the United States. A few years later when the World War I monument was complete, I also went to the dedication on Armistice Day in 1926 and saw Queen Marie of Rumania and President Coolidge.

Back in those days when such dignitaries would come to the city, you would see them drive the motorcades through the streets doing 60 mph in an effort to ward off would-be assassins. After the war was over, they had parades at least once a week in downtown Kansas City, Missouri, welcoming back all the soldiers from the war, and that continued for a very long time until all who were able returned home.

My cousin told me once that I was lucky that my foster parents were so good to me. I told him that they didn't do anything for me, that I took care of myself. All they wanted was the insurance money and what I could do for them. They even had Mary's mother brought over from Italy so they could insure her for $5,000. Zora Brunner was her mother, and she came to the United States from Italy and worked as a domestic for the wealthy Woolf Brothers family on the Country Club Plaza, mainly because she knew all the Jewish recipes that they were used to eating.

When they would visit Rome, Italy, they would take her along as their interpreter. I liked her mother very much and she liked me. We got along very well, and she even bought me a ring to remember her by. I hated to see her leave when she went back to Italy. She did not like the way my foster parents were raising me and told them to stop beating me, because I did all that they asked me to do and it wasn't necessary. She returned after a while to Italy and died there several years later, leaving a $5,000 insurance policy to her daughter, my foster mother in the United States.

They would insure everybody they could just for the money. There was a crippled old man called Scooby who was a hunchback and walked sideways. He was insured by a lot of people who would let him sleep under their porches or in their basements, and my foster parents had an insurance policy on him also.

When I was in grade school at St. John's, I made friends with a chubby little boy my age named Frankie Vesel. Over the years we became great friends, and every day during school I would wait for him to come with his little bag of jelly beans to meet me and walk the rest of the way to school. I became very fond of little Frankie and felt that he was the brother that I was never able to have because of my foster parents. We were very close and I would give him the pennies to get the candy every day. One grocery store had a cardboard box on the counter that was filled with candy. There was a circle cut out on one side of the box, and for a penny you could put your hand inside and pull out all the candy you could hold in your hand. I could never pull out as much candy as Frankie, so I just let him get the candy every day.

One morning while I waited for him to show up I knew something was wrong because he was never late and it was getting later and later, so I began wondering why he wasn't there. I decided to go down to his house to see if he was sick or something. I ran down to his house, and the front door was wide open and I saw both Frankie and his mother lying there in the doorway, and I knew when I saw their faces that they were both dead. I started screaming and running as fast as I could up Fifth street yelling "Help, help." A grocer named Speahart, who walked from door to door in the mornings getting grocery orders from the neighborhood to deliver in the afternoons, ran up and grabbed me. I

Willie at right end of top row — 1921.

tried to tell him what I saw, but I was stuttering so bad I couldn't talk, so he followed me back down to Frankie's house. I avoided looking at the bodies this time, and I noticed that Mrs. Vesel was doing the wash and had her clothes in a big copper boiler on the stove heating the water, but the water had boiled out and the clothes had begun to smolder. The entire house had been ransacked, and everything was scattered all over the floor. Mr. Speahart ran and called the police, and I just waited outside on the curb, not wanting to leave but not wanting to go back and look at their bodies again.

They never caught the guys who did that, but in those days a lot of the men in the family and in the neighborhood would hire out to go to other states like North and South Dakota on a bus to work the harvest, or down to Arkansas to cut down trees. When they came home on weekends with their cash pay, they would hide it in the house instead of putting it in a bank. Everyone just figured it was a robbery since they knew that Frankie's dad was always away from home during the week. I was able to go to Frankie's funeral and to the cemetery with some other kids from school for all the services.

I was brokenhearted for years, and even today I still have dreams of him and thoughts of that day many years ago and my chubby little friend with his bag of jelly beans. Frankie had a younger brother who was spared that day, and I kept track of him for years and we always stayed friends.

A few years later there was another murder similar to this one, but someone saw derelicts from the railroad yards walking away and the police caught up with them a short time later and charged them with the crime.

When the horses and wagons would go across the Intercity Viaduct from Kansas to Missouri, there would be a fountain there for them to drink from on each end and in the middle. It was a toll bridge back in those days with a gate you had to go through and then through this fence to proceed along the edge made for pedestrians. The streetcar would go across the viaduct on tracks along one side. The toll was a nickel for pedestrians and 10 cents for an automobile. We'd pay our nickel, then hitch a ride to the other side. Back then you could ride all over town for a nickel on a streetcar. They would give you a transfer, and each driver would punch a hole in it, and you could go anywhere in the city just transferring to other streetcars along the way.

The streetcars back then would come down Fifth Street, go about five miles and stop. The guy driving the car would take the handle out of the control panel and go to the other end of the streetcar and put the handle in that control panel and ride off in the opposite direction.

Us kids would put .22 shells and .32 shells down on the streetcar tracks and wait for the streetcar to come by, exploding them and making a lot of noise and scaring the hell out of everybody on board.

Us kids used to go around at night busting windows of businesses for the hell of it, and the newspaper called us the "Ghost Window Smashers." Windows weren't easy to bust back then; you could hit them with a brick and the brick would bounce back at you, and all you got was a dent in the glass. It always took four or five tries to actually break one.

We'd go away from Strawberry Hill to do it, like Armourdale or Rosedale. We'd bust the window and run like hell as far away as we could go to get away from it, then sit on the curb to rest up. Then someone would jump up and break another window, and we had to get up and run all over again.

There was one old guy in the neighborhood who hated us kids and would holler at us all the time to get away from his place. We had one kid who shit on his front steps, and when the old man came out to chase us, he slipped and fell in the shit and damn near killed himself.

Back then all the street lights were gas mantles that a guy had to light every night and would come around again at 11 p.m. to turn them off. You had to get off the streets then or the cops would come around and pick you up and haul your ass to jail.

When I used to get in trouble in school, the priest would line us all up and ask us to cross ourselves and have God strike us dead if we were lying. The first time I did that, I was breaking a sweat waiting to see if anything would happen to me. When nothing did, after that I crossed myself all the time, saying to myself that I should have been dead a million times. I usually was the one who did it, and I even got away with crossing myself at home saying, "I'm not lying or let God strike me dead." In those days that would beat any rap there was, they were so religious.

I got in trouble a lot of times with Monsignor Krmpotic who controlled the entire church. He was a big man who towered over all the people. He must have been six-foot four-inches tall, and all the people were afraid of him. Father Krmpotic told me once: "You'd steal a penny out of a dead man's eye." The nuns would be the ones to spank my bare butt with a hairbrush back then, thinking that would change my ways.

When I was an altar boy, I was supposed to kiss the monsignor's hand, and I wouldn't do it. I said: "I ain't kissing his hand; he wipes his ass with that hand."

I remember that when the nuns would bring him his food to the rectory they looked like a line of coolies running all the food over to him. Three times a day you would see this line of six or seven nuns dressed in their black-and-white habits running the hot food over to the rectory for Monsignor Krmpotic.

Since my foster parents both worked, it was a custom that I ate lunch at the school. I used to go over to the orphanage side and eat over there all the time because the food was always real good. Those nuns sure knew how to cook. They had a barley soup they made that was so good I would run over there every time they had it and eat as much as I could.

Standing just as tall next to the church is the orphanage (St. John the Baptist Children's Home), an original Queen Anne style home built in 1887. The 1918 flu epidemic in America left many orphans among the Croatian community. The pastor, Father Martin Krmpotic, who himself had sponsored many of the original immigrating families to America, encouraged the parishioners to raise the funds to purchase the home for an orphanage. The owners of the Electric Movie Theater originally owned the home, and they donated it to the church so that it could be converted to an orphanage. The church took care of its own during the flu epidemic and later on through the depression. No one on the hill ever went hungry, because the church would make sure they had food, shelter, and their children were attending school.

All boys had to be altar boys in the Catholic schools in those days. You served for the low masses during the week and worked up to being an altar boy for high masses on Sundays. It would take six altar boys to do the High Mass, and it was an hour long. I always waited impatiently for it to be over with, but at the same time I was so proud to be serving for the High Mass.

The altar boys sang along with the choir, and I sang so loud that I was screaming and shouting at the top of my lungs to every hymn. I remember when I was pouring the wine for the priest and I knew at any moment he would lift his glass to signal that he had enough wine in the glass. I kept pouring and pouring until the wine was level with the top of the glass. That angelical wine the nuns made was made of pure sugar, and they let us altar boys taste it. It was real sweet, but it would knock you on your ass. On Sundays when you had to be an altar boy for a High Mass, you dressed up in a red cassock. Sister Bonaventure was Mother Superior, and she did the Sacristan. She would handle all the holy objects in the sacristy. She went by the Saints on that day and knew what color cassock to lay out for the priest and us altar boys.

When I was in grade school, all the kids in the neighborhood would play a game called "Squeeze, drop and run." It was a form of tag where you would stand in a circle, squeeze hands and count to ten, drop your hands and run like hell. When you caught someone, you'd squeeze them and then they could proceed with you to find the other kids. We would run all over the neighborhood and even in and out of people's houses and down to the railroad yard where we went in and out of the boxcars.

I had a friend named Johnny whom I played with most of the time during those days, and Johnny ended up becoming a priest and then later became Monsignor John Horvat of St. John the Baptist Church there on Strawberry Hill. We would visit in later years and talk about the old days playing together, and he would always slip in the part where I should confess my sins and begin a respectful life. I was one mean son-of-a-bitch by then and it was too late.

I sat in the back of the class in school when you would stay in just one room the entire day. It would cost a dollar a month to stay in school back then, and my foster parents would give me the money monthly to take to school to give to the nun who kept the records. So I figured out how to open up the drawer on her desk that was kept locked that contained the sheet saying who paid and who didn't. I would get the sheet out every month and copy her handwriting and mark it "Paid" by my name and, of course, keep the dollar that I was given to pay it.

I also found out that the collection boxes for the holy candles in the church were kept in the basement. I used to fill my pockets with the empty boxes and walk in the church and switch them with the ones that had the money in it.

At St. John's School we would go into the classroom in the morning and wait for the nun to check us in. There was a window in the back of the class that a bunch of us guys would climb out of once we had roll call and play hooky all day. One time a bunch of us guys were shooting craps behind a big curtain on the stage in the auditorium. I saw the curtain move and knew something was up, so I left and ran back to the window of the classroom. I waited for the Skradski girl to tell me it was safe and climbed inside the window and back into my seat. It was just in time for Monsignor Krmpotic to walk inside the class room telling the teacher "that Scrakocic boy" (referring to me by my mother's maiden name) was running a crap game again. The nun said: "But my father, he is right here," and pointed to me looking all innocent sitting at my desk in back of the room.

I even enrolled in a public school called Bancroft at the bottom of Fifth street on Splitlog Avenue. They had to put me two grades ahead of all the other kids that were my own age because of learning so much more at the Catholic school. I would just go back and forth from school to school just to have something different each day. All the teachers and nuns wanted me to write the day's study on the blackboard because I had such a nice handwriting. I taught myself penmanship from a book that I brought home from the library and practiced making all my letters just like those in the book.

Sister Bonaventure, who was Mother Superior, liked me, and she had me help her paint one of the first backdrop screens that is still on the stage even today at St. John the Baptist. I painted with a four-inch brush while she did the detailing, and when I finished for the day she would give me a nickel for my work

Even today I still visit her grave at Mount Calvary in remembrance of her (1876-1947), and I can still hear her telling me to be a good boy. What a mean little bastard I turned out to be! She was a brilliant woman and a good artist. She painted a portrait of Monsignor Krmpotic on silk that is still up there hanging in the parish building today.

Once in the classroom at school another kid and I were arguing, and I said, "Fuck you," and the sister heard it. She had me write "Fuck you" 1,000 times on the blackboard. While I was writing this, every girl in the classroom covered her eyes the entire time until I was done.

Sister Bonaventure had real sharp facial features, beautiful handwriting and a wonderful personality, and I liked her and she liked me. Sister Angelica was very attractive, soft spoken and a wonderful teacher. Sister Pulcheria was sweet, funny and caring for you to learn as much as you could while in her class.

I ran with a few kids from school, and we were always getting into trouble. There was one nun who was always getting mad at me when I would do something and get into trouble in class. She would ask the class, "Did anyone see who did this?" I would tell her to ask Jesus, since he sees everything, and that would make her even madder.

We had a boarder who my stepfather was screwing around with named Anna who had her daughter Helen living with her at the house. I heard Anna tell my stepdad she worried about me getting to her daughter. Hell, I would have never done that, especially in my foster parents' home, plus I went to whores and didn't need to mess around with little girls. The daughter was only 11 years old, and she would come into my room early every morning to jump on my bed and wake me up. We played together around the house; I teased her and pulled on her braids, and she made me feel like I was playing with my younger sister whom I never knew or was ever able to play with. I really liked this woman and respected the way she protected her daughter, pampered her and took her places. She was so nice and caring I enjoyed being in her company and liked to sit with her at the kitchen table when she had coffee or breakfast. There were times I wished that she'd been my stepmother rather than the foster mother I had. I stopped playing with her daughter because it upset her so much and because in those days boys did not play with girls or vice versa.

When my foster mother got suspicious of my foster father and Anna having an affair, she told Anna that she would have to move out. I ran to Anna and pleaded, "Please don't leave; I want you to stay," and that my foster poppa really likes you and he wants you to stay, too. She moved out shortly after that, and I was brokenhearted to see her leave, but she let me visit her in her new apartment, and we stayed in contact and remained friends for many years.

When it snowed heavy back in those days, most people had to just stay inside and listen to the radio around the fire. The snowplow would eventually come and make one swipe down the center of the street. Then the people would venture out and everyone would just walk down the center of the street where it had been plowed. I loved to play in the snow like most kids, and having such a big hill like Fifth street was great for sledding. I had a piece of corrugated metal, and I would pull up the front end like a toboggan and let her rip. I would start on top of the hill at Barnett Avenue and sled down the six blocks to the bottom of the hill at Orville Avenue, then turn left into Fifth street Park through the ball field over to the other side straight down the hill of the dump and into the railroad yards, bouncing along and across the railroad tracks until I finally came to a stop. What a ride that would be and what a long walk back to the top of the hill where I started!

Looking back, I do appreciate the fact that my foster parents did adopt me and care for me, even knowing now that it was only for material things and that I was just a product, a medium for exchange, for their pleasure only. I guess they did try to give me the best home they knew how, and I was thankful for that. My foster parents continued to work along with the income of the boarding house, which made them well off.

When I would take a crap, I couldn't flush the toilet until my foster parents looked in it to make sure I had a bowel movement. If I didn't have one, I was given castor oil; then I was in big trouble because one of them would give me a soap enema and finished by cramming a piece of soap up my ass to leave there. Many a time in school I would get diarrhea from this practice and have to leave the classroom crapping in my pants. I had real curly hair back then, and it would hang down in ringlets on my forehead that my stepmother hated for some reason. She'd put starch on my hair and comb it straight back, making it flat and hard as a rock.

Every Christmas in Kansas City, Missouri, Mayor Cromwell would have a big Christmas tree set up at the Municipal Auditorium. Any kid in the entire metropolitan area would get a free ride on any bus or streetcar to go there to see a free silent movie and get a shopping bag full of toys. In the center of the convention hall there was a big square hanging from the ceiling with a movie screen on all four sides that could be seen from any place in the entire hall. I remember seeing the silent movie, "Peter Pan," starring Betty Bronson, and enjoying all the toys and candy I got in the big shopping bag.

One time a woman came over to visit my foster parents, and when she was getting ready to leave couldn't find her purse. They came up and dragged me out of my bed and beat the shit out of me for stealing the woman's purse. Later the woman said that I didn't steal it, she just forgot and left it at home. No one ever apologized to me for that beating.

Every single Sunday morning my foster parents would fight and argue with each other over all the shit that they did over the weekend. The old lady and me got into an argument one Sunday morning, and she ran me out of the house and told me to stay out and never come back. I told her that I was going to go down to snitch her off to her boyfriend, Mark, and tell him all about her screwing around with all the boarders. That did it; she ran down the street after me and brought me back and gave me 50 cents to go to the show. They were a bunch of no-good phony sons-of-bitches. They only took me for the insurance money on my grandfather and what I could do for them, and they didn't even care about me otherwise.

I was a juvenile delinquent in those days, along with other guys from the neighborhood that I went to school with. We all went before Judge Mead in the red brick courthouse up on Seventh street. The newspapers would write front-page stories on him saying how he was the "children's friend" and would dedicate even his off days for the kids. What they didn't know was all of us, about 15 or more, would go up to his chambers every Saturday, and he would play with our dicks one at a time and give us a dime. Hell, that was a lot of money in those days, and we went up there every Saturday just like clockwork to get our money.

There was this one time when all of us Hunkies were standing outside on the hill looking across the Kaw River watching the Zeppelin dirigible glide slowly in circles over downtown Kansas City, Missouri at a low altitude. The papers the next day said that the captain of the airship was Hugo Eckener.

In the late 1920s on Minnesota Avenue in Kansas City, Kansas, they had a big parade with a guy named Gunner Kasson and his 30-dog sled team that took the serum to Nome, Alaska, to prevent the diphtheria epidemic in 1925. I didn't remember seeing the famous Siberian husky lead dog named Balto. The dog team traveled 700 miles in the minus-50-degree temperatures. Kasson was wearing a big fur Eskimo coat with the hood pushed back while the dogs pulled the sled down the dry pavement of the street in the parade. I visited the statue of Balto, the lead dog in that team, in New York's Central Park years later when I was there on the lam.

On Sundays my foster parents usually gave me 15 cents to go to the movie show, a nickel for the show and 10 cents for popcorn and candy. One Sunday I did something wrong, and they made me stay at home in my bedroom upstairs. On the ceilings downstairs and the floors upstairs they had metal registers that when opened would vent the heat from the downstairs fireplace to the upstairs bedrooms. I started hearing all kinds of noise and rackets and peeked down through the register and couldn't believe what I saw. Both of my foster parents had been drinking, and my foster mother was on one side of the house with the neighbor pumping on her, and my stepfather was pumping on this woman on the other side of the house. Then someone must have realized that I was still in the house and I could hear him and her react to that possibility, so I ran back to my room. The old man came up to my bedroom, and I acted like I was asleep, so when he shook me to wake me up he just gave me a quarter to get my ass out of the house and go to a movie. The Electric Theater in those days had five vaudeville acts every weekend, and the theater would always be jam-packed.

Then it became a normal process that I would leave the house with Mary two or three times a week for her rendezvous with her lover. She would give me 50 cents and drop me off in front of the movie theater, picking me up on her way back home. Now the old man, Isaac, was cheap and only gave me a quarter when he dropped me off at the movie show for his little escapades. I became accustomed to being paid off to keep my mouth shut and liked it because of the easy money I'd make. I was getting spoiled from the payoffs and just figured this is where the larceny began within me wanting more and more.

I worked on weekends with a farmer who would come to town with his chickens and eggs to sell to homes and businesses. I would make the deliveries for him while he sat in his truck. Then we'd go to his place to "candle" all his eggs. You'd have to put each egg in front of a light to look inside for blood or baby chicks that couldn't be used to sell to customers. I made 15 cents a day, and my foster parents got all of it.

On weekends I also sold the magazines, *Ladies Home Journal* and *McCall's* for 10 cents a copy. I would make three cents on every magazine I would sell. I wanted to make more money, so I'd go to drugstores, steal their magazines, then take them door to door to sell them, making the whole dime per copy.

I found out that back then people didn't trust banks, so they hid their money in their rooms. I started by going into all of the boarders' rooms looking for money. I found out that they kept cash in the brass bedposts, so I would unscrew the top off and only take a little of the money so it wouldn't be too noticeable so I could return again and again. I guess you could say this was the start of my criminal career because I wanted to make more and more money, which only increased my thirst for stealing and being sneaky as I was taught to be.

Hell, my foster parents had about $20,000 hid in the house, and I always knew where it was, and I'd only take a five-dollar bill at a time so they wouldn't get suspicious. One time these two young boys were orphaned and had no place to go so my foster parents let them live at the house with free room and board and, of course, two life insurance policies on them. They found one of the hiding places for my foster parents' money and took it, and I got the shit beat out of me for it until they found out it was the boys' and they made them leave the house. I remember that they went to the Salvation Army and got a place to live until they finished school and got a job.

Growing up with my foster parents' I began to stutter so badly I could hardly talk. If they sent me to the store' I had to put it down on paper because I couldn't talk without stuttering long enough to tell the butcher what I wanted. My foster parents would hide behind the door and pounce on me and beat me when I walked into the house. My foster father said, "I give him everything he wants except a good whipping." They said they just did this to stop me from thinking about doing anything wrong before I did it. Later on, they thought that scaring me and beating me every day when I walked into the house would also stop the stuttering, but it didn't; it just made it worse. My foster father told me he didn't have anything growing up as a boy and believed I shouldn't have anything either.

I used to ask a friend of mine named Zonny to go over into Missouri on a streetcar with me and go to a burlesque show to get away, but he wouldn't go. He wouldn't leave the neighborhood; he was scared. Hell, I was scared the first time I took a streetcar over into Missouri to those honky-tonk joints over there. It was like another world so strange compared to the isolated ethnic neighborhood we lived in.

During school vacations my foster parents would send me to my Aunt Mary and Uncle Alex who lived on a 60-acre farm two miles outside of Lawson, Missouri. My aunt tried to teach me to milk a cow, and the cow kicked me. She said that I must have hurt the cow, and she showed me how easily she could fill a bucket up without any problems. I told her I would rather work out in the field instead of milking. On Saturday nights we would get into the old buckboard wagon led by one horse and go into town to the town square. A guy traveled around to small towns with a projector and showed silent movies that were paid for by the merchants of Lawson. They projected the movie on a sheet that had each corner tied to a branch of a tree. As the wind blew, the picture distorted when the sheet went in and out, but nobody seemed to mind. Later on, they projected the movie on a painted wall instead. At my uncle's farm their outhouse was a small building with a "two holer." They'd dig a hole and put the building over it, and when it would fill up, they would dig another hole and move it to another spot, covering the full hole in the process. You could sure tell where the holes were dug and filled because they had the most growth in the entire pasture from all the fertilizer.

Just a few miles from Lawson was a small town named Polo, Missouri, and that is where the movie star Steve McQueen was raised.

My foster father always parked his car out on the street, so one day I came home from school and drew a bull's-eye target on the garage door. I shot off my .22 at the bull's-eye for a while, then left. When I got home later that evening, I found out his car was parked inside the garage and it had a bunch of holes in the radiator, leaking water all over the ground.

When the Amos & Andy show was on the radio at seven o'clock every Saturday night, everything would shut down to listen to that radio program. Every business place in the city would all stop until after the show was over. It was a good comedy, and nobody wanted to miss it.

In the house that my foster parents acquired after my grandfather's death there were many rooms that they rented out to boarders for $5 a week. All the rooms had big four-poster beds, and I was walking by one room and saw that a guy had rope going from one bedpost to the other bedpost and across the top with about five or six pairs of long johns hanging off the rope all around his bed. I told my foster mother that the guy was doing his laundry in his room. She told me to mind my own business and don't say anything to anybody about it. It wasn't until later I found out that it was to protect him from witches grabbing him outta bed at night while he slept. If the witches fly into your room to try to get at you, they would get entangled in the hanging long johns instead of grabbing you and flying you off somewhere.

All of the people who came over from the old country, Croatia mainly, had strange customs and ways that they brought with them. When it thundered outside, they would say: "The devil is coming after one of his own." When the old women would butcher a hog, they would drain the blood and mix it with cool water so there wouldn't be sediment in it. Then they would all drink this warm blood for health reasons.

On Saturdays when I was out of school, it was my job to clean that big two-story house while my foster parents were at work. I had to mop, clean and wipe down all the wood with cedar oil and have the kitchen and all the bathrooms, plus the boarders' rooms sparkling clean when they got home. Some of the boarders were nothing but filthy bums when it came to their rooms. It always took me most of the day to complete the job, but it was to help out my foster parents. That way they had a clean house to throw their weekend parties since they didn't have to be at work until noon on Monday. I felt that they were raising me like a girl teaching me how to cook, wash and clean the house.

They had the biggest bar-b-q pit anyone had ever built in the back yard. They cooked pork ribs and roast beef and even a whole pig for the big parties they had every weekend with all the wine you could drink. Every morning my foster mother would say, "If I could only put some food on my stomach, I would feel better." Then she downed a big swig of homemade whiskey and followed that with a bigger glass of wine.

The Radkis made homemade wine in a giant wine press that included the grinder that was a work of genius. The elderberry wine was so strong it would knock your socks off. We think that's what gave the old man a heart attack when he died. The basement was always full of at least seven barrels of homemade wine for all the parties they had on weekends. I used to have to break down all the empty barrels and wash them and let them dry in the sunlight. Then I would have to put them back together again, placing a piece of straw between each slat of the barrel. I would fill them with water to let the wood expand, sealing the barrel and getting them ready for more wine to be placed inside. My foster parents beat the shit out of me a lot of times because I didn't come home in time to play music for them when they would be drinking and drunk on weekends.

After making the elderberry wine, they would take it and run it through the still, making a drink that was 140-proof alcohol.

2

Young Man

THEY ALSO RAN a still that was a copper boiler that a tinsmith put knobs on, along with all the coils that sat inside. Two or three times a year my foster parents would take me out of school to stay home and watch the still when they would make their own booze. The still was in the bathroom where the water line would run cold water into it to keep the coils cool that made the condensation of the booze to drip down into fruit jars. One time I was screwing around not watching it like I should have, and a raisin got caught in one of the coils. By the time I walked in the bathroom, the boiler had enlarged and was expanding and retracting like it was ready to blow up. I cut off the flame just in time, then had to clean the stuck raisin out of the coil before I could get it going again. All the Hunkies on the hill, including us, would go down to Asner's Salvage to buy old bottles and fruit jars to fill up with booze.

The Radkis, my foster parents, would take away my condoms because they said that I was too young to be screwing around. When I was 15, I got a case of the clap from screwing around with the whores, and that's why I used condoms. In those days, if you saw a woman walking down the street with a newspaper under her arm, you knew she was a hooker. You would just walk with her into the alley or behind the billboard, and all it would cost you was a quarter. I fondly remember one whore Red Bodner and I went to, which was my first piece of ass that screamed out in pain: "Oh, Daddy, you're hurting me; oh, Daddy, you're hurting me." I gave her 50 cents and walked away pretty proud of myself, but now I just laugh thinking about it.

I have been in every house on the block and a lot of houses in the neighborhood. I would go in just to steal something I could sell or take money if they had any. I went into one house and found a .32 pistol in a drawer and took it. I took this .32 pistol to school and shot it off in front of the class when we went out for recess.

Meanwhile, the neighborhood had been complaining about a group of men who looked like derelicts who were going door to door through the neighborhood leaving flyers inside the screen doors or on the door-knobs. Very few people spoke English, so without their children who knew English they had no idea why the men were there, and it was upsetting to them. I went up to these guys and told them to leave the neighborhood and fired several shots up in the air to get them moving and on their way. Every time I fired the gun, the shells flew out and the cylinder flew up in the air, then scattered onto the ground, and I had to put the gun back together over and over again every time I shot it. The derelicts called the police, and the police came down to the neighbor-hood to investigate, but no one said anything about seeing or hearing a thing in relation to what they reported had taken place.

When they took me out of school before my graduation, they told me that it was time to get a job to take care of them now because they took care of me. I was working with a guy on a truck loading and hauling stuff 12 hours a day six days a week, and I made a dollar a week. They took the dollar, saying I didn't know how to handle money.

On Ninth and Minnesota Avenue back in those days was the old Kansas City High School. They used to have a tunnel under the street that led from a warehouse building to the school. We used to sneak into the warehouse building and go over to the high school through the tunnel and swim in the pool like we belonged there and went to school there. When we got older, we used that tunnel to burglarize the ware-house building and got away through the tunnel and out at the high school. They later moved the school to 18th and Minnesota and called it Wyandotte High.

One whore who I would see all the time became worried that her pimp would try to rob me, so she gave me a .32 pistol to protect my-self. Little did she know when she handed me that gun it was like telling me to go rob a drugstore or something, kiddo.

The first place we robbed was the Western Auto store at 29th and State Avenue in Kansas City, Kansas. We were as nervous as hell; all of us were scared to death, but when I entered the place and brandished my new .32 caliber pistol, I yelled at the top of my lungs, "Reach for the Rafters." We got $200 in that robbery and thought we were rich. It wasn't until I picked up that gun that I got my courage back and stopped stuttering and haven't stuttered since.

My two buddies and I went into Montgomery Wards in Kansas City, Kansas to rob the place, and when we announced that this was a robbery, hell, we were shaking just like everyone else in there. Back in those days, all of the salespeople were women, and each department had their own cash drawer. We were running around trying to get all of the money from each drawer, spilling coins all over the floor as we ran from one department to the other, trying to get out of there as fast as we could before the police came. The entire department store yielded a total of $121.

I used to sell newspapers for a Jew along with two other kids on 12th Street in Kansas City, Missouri. It was called the *Kansas City Journal Post,* I sold the papers for three cents and I got a penny. I sold these papers right in front of the place where Harry Truman worked, which was called "Jacobs Haberdashery." I used to make enough money to go to the show and have some popcorn and candy. The movies cost five cents, and I really enjoyed watching the weekly "Green Archer Serials." Later on, I'd go right in front of the guy's newsstand on the corner of 12th Main where he sold newspapers and yell: "Get your paper, get your morning paper." He'd get pissed off and start chasing me off his corner. While he was chasing me, the other two guys with me would steal all his papers so we could sell them later on another corner. Wallace Berry and his brother, Noah, sold papers on the corner of Eighth and Grand in Missouri at the same time we did and we were friends, so sometimes when we had to get back home we'd sell them the papers we had left over.

I was walking through this alley once and a kid told me: "You can't come through here," and he hit me hard and knocked me down. Well, he shouldn't have done that because I went home and got a baseball bat, came back and hit him harder and told him, "I'll walk anywhere I want to."

One of my school buddies named Dusan came from a family of

nine. I knew that his family could never afford to let him go to the movies on the weekends, so I would always pay his way, and we'd walk all over town to go to all the movies showing that weekend. We always stopped at the "Den of Sweets" and got a gigantic banana split for 35 cents. I would sometimes steal bicycles and scooters and give them to my buddy Dusan and the other kids in his family. I also kept mine hidden in his garage so my foster mother wouldn't find them.

The Radkis trained me for everything that they wanted done. They had me go down to Fifth Street Hall, and there was a guy down there who taught me to play the tamburitza. They are like mandolins but with a longer neck. I played in the band with a guy named Zonny Quaternick, who later went to Kansas University and became a famous football star. I made a dollar a week and didn't see a penny of it; my foster parents took it all. The name of the band was the "Young Junior Tamburitzans."

I felt like a chained animal at times with them and the control they had over me. My mom knew how they treated me, and she would cry, saying she wished she'd never let them talk her into putting me up for adoption so they could raise me. She told me that I was born under an unlucky star. She thought that since the adoption took place in a courthouse and was legalized it could never be reversed and she could never have me back.

Our band started to get pretty popular, and when we would just rehearse, crowds of people would gather around and start dancing. We knew a guy in Cincinnati from whom we got all our sheet music, and he would take the popular songs by the big bands and favorite singers of the day and write them out for our band to play. I played the horn section with my tamburitza, and I have to admit we sounded great. We even cut a few records back then at the Huron Building where they broadcast KCKN radio station at the time and where we'd play on Saturday nights. I also liked playing bass when I played "Beer Barrel Polka." We started getting so popular we traveled all around with our band. We drove to Pittsburg, Girard and Arma, Kansas, where the crowds just waited for us to perform on weekends. One time our Model-T blew a piston right outside of Arma, so a family named Murn put us up for the night.

The Murn family had a cute little daughter with blonde hair that was cut in a 1920s bobbed hairstyle. She was one year older than I was, and we became good friends. They lived right along an active coal pit, and that night after everyone went to bed in the house I spent my time reading the Sears catalog to pass the time. They didn't have a radio, newspapers or anything else to read but that catalog. The next day we just pulled the piston out of the block and drove the Model-T back home to Kansas City on three pistons. You just had to cut off the oil to the one piston so it wouldn't leak since it wasn't working anyway.

I wrote to Christine Murn often and saw her every time we were in Pittsburg, Kansas. We drove down a brick road they called the "S-L, the Slim Line," which they later named 69 Highway. When we had a performance in Kansas City, I invited her entire family to come up and watch us play. Her family and my foster family got together and wanted to make plans for the two of us to get married. She was sweet, but I wasn't ready to settle down and liked to visit all of my whores when I wanted to. She was so pretty and so nice, I made several trips down to see her.

There were eight of us in the band called Junior Tamburitzans. I started playing when I was nine years old, and we traveled to small towns to entertain on weekends when I was 16. We played at a hall at 10th and Main in Kansas City, Missouri, and it was a sell-out. They had me play solos all the time when I got older.

Somebody has those pictures of us with the whole tamburitza band together. I don't know who would have it; I don't know who would be alive today. I think I'm the only one left; everybody else in the band is dead.

My foster parents loved to slap me several times a day, and when I started stuttering, they slapped me more. They said that they had to hit me and slap me to get my attention. They would wake me up at two in the morning and drag me outta bed when they were drinking and wanted me to play the tamburitza so they could dance. My confirmation sponsor, Mary Novesel, knew how mean they were to me, and she kept an eye on me for my mother. She also thought there was nothing they could do to change the situation because the adoption had gone through a legal court in front of a judge.

All the Hunkies went to a place on 12th and Jefferson in Missouri to drink and party. They got kegs of beer and drank them until they were gone on the weekends. That would give me the time to case a lot of places to rob since there was no supervision at home, and I liked it that way.

There were big copper cables on all the steel bridges back in those days for electric streetcars to be grounded as they drove across. We'd cut the cable from the bottom to the top of the bridge, clean off the outside rubber by burning it and take the copper inside to the salvage yard. The cable itself was about a two-inch circle with four individual rubber-covered pieces of copper.

When they closed the Eighth Street tunnel, we got the mother lode of copper ground wire from inside the place. Several times when we cut the ground cable at the top inside the tunnel, it fell down on the tracks and sparks flew and the cable whipped back and forth for a while hotter than hell, and we'd run out and wait until it slowed down so we could grab it again. The place where we took all our copper was called Asner's Salvage down on James Street right across from the Armour packing house. We sold the copper for 27 cents a pound then. I knew the old man Morris and his son, Louie, but didn't remember ever meeting the youngest boy who went to Wyandotte High School named Ed Asner (TV and movie actor who played Lou Grant in the Mary Tyler Moore show). Asner's Salvage was selling thousands of bottles and jars to all the bootleggers, and you could even sell the emp-ties back to them. My foster parents bought bottles for booze all the time, like all the others on the hill.

I bought a Model-T for $25 that didn't have a top, no tires and no rear end. I didn't care because I could just steal everything it needed. Just jack up the back end of a model-T and remove two bolts on the rear end and two on the spring and carry it off. We got the top the same way; it took only four bolts to remove it from somebody's car on the street, and after that it was ours. One time we ran out of gas in our Model-T and saw a barrel in a guy's back yard. We thought it was gasoline, so we stole it, putting it in our gas tank. We started noticing a big trail of black smoke coming out of the exhaust, and the car start-ing to chug, chug, chug along. We figured out later we put kerosene in it instead of gasoline, but the damn thing still ran for us.

When Henry Ford sent out his Model-T to the car dealers, he would pack the windshield in wooden planks that were later converted to the floorboards when unpacked. The Hudson automobiles they made back then were naturally bulletproof because they were so big and heavy that bullets would just bounce off, never penetrating the metal body.

The local hockshop on James Street belonged to a guy named Shaffer who was a cousin of the Asners who owned the salvage yard. They sold .410 double barrel shotguns for $9. They had a 12-gauge revolver that held five or six shells and a .410 revolver in the window that sold for $5. They even sold sawed-off shotguns for $7 until the law said that they were illegal and made them stop.

We would go there to buy our guns and ammunition all the time. I was riding on a streetcar one night, and a guy came over to me and asked me if I was Radkay. I recognized him as Louie Asner when he started talking, and he told me to come to the hockshop, that he had something to show me. I went with him inside the place, and he pulled out a writing board on the desk that revealed three mug shots of my two buddies and me. I asked him what the hell this was, and he said that the police had been there and told him not to sell any guns or bullets to any of us guys and to call them when we came around and let them know if we tried to buy anything. I always made sure Louie was working when we went in there to get shells so no one would turn us in. His family lived in Mission, and I was lucky to meet with him on that streetcar that night when he was heading home.

We thought about getting our guns at the hockshops in Kansas, but found out in time that the guy was a rat who sold them to you. Sure, he would sell you as many guns and bullets as you wanted, but he would wrap them in blue paper and then call the police. The station was just a couple of blocks away, so they got there in time to see you get into your car with the blue package and drive off. Then when you walked inside your house, they would nab you and search your house, then haul your ass to jail.

Back then, all nationalities had slang names, and nothing racial or offensive was ever thought of when they were used. I was called a "Hunky," which is the slang for Croatians, and as long as they wouldn't put "son-of-a-bitch" in front of it I didn't mind. I would rather be called a Hunky than "Hey You."

There were four Catholic Churches within just a few blocks of one another in our neighborhood, and all of them were different nationalities. St. John the Baptist was the Croatian church, and we were called Hunkies. St. Mary's was an Irish church, and they were called Micks. St. Anthony's were from Czechoslovakia and called Slovaks. Holy Family was from Slovenia, where in the old country it sets along the edge of Croatia, so they were called Kranjnac, which meant "edge." Back then, the blacks was all referred to as the "N" word. In those days, that or any slang name was used without any offensive, disrespectful or insulting intention. We were all labeled by slang names and were proud to be labeled by our own personal nationality and race.

My foster father worked in this foundry and spilled hot molten metal on his leg. The company's doctor told him that his leg would have to be amputated, but he refused to let the doctor do it. He went to another doctor, Brathaway, who was Jamaican and had an office down on James Street that all the Hunkies went to. Doctor Brathaway would come to the house every day and treat my old man's leg by packing it in Vaseline and wrapping it up with a clean rag. Dr. Brathaway healed his leg, and he didn't have to have it amputated like the other doctor said. We had an old dog named Bebba at the house that disappeared one day. Doctor Brathaway was making his rounds around the city, and our dog recognized his Model-T and jumped right into the back seat. Dr. Brathaway recognized our dog and brought him back home to us on his next visit.

I learned to drive a Model-A that had three pedals to regulate it. Our neighbor ran his Model-A in only one gear, and you could follow him around town by following the smoke. Back then, the Flint car by Maxwell had the gearshift box on the floor next to the driver, which was unusual back then. You would have to insert a handle into the box, change gears, then you could remove the handle making more leg room in the car. We stole a Cord automobile once and didn't know that the gearshift was on the dashboard. We hardly got it started in time to get away because no one knew or could figure out where the gearshift was in the thing. Stole a Cadillac once and opened the gas tank to see if it had any gas in it, and all this air spewed out. We had no gas gauges on cars back then, so you had to look inside the tank to check it. Also back then, you didn't have fuel pumps either, and you had to use a pump to keep air in the gas tank to push it up to the carburetor to drive. You had to use the pump every 40 miles or so. Some of the cars needed only a ballpoint pin to start the engine or a piece of foil; it was so simple and so convenient to just keep getting different cars.

The Governor of the State of Kansas was in Kansas City for a big parade, and they had all of the parade cars parked in this big garage at Sixth and Tauromee Avenue. A kid named Iggie who was with us jumped into a big limousine that the Governor was going to ride in while we jiggered for him. The keys were in the ignition, so he just started it and took off. He picked up Red, Harry and me and drove it out of the garage at a high speed. It was a big LaSalle limousine that had the front section where the driver sat surrounded by glass, and the entire back end was open so the Governor could be seen by his public and wave to the crowds as they drove down the streets. Us kids drove that limousine all over the city plus up and down Central Avenue, showing off the car to everyone we knew. Every kid we saw and knew got a ride in that limousine that day, and we had a great time until it started getting dark. We knew we had to get home, so we just dropped it alongside the road not far from where we picked it up that morning. Back then, most of the people just left their keys in the ignition because all of the cars were so easy to hot wire, start and take off with anyway. They didn't see any sense in taking the keys out of them.

Never once in the entire time that I lived with my foster parents was there any kind of affection shown toward me like a hug, kiss, or even a hand on the shoulder in a friendly way. What a crazy, messed-up house I lived in. I couldn't get any affection from them, so I started frequenting prostitutes for pleasure and affection that was pretty darn good, now that I look back on it all.

There was an empty lot between our house and the house next door, and the old man went to the neighbors and I went along with him. They were drinking and partying, and I was playing the tamburitza. My foster mother didn't go over there to the party and we wondered why. Barto, who lived there, disappeared from the party. Everyone asked, "Where's Barto?" I knew where he was. So I ran down to our house, and he was just coming down the stairs from the upstairs bedroom. I told him that everyone was looking for him, so he ran out the back door. Just then the old man walked in the front door, and I told him that Barto wasn't here. I saved that son-of-a-bitch; you know that he was screwing my foster mother.

It wasn't long after that my foster mother took me up to a jewelry shop on Minnesota Avenue right next to the Electric Theater. She pointed at everything in the window and asked me what I wanted. I picked out a Benrus watch for myself that cost $55, which was a hell of a lot of money in those days. I was the only 14-year-old kid in the neighborhood who owned a real basketball and a wristwatch when most adults didn't even own a wristwatch. My stepmother was better to me than my stepfather in giving me material things. He was too cheap and said I should work for everything I got and have nothing given to me in life.

My foster parents yanked me out of school when I was 15 because they didn't want me to stay in school to graduate because by then all the good jobs would be taken. They wanted me to get a job before all the other kids went and got them. That's when he had me, a puny little 15-year-old just a little over five foot tall, stand in the lines at five in the morning down at the Cudahay's Packing house trying to get hired. There were guys there over six feet, big and husky weighing 200 to 300 pounds, and he thought that they would pick me. I eventually got hired down there and worked 12 hours a day and six hours on Saturday. I made nine cents an hour, and my job was to wash out pig bladders in salt water that ate the skin off my hands. I was given only a quarter from my paycheck every week, and the rest would go to my foster parents. My godmother found out about this and demanded they give me at least a dollar, which they later did. I would go to this pool hall and shoot craps with loaded dice and win some money to spend.

The school had them bring me back to class to graduate and get my diploma. I sure got a beating on that day that I will never forget. I need to get that graduation picture, and you'll see how black my eye was. They didn't whip me; they "beat" me. My hand was all blue from trying to protect myself from the old man while he was beating me and beating me, and this time he just wouldn't stop. That's the only time I ever hit the old man; I hit him right in his mouth as hard as I could. He backed off, and I waited with fists up ready to do it again, but it worked, and he stopped beating me and never hit me again after that. I'd just finally had enough of his abuse and beatings.

In 1927 when I was 16 years old we went to a small airport in North Kansas City that was just a dirt runway back then. My buddies and I climbed over a wire fence and walked right up to where Charles A. Lindberg was standing alongside the "Spirit of St. Louis," the plane he flew solo across the Atlantic Ocean. While all the reporters were interviewing him and many were taking pictures, my two buddies jiggered for me while I jumped into the cockpit and went through his plane. It was sure small and tight inside that plane, and the only thing I found to steal was a magazine and a package of Lorna Doone Cookies that we all ate on the way back home.

Uncle Mike lived in Gary, Indiana, on Alcott Avenue, and their house was way off of the road. It took 12 hours to get there on a train. My stepmother was in love with my uncle, and that's why she always wanted to go up there and I went with her as a decoy. I remember that she argued with my stepfather before we left and he didn't know if she was going to come back or not. I felt pretty bad all the way up there after they had that big argument. The train was the "Chicago Western," and it was a coal-burning locomotive with a big smokestack and went chug-a-chug all the way. It had double windows and I was wearing a winter coat, but when I took the coat off I had a "V" on the front of me from the coal dust that came in even through those closed windows. My face was dirty with coal dust, and every other part of me exposed was coal black. These were the trains before diesel engines came in. The cost of the fare from Kansas City to Chicago was $10. When we got to the Chicago Union Station, I was standing on a bridge looking out at all those big buildings of the skyline and how amazing they were. Back then, going to East Chicago you see Lake Michigan and how outstanding the green color of the water was. I remembered when we lived up there you didn't see anything but the dazzling green water of the lake on the horizon. There was something funny though, because it had a canal running right alongside it that was filthy and dirty and had all kinds of crap running in it.

On the same block as my Uncle Mike in a house on the corner was a family we knew very well. One of the kids in that family was named Mladen Sekulovich. He later became a movie star and television star, changing his name to Karl Malden. His father even tried to become a movie star along with his son, but never made it.

I visited my Uncle Mike in 1929 in East Chicago and I was able to find my dad's grave without any trouble at all, seeing his big stone from the road when driving up to the cemetery. When I visited with my Uncle Mike, he had a good business that he built up over the years running routes for the brewery and also hauling ice and coal. They had people working for them instead of them doing all the work as he and my dad did. If my mother had stayed up there, we would have been well taken care of and all of us kids would have been together.

Back in those days the police had only one-way radios. They received calls in, but couldn't call out. To receive these calls, they had to have a big 10-foot antenna that was hooked on the back bumper. When the cars would drive by, all the old people would say, "Shut up, they can hear what you are saying with that antenna." I used to go up to the police station's garage and try to bend them off and break them, but they wouldn't break; they would just snap back to the original position. I would go snooping in the police station garage to look for something to steal. In the corner of the building one night I saw a big motorcycle that said "Police" on it and had a siren and lights all over it. I jumped on, turned the key on and drove it away. I drove it only at night to case places and had one particular place I would park it during the day in a neighbor's garage. It was a big Harley motorcycle that balanced itself like a car when you drove it, and you'd get 80 miles to the gallon on it. One night I was riding it down in the Fairfax district and made a turn off the main road onto a back road. It was pitch dark, but in the nick of time I saw a reflection of light on a ground wire that was leading from the ground up to the side of the pole. I was able to swerve and bend my head down just in time to keep from cutting my head off. I went home and parked it just like I always did in this neighbor's garage, and when I returned the next night to head out again, I noticed it looked like it had been moved. I was suspicious that it had been moved, so just left it and never went back. I found out later the neighbor said he just found it in his garage and didn't know where it came from and called the police. The police parked outside the garage and waited and waited for someone to go inside to get the motorcycle and ride off, but I never did.

I stole an Indian motorcycle later that was a lot smaller than the Harley but served the same purpose for me, and that was driving around casing places to rob. I just parked the bike in a corner inside of the DeCoursey's Dairy parking garage until I needed it. Some guys who worked at the dairy that I went to school with watched it for me and kept it out of sight.

My foster parents took a life insurance policy out on my mother, but she would only agree to sign for it if I was made the beneficiary. My foster parents both agreed to the policy, thinking the life of crime I was living would get me killed at any time and they would take over as beneficiary on that policy. Of course, they also had a couple of insurance policies on me.

Back in those days when people would be making their own whiskey, you could sure tell who had a still in their house. Just look up on the roofs and see who has the exhaust vent all clogged up, and you know they had a still. They thought that the smell would attract attention, so they tried to conceal it.

When you walked by the houses, you could also listen to who had the water running, and you knew it was to keep the coils on their still cool. Some of the people just had big copper boilers out in the back yard. There was one guy who had a 200-gallon still. It was the biggest still I'd ever seen and was five feet in diameter. It was built through several floors of his house and went all the way up to the top. He had the biggest operation around. He would ask the people in the neighborhood to make him two gallons each to sell, in addition to what he made in that big still. He pushed more whiskey than anyone did. He would get two gallons from this house, from that house and, hell, every house was making whiskey.

We stole his whiskey once; then we called the cops. When the cops came and busted him, he thought they were the ones who took his whiskey, and we got away clean. Four of us guys hauled it off, hid it, then came back with a few jars and sat on the curb and got drunk watching all the action.

We would take truckloads of whiskey up to Lawrence, Kansas where Kansas University was, hoping to sell it. A guy told us that we could haul all the whiskey that the entire state had and it still wouldn't be enough whiskey to satisfy that college town.

We robbed a place called Midwest Liquors, which was one of the biggest distributors around. We rented some white uniforms for 15 cents a day, then stole a grocery truck in order too not look suspicious as we waited for them to drive their whiskey truck past us out on K-10 highway. With guns drawn, we pulled them over and got away clean, and it was all "Bonded" whiskey. We then sold it to one of the major bootleggers, Carl Ruben, in Topeka, Kansas.

When we would steal homemade booze from all the bootleggers, we would make what they called "Needle Whiskey." You put a hot soldering iron down into the booze that you have in a metal container, and the heat from the iron burned the sugar and it would turn dark brown, and then we would get 25 cents more on the pint because we could sell it as "Bonded" whiskey. People didn't know any better back then; they just wanted alcohol to drink. I was burning whiskey one time and kept laying the hot soldering iron down on the floorboard of my car. We saw smoke and knew I had set the car on fire, so I had to pour the whiskey we just burned on the fire to put it out.

The way that our neighborhood area became what they now call "Strawberry Hill" wasn't because they grew strawberries on the hills. A guy was doing a story in the newspaper about the immigrants moving into areas of Kansas City, Kansas, with strawberries growing behind the houses on the hills. The real explanation was they would throw out their mash from the stills in back of their houses which were hills, and little plants would be growing up through the discarded mash and the reporter thought they were strawberries. Like neighborhoods from the old country, he saw what looked like a field of strawberries. When most of the neighborhood would be running their stills, they would throw the used mash in this dump area that would draw more rats than the dump already had. A lot of us kids in the neighborhood would get .22 rifles and go down to the dump to shoot the rats. The rats were so thick at times you could kill at least two and sometimes three with each shot.

There used to be a big empty lot on Sixth street between Sandusky and Elizabeth Avenue that would fill up on Saturdays with farmers selling everything they grew out of the backs of their trucks. Everybody in the neighborhood would gather to that spot on Saturdays, so we were always right in there casing everything, looking for something to steal out of the cars.

From Strawberry Hill I watched a tornado hit and destroy a lot of the Rosedale district one evening. Almost the entire neighborhood and I were watching the black swirling cloud throw around all the debris of what were once houses in the Rosedale district. There were deaths from all the destruction, and the area had a lot of devastation from the tornado.

Kvaternik was the name of the restaurant at the bottom of Fifth Street where everyone went to eat the best chili in town. I used to play pool in there with the guys in the neighborhood. Someone shot a pool ball off of the table, and I went to pick it up off the floor and noticed there was a shelf underneath the pool table. Later on, when I found out that Kvaternik was selling illegal cigarettes for $1 a carton, I went in to eat a bowl of chili. So one evening when I finished eating in the restaurant and no one was looking, I slid under the pool table and got up on that shelf and lay there until closing time. When everyone was gone, I slid out, got all of the cartons of cigarettes he had and left out the back door. Us guys sold them all over town for a dollar a carton.

When I would go to the movies when I was young before there was sound with the pictures, the projector was in the middle of the aisle and you could hear the "cluck, cluck, cluck" of the film running through the reels. The guy would tell you that he had to stop, turn the ceiling lights on and reload another roll of film into the projector. In those days they didn't have lights or bulbs behind the film to project it on the screen like they do today. They had an arc (like a welding torch), and when the picture would start to get dark, the projectionist would open up the box and the whole room would light up while he adjusted the screws to get the points together for more light.

Then when the talkies first came out, they would have a record that was about two feet wide on a record player alongside the projector. The guy would either hold it to slow down the record to adjust it to the words the actors were saying or speed it up to try to catch up to get it all in sync.

There was one theater in Kansas City, Kansas where during the summer the fans were so loud I was glad that they were silent pictures because you wouldn't be able to hear anything. They would put blocks of ice on the roof in these openings and blow big fans down into the theater to cool the patrons off; just don't sit where the ice was melting and falling down into the theater. On 10th and Central Avenue they had a theater that was outside and a great place to go in the summertime. The movie was projected onto a brick wall painted white for the people to watch.

At the *Kansas City Kansan* newspaper building on Minnesota Avenue, people would gather around and listen to the ball games that they would announce over big speakers outside the place. Minnesota Avenue was the main drag of Kansas City, Kansas back then, and couples would window-shop up and down the Avenue on the weekends. It was a meeting place for both young and old. The ball games would draw big crowds of people who were just standing in the streets listening to the game. I recall that the streetcars would clang their clangors wanting to get by, but the people were too interested in listening to the game to move. Below one of the speakers they had a big baseball diamond made of wood, and behind the diamond was a man who would move a ball on a string, letting people know where the ball was hit and where it went on the board. When it was at the pitching mound, it would sit there in the middle and go around and around, getting ready for the wind-up and pitch.

My foster parents acted like if I got married that they would be there to put it in for me because they thought that I didn't know how to do it. They even had the girl picked out that they wanted me to marry. In fact, they said that they wouldn't put my name on the deed of the house as beneficiary until I married her. She was pretty, and Sharon Stone has nothing on her; she was really a good-looking little gal. They all called her Jean after the movie star "Jean Harlow" who she looked a lot like. I didn't care for that gal because she told me what I was going to do when we got married. She said the first thing I was to do was to get rid of my friends and all my flashy cars and instead of my expensive suits to just wear work clothes. Hell, I was going with whores who taught me how to dress by showing me *Esquire* magazines and telling me to buy this kind of a suit or that. I had them pick my clothes for quite a while; then later I just picked out the style I wanted to wear instead. I always had four or five $300 to $500 suits hidden from my foster parents back then.

Red Bodner and I were walking across the intercity viaduct heading for a whorehouse in Kansas City, Missouri one night when the cops stopped us and asked where we were going. We told them that we were going to 14th and Main to a whorehouse. They searched us and we had no money at all between us, and the cop said that either we had something special for the ladies or our credit was damn good.

Another time when we were walking over the bridge to the whorehouse, we could hear the cops driving up behind us with the police cars that were Dodge motor cars that had an engine that made a noise like "pop, pop, pop." It gave us time to ditch our guns, and when they searched us, they took my $60, then just let us go. So we went back to retrieve our guns and had to rob another grocery store to get some money so we could continue on the way to the whorehouse.

I remember running from the cops down on Central Avenue when one cop caught up with me and told me to stop or get shot while he was pointing his gun out the window at me. I hated to get arrested because when they take you to jail you have to go to a lineup, and that's where you get accused of all kinds of shit that you didn't even do. I handed him a $20 bill and asked him if I could buy him breakfast. He took the $20 and got back into the police car and left. Twenty dollars back then was as much as some people made in a month and I think the cops made less. One dollar was worth the equivalent of about $10 back then, and most jobs only paid 50 cents a day.

Back then, you wouldn't be able to make a phone call from jail unless you had money and could pay off the cop who arrested you first. That's where I made a lot of extra money on weekends on my way to the movies. I would walk by the old city jail at Sixth and Ann on Sunday mornings, and all these guys would start yelling out the window at me, throwing money to contact their families to let them know they were in jail. Mostly just quarters, but when the jail was full it added up to a little chunk of change.

The Central Avenue bridge that also went into Missouri from Kansas had an elevator in the middle of the bridge for the horse-drawn vehicles that carried heavy loads for delivery like kegs of beer up from the Central Industrial District. There were two ropes to operate the elevator — one you pulled on to go up and pulled on again to stop and the other you pulled on to go down and pulled on to stop. We would go down there to the National Biscuit Company (NBC) that was called Loose-Wiles, the bakery with a thousand windows. We knew a lot of the girls who worked there, and they would throw cookies at us out of the windows.

Down on James Street there was a factory that made Baby Ruth candy bars. I went to school with a girl they called "Dirty Aggie" who worked there, and she would throw the unwrapped candy bars out the window for us kids. They had to wrap the candy bars by hand back then, and it was that piecework that made their paychecks in those days.

On Sixth Street there was a place named Kopps Bakery that made delicious pies. In the summertime we'd go around to the back window that was wide open, and when the pies came out of the oven, they would run along a conveyer belt that ran just inside the window. All you had to do was reach inside and grab the hot pies as they went rolling by and run like hell.

In the 1920s in St. Joseph, Missouri, a black man raped and killed a white school teacher. The man was arrested and taken to the local jail by the sheriff. It wasn't too long after he was locked up at the jail when a mob of citizens from St. Joe turned up at the police station wanting to take him out of his cell. The sheriff told them, "Come on, you know I can't let you do that. I can't turn the prisoner over to you." The mob kept backing the sheriff up inside the jail and told him that they were taking him out and he couldn't stop them. The sheriff kept trying to get them to leave, but they pushed him around a little and threatened him, so the sheriff ended up just throwing them the cell door keys to keep from getting himself hurt. The mob opened the cell and dragged the black guy out and took him to the schoolhouse building. They tied him to the top of the school and set the building on fire. The black man was screaming and crying while he was burning alive. The entire mob watched the schoolhouse burn to the ground, then just walked away.

Back in those days, it wasn't uncommon to see a black man hung from a light pole every week or so. The police said that they just did it periodically to keep them in line in case they strayed. You didn't know if they actually did it or they were just scaring you and someone else had done it.

I had a crippled cousin named Tommy who I used to carry around with me because he couldn't walk and I felt sorry for him. I changed his pants and kept him clean and took him with me whenever I would go to play with the other kids. His parents took him to a guy in Olathe, Kansas who was supposed to be able to do some healing on the affliction he was born with, for a price. I went along and watched the guy take the lid from a copper boiler to which he had attached dials and wires all over the top and proceed to bounce it all over Tommy's body. The guy would tell you where the pain was in your body: "It's here, and now it's here, and here." Then he would sell you a bottle of "Vitola" to help you get better. They paid $10 for that bullshit plus the bottle of Vitola. Tommy later got leg braces and was able to walk by himself and even got a job at a bowing alley setting the pins above Katz Drugstore on Minnesota Avenue.

The old man loved cowboy movies, and his favorite cowboy was William S. Heart. He was a cowboy who wore a short brim cowboy hat. The old man couldn't read, so he would take me to read the captions to him because the movies were all silent in those days. After a while, all the theaters would throw away the movie tapes in the local dump. Us kids would pick up all of the tapes and I would take them home. The first movie projector I bought for $5 had an oil lamp inside that provided the light to see the film. Then later I bought a Keystone movie projector with a light bulb for $15 that you had to crank to move the film from reel to reel for viewing. All the kids in the neighborhood would come around to watch us crank up the movies on this old projector using our garage wall as a screen. We would crank fast for some scenes and slow down for others. We would watch them over and over and over with as much enthusiasm as if it were the first time. One afternoon while several kids and I were watching a movie, my foster mother walked in and saw us. Without any explanation, she said what we were doing was wrong, and she destroyed all of our film and carried off my projector.

I ran away from home all the time after bad beatings, and at first I would run down to the railroad yards, get into the box cars that contained trash and hide. You'd see a lot of guys hiding there running away from home. In particular, there was a boy named Mufich who I'd see all the time, and they told me later he was smoking and his cigarette caught the trash on fire and he burned himself alive in one of those box cars.

When I would run away from home after getting a beating, I'd go down to the railroad yards and sleep in a caboose. I slept there when I was afraid to go home because I knew I'd get another beating. There were mattresses in the caboose with blankets and pillows. An engineer caught me and asked me if I had run away from home. I told him I got a beating and just took off from home, and he said it was okay for me to sleep there, so I kept it up for quite a while.

I always walked through the alleys back then because you could see a lot more things that were going on. I saw who was running out the back door of whose house and different stuff lying around in the yard to steal later on. I remember once seeing an old woman leaning over a burning trash barrel throwing paper money into the fire. I found out later that they said she was just going through the change and acting funny and weird.

My friend Jimmy and I were running away from home one night and just hopped the train, jumping right on behind the coal car. We fell asleep and ended up in Omaha, Nebraska. When the train finally stopped and we got off, we had to laugh at ourselves because we were solid black, covered with the soot from the smokestack from top to bottom. When we got there, we ate a big stack of flapjacks and all the coffee you could drink for a dime. We stayed in Omaha until Sunday night with a Croatian family Jimmy knew, then headed back to Kansas City by hopping another train so we'd get to work on time Monday at the packing house. Jimmy's dad was my foreman, and he timed us both in because he knew that we were together and we were going to be late.

We made fifteen cents an hour at Armour's packing house where Jimmy's dad was our boss. We worked alongside a black couple who lived nearby down on Central and James Street. A couple of times when I had too much heat on me, they let me stay at their house until things cooled down.

One night I ran away and walked across the intercity viaduct to Kansas City, Missouri to a "flop house" called the Workman's Hotel at 10th and Main. For 10 cents a night you would get one blanket and a mattress on the floor. During the night a guy with a stick came along, and he'd hit you with the stick if you got off your mattress and onto another guy's mattress. For a quarter you could get you a real bed with two blankets on it.

St. John's Catholic Church at Fourth and Barnett Avenue is a very steep hill in the center of Strawberry hill. The street used to be nothing but mud with huge stones and rocks that had grass growing around them that people carried and placed in the dirt themselves so they could walk up and down the hill. The rough rock made it impossible to drive a vehicle on those streets. So when the cops chased us, we ran down the hill to get away, knowing they couldn't drive on it, and they wouldn't get out of their car and chase us either.

The Croatian women would tie a rag in a crown on their heads and with empty feed sacks go down to the railroad yards and pick up grain that had dropped from the grain cars to feed their chickens. They would balance discarded railroad ties on their heads, putting their hands on their hips, and carry the ties back up the steep hill in a path that would zig-zag like a trail up a mountain. One old man would get the creosote railroad ties and cut them up to burn as firewood in his house.

One morning we were driving back to Kansas from stealing over on the Missouri side the night before when the cops stopped us. They searched the car and found our guns, and one was a .457 Magnum. One cop asked, "Where's the wheels to this thing? It's as big as a cannon." Red popped off and told him, "I'm the wheels to that son-of-a-bitch." With that remark, they hauled our asses off to jail. When we got to the police station, I asked if I could use the restroom, and I guess the cop forgot about the window in there and that was the last time that guy saw me.

I was sitting in the house when the front doorbell rang. I went to the door and saw no one there. It happened quite often, and I just thought that it was kids in the neighborhood playing a prank. One afternoon I was pulling up in front of the house parking my car and looked up on the porch, and there was our big yellow house cat the size of a small dog sitting on the bannister. He would take his paw and ring the front doorbell, then run into the nearby bushes. My foster father opened the door and looked out, saying, "Is that you, kitty cat?" Then the cat jumped out of the bushes and ran into the house.

Cops were always on the take back then because they never got any real pay in those days; all they got were grocery scripts to live on. I remember when they would even let the high yellow whores work on 12th Street in Kansas City, Missouri, just so they could get their cut from her profits, and that was something back in those days since they didn't let black whores work downtown at all.

You'd see a cop sitting in his patrol car talking to a hooker, but when she got a customer she'd leave, then she'd return in a few minutes, give the cop his cut, and they would just continue talking again.

There was one robbery that we did, and it came out in the newspapers that it was a well-planned job. Hell, we didn't plan anything; we just went in to rob them. Glenn Holmes was a big supermarket at Seventh and State Avenue in Kansas City, Kansas. We had a Studebaker; it had a slow pickup, but once you got it going you could go like hell. It was a big long car with 8 cylinders and all 8 cylinders were in one straight line on the motor. We walked into the store and we were going to rob the cashier, but there was a guy sitting at the desk named Glenn Holmes. We knew he had two other stores, but didn't know he had just picked up the money from both of them and was coming to this store for its money, then heading for the bank. I picked up a package of money wrapped up in newspaper lying on his desk in front of him. It was $2,000 and we couldn't believe it. They kept saying in the paper that it was a well-planned job, but hell, we just got lucky. We hopped into the Studebaker, and it was so damn slow we barely got away. We were rich and headed for a whorehouse over on the Missouri side to count up the money and make the split.

I went out and bought myself another new car at Simon Wiles Buick in Missouri, and it wasn't worth a shit. Big luxurious car, but it had no pickup and go, and I needed something fast to make my getaways.

In those days no one had money, and the car dealers tried to get you to put 50 cents down to buy a used car. Some of them I bought were only $50 up to $150. The dealers had them sitting in the car lots and wanted to get rid of them, so they sold them to anyone who had the 50 cents to put down, because they knew that if you missed a payment they'd get it back and sell it over again.

There was a guy named Frankie Kovach who was a good friend of mine, and there was an optical shop in Kansas City, Missouri at 10th and Grand Avenue where he worked. I can remember when he would bum rides from me across the Intercity Viaduct every day to go to work. He was working for $2 a week at the optical shop. He worked there so long that when the guy quit the business he gave the optical shop to Frankie. When I needed glasses, he just gave them to me. He has a copy of our graduation picture, and I had a black eye in that picture, and my hand and arm was black and blue where I held it up over my face trying to protect myself from the old man's beating.

Red Bodner, Sam Ricketts and I dressed up like clowns on Halloween one year and had our shotguns hidden inside our costumes. We robbed Montgomery Wards and a few other places on Minnesota Avenue in Kansas City, Kansas and made a pretty good haul. We ran through the back alleys to make our getaway with all the loot from the scores. We were in an apartment lying low — Red, Sam and I — and all of a sudden there was a knock at the door. We were all startled because no one was supposed to know we were there, and our first thought was "cops." I boosted Red up to look out the transom above the door to see who it was, and it was a little kid with funny glasses and a cape dressed for Halloween trick or treating. He scared the shit out of us, but I gave him a couple of bucks and told him to get the hell away from our door and don't come back or send any friends.

Back in my day, you didn't need to have a legal driver's license; all you needed was a bill of sale. If you did go to the courthouse for a license, there was no test — you just asked for a driver's license showing the bill of sale and they'd give it to you.

Salvation Army was always around to help the guys in jail back then when they would visit the jails on Saturday nights for prayer meetings. One guy from Leavenworth had been in jail for a couple of months and his family didn't know where he was. He didn't have any money to give to the cop who arrested him, so he wasn't allowed a phone call. The guy asked Salvation Army visitors to please notify his parents of where he was. Salvation Army drove directly to Leavenworth that night to his parents' house to let them know where he was, and it wasn't long after that when his parents paid his bond and got him out.

I was in jail with a guy who stole big dump trucks all over the city and used them to get a contract with the state of Kansas to fix and repair Highway 7. If the heat came around the construction site, he just took off and left the poor workers who were driving the hot dump trucks there to face the music.

When you walked down Main Street in the late 1920s and early '30s, you'd see all these hustling broads sitting inside the front windows of every building on the block. They would start tapping on the glass with a quarter as you walked by to get your attention to get you inside for your business. All the windows had one spot that was scratched and marred where they tapped so consistently to get your attention at you walked by.

In those days, Eighth and Walnut was wide open and they had women hustlers walking the streets in front of a group of picture studios that you could take one into. She would lift up her skirt and take a picture for you and with you for a buck or two.

Back in 1929, three Dagos robbed the City National Bank and were making their getaway down a crowded street. There were no street lights, and traffic cops stood out in the middle of the street on a little stand and would signal you to stop or go. Well, the driver of the getaway car hit and killed the traffic cop named Happy Smith while speeding away. Happy Smith was a popular guy and would bring a lot of smiles to both pedestrians and drivers alike every day while on the job, and the entire city loved him. The door handle fell off their car when they hit him, and it had serial numbers on it, and that's how they were able to trace these guys. The Johnson County jail used to be in the City Market district, and it had no round bars at that time; it was flat steel slats instead. Anyway, they hung all three of these guys in this big room in the county jail at the same time. There were a lot of stories in the local paper about it at that time because of the popularity of Happy

Smith. Everyone thought that the entire Italian community would have an uprising over the hangings, but nothing ever happened.

I was getting ready to do a score by myself in Olathe and wanted to steal a car for the getaway. I was working on starting the car in a driveway when the guy and his kid came running out of the house, and he was holding a shotgun. He led me into his garage and told me to stay there until he called the police. I have a hard time standing still hearing those words and having a shotgun pointed at me, so I looked around and spotted an open window. I took a chance and leaped past the guy and dove right out of the window. As I was running away, I could hear the police sirens coming from all directions, so I stayed off of all the main roads. I knew my directions, so I ran through the woods toward the railroad tracks. Once I got on the tracks, I walked 25 miles back to Kansas City along those tracks. It's awkward as hell to get started to get the rhythm to run on the railroad ties at first but, believe me, I got good at it by the time I got home.

Another time Harry Savage and I were driving around in this hot Oldsmobile with hot tags in Olathe, Kansas. We came up to this square, and two girls were singing: "I'm in love with you, honey." We picked them up and drove around and tried to put the make on them, but they wouldn't go for it. So what we did was drive down to the Country Club Plaza and left them sitting in that hot car. We told them we'd be right back, but we left and caught a streetcar and went home.

Back in those days, there was a car named REO. What that stood for was Rand E. Olds. That was the guy who invented and built all the Oldsmobile cars back then. The 16-cylinder Cadillacs made at that time had jump seats in the back. A Franklin automobile had a water-cooled engine that was so silent you couldn't even hear the motor when the car was running.

There was a store on 18th and Central Avenue in Kansas where you could buy a cop uniform for a couple of bucks. Hell, you could get a three-piece suit for $9. We got the cop uniform and a big brimmed hat just like the highway patrol wore, along with phony badges, and headed out. We started hitting joints in Lawrence, Kansas, first because we knew they all had illegal slot machines in the back rooms or basements. We'd storm in like we were cops, telling them to step aside while we removed the illegal machines. They were so heavy we had to tip them over and dump some of the coins out of them before we could haul them off. There was a plumbing store in the Italian neighborhood that was a front for the largest quantity of slot machines in the city. We'd take all the machines over to them to put in bars and places all around the city. All the coins we got out of the machines were nickels, and we had bushel baskets of them, and they were heavy. We'd make good deals for stores and bars to take them off our hands, and everyone took them without hesitation. I even got $125 in nickels out of just one machine, and all the others had a lot of money in them, too.

I went to the Harvey House at the Union Station one morning to eat breakfast, and while I was looking at the menu, someone said, "Hello, Mr. Radkay." I looked up, and it was Helen Cigich working there as a waitress. Her father was Captain Joe Cigich of the Kansas City, Kansas police department and a good friend of the family. I asked her what time she got off, and she told me noon, so I waited around to take her home. We started dating, and I took her to work every day so she didn't have to wait by the curb at four a.m. in the morning to ride the streetcar, and I would pick her up at noon and take her home.

Helen was known as a beauty queen because she won the contest for being the prettiest girl at St. John's School. Her father didn't resent me dating her and became quite a friend when I got into trouble. When I went with Joe Cigich's daughter, I took her brother with me to the wrestling matches every Monday night. A guy who worked with us at the packing house named Shaster promoted tickets to Memorial Hall wrestling matches. I would get the tickets, and my buddy and I would take Henry Cigich, Helen's brother, with us every Monday night. Ed "Strangler" Lewis was world champ at that time. Most of the guys who wrestled were champions. Jumping Joe Savoldi, who used to play football for Notre Dame, kicked like a kangaroo with both feet into a guy's chest, knocked him backward, then pinned him down on the mat. One Indian guy from the Haskell School that they called "Roebuck" split his head when he was thrown right into the corner post and died right there on the mat.

Jo Cigich, the captain of police in Kansas City, Kansas, would not let any cop put me in a lineup unless he was present. Then he would tell the robbery victims who were there to try to identify the thief that the robbery itself only took a couple of minutes and what do they want to do, look at these guys all night? They wanted to see the guy in a lineup with a different hat or coat, and Joe would get mad and tell them the lineup was over. Sometimes he would even put someone else up in the lineup, using my name and keeping me from getting picked.

There was a guy named C.A. SaLee who owned a drug store at 18th and Central Avenue. He would always say he was robbed and in front of a lineup he always picked out a kid who he said did it and the poor kid would do time for the robbery. They finally arrested SaLee and found out he was the one taking the money and all of the drugs and just pinning it on some poor innocent kid in the lineup.

Cops had 10-gauge riot guns with short barrels in all the police cars back then, and at night they just put them in a metal box that was between the seats and put a padlock on them. They used to park the cars in the alley behind the police station until we broke the locks and got about three of the riot guns. Then they started locking the guns up in the police garage and kept the garage locked up at night.

I was in jail this one weekend, and my foster mother made a call to the Captain Joe Cigich and asked him if there was anything he could do to help me get out of jail. He made one phone call to city hall, and within minutes they had me out of there and back home. When I had charges on me, Captain Cigich would never let me show up in court; he always took me back to the judge's chambers to work things out. Captain Cigich hoped that I'd straighten out one day, continue to see his daughter, and some day we'd get married.

My first cousin, John Carr, was the district Judge for Wyandotte County back then. When I went before him in court one time, he actually pressed perjury charges against the cop who arrested me and cut me loose.

I was in Kansas City, Missouri on Prospect and Independence Avenue at a corner drugstore where we used to just hang around. You could buy cheap soda pop by the gallon down there. I was hanging around down there, and a guy named Smitty saw me and set me up and snitched me off by calling the cops.

Back then, upstairs from the Roma Bakery they sold what they called "Policy Game." It was a penny lottery that you could win a dollar, five dollars or ten dollars. All the blacks and everybody else in the neighborhood would buy those tickets, and they were as big as a grocery receipt is now, and the next morning you'd see thousands of them on the sidewalks. What happened was I saw the cops coming toward the drugstore and took off running and, hell, there were cop cars everywhere. I kept running until I saw a little boy playing in front of the steps to this apartment and ran over to where he was. There was a broom leaning up against the steps, and I picked it up and started sweeping. The cops were flying by left and right, and I wanted to crap my pants, but kept cool and just swept the sidewalk with my head down. People started to gather around watching the police drive by back and forth, and I heard some woman say, "I wonder who they are looking for." The little boy that I was standing next to pointed to me and said, "I think they're looking for him." I just smiled and walked away calmly, then took off in a run to get back to the Kansas side. I was just glad it worked and I got away from cops again.

I was walking down Minnesota Avenue heading for the drugstore when a woman came running up to me asking for help. She was covered from head to toe in these big red bumps that had scabs on them. She said that she had no money and the druggist would not give her anything to help. She pleaded with me to help her, so I walked inside and told the druggist I didn't know her but I sure felt sorry for her and would gladly pay for some medication that could help her out. She had both poison ivy and poison sumac and had been suffering for days. They gave her all the medication she needed, and hell, it wasn't but a few bucks to help her out and get her well. She wanted to give me her address so I could go to her house for her to pay me back, but I told her that I didn't need it.

When we would visit whorehouses, we'd usually check in our guns at the desk before seeing the girls. I was so proud of my little .32 caliber pistol as I laid it up on the desk for the madam to see. She said, "Oh, that's such a cute gun." Then she said, "But this is a real gun," and she pulled out a .41 Colt and laid it on the table alongside my little .32 revolver, and that son-of-a-bitch was so big it looked like it needed wheels to haul it around.

In those days the madams would take the money from the girls working for them and fold it up and put it in their cotton hose that were rolled down just below the knees. The better the madam, the more money that was sticking out of her stockings. So my buddy and I were going to rob an old madam who did a good business and get all the money hanging out of her stockings. We went up the steps to her place with our guns drawn and told her to give us all her cash. She started screaming at us, calling us little sons-a-bitches, and told us to get the hell outta her place before she killed us. She took off her high-heeled shoe and began beating us both on the head. As she chased us down the steps, we were running for our lives, trying to get out of the place. She kept knocking us in the head with her high-heeled shoe, and we'd bounce from one side of the wall to the other, smashing the plaster-board on the way down and taking big chunks of the plaster with us, exposing the wooden slats left on the wall. You can bet we never went back to that whorehouse again and were just glad we got out of there with our lives. We were both 15 years old at the time.

Red and I were sitting at the bar in a gambling joint, and a black whore sat down next to us and started counting her quarters. Red grabbed all her quarters and ran and, hell, I had to run out with him. The whore chased us both down the street after her money. Red said he scooped $25 in change off the bar on that one.

Another time Red and I were sitting in the pool hall when a guy walked in wearing a raccoon coat. He took it off and hung it on a hook on the wall, and just about the time he finished the lights went off. Seconds later when the lights came back on, both Red and the raccoon coat were gone.

During the depression, even housewives had to prostitute to make money for food. I remember one woman who would lay all the family pictures face down on the dressers at her house until after we left. She said she would only do one at a time and the price was 50 cents, which was a hell of a lot of money back in those days. We even had one old lady who would let us stay at her house for 15 cents an hour when we had heat on us and couldn't go home. We'd sit around and play cards until it got dark, and then we would head for home.

A bunch of us kids had a lot of heat on us one time, and the cops were driving all around the neighborhood looking for us to take us to jail. I got tired of jumping from one place to another trying to keep out of sight, so I went through the back alleys, staying off of the main streets and sneaked inside the police garage. I went to a far corner, rolled underneath an old police truck parked there and went to sleep until dark, then went back home when the coast was clear.

Times were tough back then and people had no money. The people who couldn't make it would all go up to a market up on Sixth Street between Sandusky and Tauromee Avenue. The market had a big over-hang roof, and I saw them pass out free food bags of flour and oatmeal to those in need. It was rough in those days; the only places that had money were the bootleggers. The only reason I had money was be-cause I was stealing it from the bootleggers.

My mother and stepfather, Steve Tomasegovich, bought a Studebaker car with disc wheels back in the 1920s. They moved to Independence, Missouri, and they always let me drive the car when I would go visit them.

After a trip to visit relatives in Kansas City, Kansas, they were heading back to Independence when the car ran out of gas. My stepfa-ther didn't know that you had to put gasoline in a car to keep it run-ning. It was quite an ordeal being stranded on a country road back then, so he sold the car soon after that.

I remember once we went up to Lawrence, Kansas to sell some bootleg whiskey and stopped at a carnival show with a big ferris wheel. They had a revival tent, and we went in and watched how one guy was in a wheelchair on stage. Then they gave him some "Vitola" that they were selling for a dollar a bottle, prayed over him, and the guy got up outta the wheelchair and started to walk, which made everyone stand and yell, "Halleluiah! Praise the Lord." A few weeks later we noticed that they were setting up a carnival right at the bottom of Fifth Street in our neighborhood with ferris wheel and all. We went to the revival tent, and we saw the same old guy in the wheelchair get up and walk again after drinking the Vitola. Everyone would be buying that Vitola for a dollar a bottle, thinking it would heal and cure everything. Back then, they only had gaslights at the carnivals for lighting. They had a can of gas with a big metal reflector behind the two-foot flame directing the light toward the main attraction. We'd show up every evening and tell the guy we saw him do this same thing in Lawrence, Kansas. He'd throw us guys some quarters and tell us to get the hell outta there.

We would hit up to three drugstores a night, and the takes would be about $15 to $20 each. Once during a holdup at a drugstore in St. Joseph, Missouri, some guys shot and killed a druggist. They took me in, but I was cleared, and three guys from Missouri were all charged for the crime about a week later.

We cased a guy on the way to the bank every day for over a week with the money from his two movie theaters. He always had a brown paper package with him on the way to the bank, and we just knew the money was inside. We went to rob him, so we just drove up alongside of him walking to the bank, and with our guns drawn on him told him to just throw the package into the car. He threw the package into the car, so we made our getaway and drove to a safe place to open up the package. When we opened it up to split the money, all it contained was a cut-up bloody chicken with no money in it at all.

The Midway Theater in Kansas City, Kansas was called the "Garlic" theater because of the smell. I remember selling bootleg liquor to the owner and bringing it in the back door of the theater while the movie was going on out in front. We would stack all the five-gallon jugs right in back of the screen from the floor to the ceiling.

I used to have a lot of money on me, and the old man and old lady would always search my clothes or try to find where I'd hide the money in the house so they could take it. They had a religious statue on a little shelf on the wall, and I would hide some big bills behind it. I would also roll back the rug under the dining room table and place big bills on the floor and roll the rug back out. They never knew that they had so much money at their feet while they ate, and once I even hid about $9,000 under the rug. I tried to bury my money at first, but had so damn many spots with money in coffee cans I couldn't remember where in the hell they all were. Then I started paying a neighbor kid I went to school with a dollar or so to hide maybe $200 at a time. This worked out pretty well, so I got other kids from school to hang onto my money or hide it for me.

The neighbors would all tell me when the police would go into a neighbor's garage nearby and sit and watch my house, waiting for me to come out and take off. What they didn't know was I was able to scale the outside wall of our garage and creep across the valley between the two sloped roofs. Then I'd jump over to the neighbor's roof where I could climb down and take off undetected. I always came back this same way in case they were still watching for me. The valley of the two sloped roofs connected the house to the garage, and several times when the cops came looking for me I'd just climb up there and lay flat until they left because you couldn't see me if you were walking around the house on the ground.

The fireplace in the Radki's house was huge and opened up on both sides to heat the front room and kitchen. I got trapped in the house one time when the cops were coming in to search for me and scaled up inside the chimney and held myself there, waiting until they left.

Back in Kansas City, Kansas, past Fifth and Central Avenue, there was an area they called a "hollow" where little shacks sat on stilts on muddy slopes. There was an old lady named Simmons whom we would go down to see, and she would let us hide our booze at her place for a couple of dollars. She was an old whore, and one time she had a guy in the back with her. Her son was sitting out on the front porch drunk as hell, yelling out, "Hey, Mom, when ya gonna give me some?" We hid our booze around her place, then beat the shit out of her son for what he said about his mother and left.

The newspapers had a story of a guy who kidnapped a little 12-year-old girl, took her into the woods and raped her. When the cops found him, he was still on top of the little girl. With all of them surrounding him, with their guns drawn, he calmly got up off the little girl, laughing and saying, "I guess you're going to haul me off to jail, aren't you? I know I can beat this rap in court." With that comment, one of the cops just fired off a shot right between his eyes, and the newspapers said: "Judge and Jury, case closed." They never did a thing to the cop who shot him.

All the girls in the neighborhood put the word out that they should go on a date with Willie. They all say that he takes you out and shows you a good time at the best places in town. He doesn't mind spending a lot of money on a gal, and later he doesn't try to get it out of you. The other guys who just spend a quarter on them will try to squeeze it out of them later.

If a gal gets too drunk when she is with me, I just make sure she gets home safely and never touch her, because I believe you should never take advantage of any woman in that way. If she don't want to, she doesn't have to, and there are many of them out there that would, so it didn't matter to me.

We met a guy who was pimping for his two sisters. He'd get them sloppy drunk, screw them himself, then pimp them out and keep all the money, not even sharing it with them. We beat the shit outta him every time we saw him. We hated any guy who had to get a girl drunk to screw her, especially his sisters.

Dago Dan, a buddy of mine, used to go with me to a whorehouse on 12th Street in Missouri. The two girls had just let us in the room when someone knocked on the door. It was their pimp, and he told us to leave and said the girls had to stay. Dan and I walked out into the hall and saw the scared look in their eyes as they shoved the pimp out into the hall toward us and slammed the door. It's illegal to carry brass knuckles, but I carried a padlock in my pocket for the same purpose. We really worked the guy over and told him to leave the girls alone and get out of town. Months later, Dan and I saw the girls working down on the Country Club Plaza, and they thanked us for helping them get away from him. They said we really worked him over pretty good and knocked out all his teeth.

I wanted to learn how to fly a plane so if we needed to make a getaway we could stay off of the main highways and still get out of town. I went down to the Fairfax Airport, which was just a blacktop runway back then, and got a flight instructor. The plane was a DeHavelin gasoline single-engine plane that had an automobile motor in it. The plane was a salvaged reject from World War I, and this is what was used before the rotary engine. I paid him $600 for a book of coupons that were my lessons to take to finish the course. Hell, it's easy to go up, but the landing is a bitch. You're supposed to make a three-point landing — that's putting all three wheels down on the runway at the same time. The instructor and I were in the air, and he tapped me on the head. Hell, I thought that meant for me to take over the plane and I did. I was heading straight for the ground and pulled back to go straight up and then went into a spin that I didn't expect and headed for the ground again. I flew out over the river, then tried to kill my speed to come down for a landing, but I just couldn't do it. I could always make a one-point landing and nothing else, so that's how I finally landed the plane. After several lessons my instructor took my book of coupons and ripped them up, throwing them into the air, and told me to stay on the ground and give up trying to fly. I took his advice.

Across the street from the Kansas City, Kansas Public Library was a Kresge's dime store on Minnesota Avenue. I wanted to burglarize the place one night, so I went up to the roof and opened the air vent and was about to drop down inside, but stopped when I heard a noise. I closed the air vent back down and walked to the front of the store, leaning over the roof, and saw a burglar alarm on the wall going off with a loud, bong, bong, bong, bong. I ran to get down from the roof and went across the street to the library's park and lay down on the grass to watch and wait to see what would happen and how long it would take the cops to get there. About 45 minutes went by and no one had showed up yet, and the alarm was dying down to a bong … bong … bong. It got so low you could hardly hear it; then it finally stopped. No one ever did show up, but I postponed the score for another time.

The Old Soldiers Home was in Wadsworth, Kansas, and all the old guys got their pension checks on the third of the month. There was a streetcar called the String-line that would go from Kansas City, Kansas to Wadsworth for 30 cents. You would see the streetcars filled with whores from the city riding up to the Old Soldiers Home to help them spend their checks and have a good time. This ritual went on every month for many years.

Armour's had a place called Moore's Packing Company just south of the Central Avenue viaduct. It was a big plant, but separate from the main Armour's packing house. We watched a guy for weeks, and on Mondays he would haul all the money back to the main plant. Red Bodner and I caught the Armour Packing Company messenger down on Central Avenue and James Street. He was a black guy who thought he was a hero and came out with a gun. He thought he would stop us by flashing it, but we tricked him and started shooting up in the air first. All the streetcars and cars going up and down the nearby streets even stopped to watch the shooting and robbery. We just started firing first; we didn't mess around. We were just shooting outright, but this guy still came out with his gun in his hand over his head, and we continued shooting and that's how we took his gun away along with the money. We took the money, and it was $19,000. It would be in the old newspapers; we need to go look at those old reels in the library. In the paper they said that we had a machine gun, but hell, all we had was a sawed-off shotgun, not a machine gun. We knew all about the black security guard and messenger and how he had shot a couple of guys trying to rob him before, so we just started shooting right from the start because we didn't want to get shot ourselves. We went down to a place on Kansas Avenue to split the money and we were rich again.

After the armored car robbery, I went to Kelly Repperd Ford in Kansas City, Missouri and bought myself a brand new 1931 Yellow Ford Roadster for $550. I told everyone it was a $500 car with $5,000 worth of extras on it. I had them put on a Frontinac head with over-sized valves and front gear. They had to take the fenders off and put on balloon tires with the center hub as big as a volleyball. We wanted to take off the Ford tires and replace them with the Chevy tires and springs for racing because they would ride anywhere in mud, water and more. I bought the most expensive wire wheels possible to put on my new Roadster. The grill was even changed along with the headlights, plus an extra battery and extra voltage regulator installed. It had two spare tires, one on each side that was low into the fender running board; they called them fender well spares. The hood couldn't be opened until the spare tires were removed from each side. I also had them install some brand new "Wood" headlights shaped like a football that were about 12 inches long and three inches wide and brighter than anything they had in that day. No cars had radios in them back in those days, but I had one put in my yellow roadster and even in the rumbleseat. I never needed to put a police radio in my car because all I ever had to do was look in the rear view mirror, and there they were right behind me.

When you wanted to buy your car tags back in the '30, all you needed was a receipt of purchase for the car. What they used were the order pads that a waitress would use in a little cafe or coffee shop when she wrote down your order. You just fill it out and take it to the courthouse and get the tags. They didn't even care if you had a driver's license back then to get the license tag. In those days you could steal a car on Minnesota Avenue and drive it all around on Central Avenue (about a 10-block difference) without any trouble or worry of getting caught.

Back in the 1920s and '30s there were at least a hundred homes on

This picture is from the Ford Motor Company Archives. It is the same 1931 Ford Deluxe Sport Roadster that Willie purchased, but his was yellow.

the hills surrounding the church on Strawberry Hill. All of the houses had the view of the river and the intercity viaduct that spanned the Kaw River into Missouri. It was possible for anyone who looked up toward the intercity viaduct to see my bright yellow Roadster going across the bridge in either direction.

None of the cops from Kansas City, Kansas or Kansas City, Missouri could ever catch me when I made a getaway in that Ford Roadster. It was the fastest thing on the road anywhere. Every night just for the fun of it I'd travel out to 32 Highway or old Muncie Drive which was a dirt road south of the city and race the El Capitan train that ran along the tracks adjacent to the highway. There was never any doubt in my mind about beating that train, even though it was running at full speed. I loved to race against that train, throwing the transmission into gear and going as fast as the Roadster would go down the highway, leaving the train as a small disappearing object in my rear view mirror.

My foster parents would drive all over the city looking for my bright yellow Roadster and stop and ask me for money all the time. I was at my brother-in-law's sister's house on Seventh Street, and here they came wanting money. I finally gave them a small wad of bills just to get them off my ass and leave me alone. They ended up buying themselves a car and even had a stone garage built for my new yellow Roadster. I also had them keep $5,000 for me in the bank just in case

I needed some bond money. They always got me out on bond when I went to jail because they knew that I would pay them back and more.

In 1931 you could buy the hit song of the week for 10 cents. It was a paper record that would play on the record player at least four or five times. Records were real expensive back then and were about a quarter-inch thick and only one side could be played, plus most people just couldn't afford them.

We were getting so daring in our robberies, it was just a matter of time before we got caught. What did me in was the time we robbed Leaders Clothing Store up on Minnesota Avenue on a busy Saturday afternoon. There was no place to park out in front of the store, so we parked across the street in front of the public library. A witness put all three of us in the store that afternoon; we didn't wear masks or anything, just boldly walked across the street and into the store, and I yelled, "Reach for the rafters." We were getting so bold by that time we thought we were so invincible and that all those stores were just there for us to rob. Red Bodner, Charlie York and I got $3,000 from that score that afternoon. Red took the money for us to split later, but I got pinched before I got home and taken to jail and thrown in a lineup and was identified by quite a few people who were able to put me inside the store during the robbery. When I was sitting in jail, I couldn't believe it, but my lawyer said my foster parents weren't willing to pay for my bail. I found out later that the old man was driving my yellow Ford Roadster and damn near killed himself a couple of times because of all the speed and power it had, and he couldn't handle it. My foster parents ended up selling my Ford Roadster and didn't even consider using that money from selling the car or the $5,000 I had in the bank for bond money to get me out.

Red and Charlie brought my split of the take up to the lawyer, and he did as much as he could. The lawyer said I didn't have a chance; they wanted to lock me up real bad, and I would have to do some time in the Kansas State Reformatory in Hutchinson, Kansas.

3

Kansas State Reformatory
Hutchinson, Kansas

IT WAS A Godsend when I went to the Hutchinson Reformatory and was able to get away from my foster parents. I was able to see and realize then what control they had over me.

I went to the Hutchinson Reformatory when I was 19 years old. I remember an old nurse in the reformatory who told me, "Drop your strides." I dropped my strides because I figured the old lady just wanted to see what God gave little boys. The old bitch had broomstick legs and a big fat ass. I had been to whorehouses, so it didn't bother me to show her everything I had.

On arrival they gave me a big gunnysack filled with straw that had a piece of string tied around the top. I was led to the cell house, and on entering my cell was told that the wooden bench was my bunk and the sack of straw was my mattress. Hell, it was a big round sack, and you had to stomp on it and roll on it to flatten it to make it a half-ass mattress to sleep on. You didn't know where they came from, but the son-of-a-bitch was always full of bugs and fleas, and they were always crawling all over you. Periodically you were given some stinky shit to rub all over you to kill the bugs, but hell, it only worked for a short time.

The dining room ran on what they called a silent system, which meant once you entered and sat down they would ring a big bell, which meant complete silence during the entire meal.

Hutch is where I met Alvin Karpavicz, a Slovak who later became known as "Creepy" Karpis on Alcatraz. He came to Hutch the same year I did and began working in the kitchen and became a baker's helper. He was born in Canada and was a Canadian citizen, but it was only because his mother was visiting Canada at the time. The family is actually from Topeka, Kansas, and that's where he grew up and got into trouble and was sent to Hutchinson Reformatory.

I worked on the machines in there, and I'm the guy who made the highway signs, the big stop signs. When I came out there to the factory, I saw a bunch of guys with bandages on their hands, and I found out later it was from trying to make their daily quotas on the press machine that drops the big blade down and cuts the metal. They would get in a hurry to pull the cut metal out and put the next one to be cut in before the blade came down, and some guys didn't make it. It was mandatory back then you had to make a daily quota for any kid to get five days of good time a month taken off their sentence. I met a kid named Steel and another named Anthony who had their hands all bandaged from losing their fingers. In later years after I got out, it was a big scandal in all the newspapers about the public forcing the state to shut the presses down to prevent from maiming any more kids. *The Kansas City Star* newspaper talked about all those big presses and the fact that a lot of kids lost fingers and hands working with them. When they lost a hand, the state would give them $1,000 and a parole back home.

When I would make highway signs, it was different steel. I had to cut with two dies that they called male and female. The male die cut the letters out, and the female cut them out of the big sheets of metal. Then you riveted them in there and they went down to the presses where it pressed them out. I also made motorcycle tags when I was down there, and I saw lots of kids get their fingers and hands cut off from working on them. They were small vertical license plates back then, not horizontal like today. Hutch superintendent of the tag factory was a guy named Fuque who wore a 10-gallon cowboy hat and cowboy boots and was from Medicine Lodge, Kansas. He said that when I first came in that I was to be watched because he was told I was violent and an escape risk. He ended up liking me, and since I had a good handwriting, he made me his clerk in the machine shop office. So when the hacksaws would break, the guys brought in all the pieces to me to record their return. I always took just one of the broken pieces and passed it around to the guys who said they wanted to try to saw through the bars. Like I said, everyone in the tag factory had to make a daily quota to receive five days of good time every month. With me as the clerk, I made sure that all the kids were written down for hitting the daily quota so they didn't have to hurry to try to get it by losing fingers and hands in the process.

I never tried to break out of Hutch because they had us securely inside the building locked up in our cells, plus they had so many guards and snitches down there it would be stupid to try. The convicts were the worst snitches of all, and you had to watch yourself every minute.

There was one guy from Arkansas who worked out on the farm until the guards found him screwing the hogs. They brought him back inside, and every time he walked in the dining room, someone would holler out, "Here, piggy, piggy, suey, suey!" I walked in on him in the bathroom one time; none of the stalls had doors and I saw that his feet were on top of the toilet seat and he was squatting down taking a shit. He saw me and just got up pulled up his trousers and walked out, and I doubt that he even wiped his ass.

I met a kid named Leo Stern in there, a good-looking, blonde, curly-haired kid that was crippled. I made friends with him while we were in there, and later I saw him in Kansas City waiting on the corner. I asked him if he wanted a ride, and he said yes, that he had to go check his girls out. I found out later the guy was a pimp with a couple of girls. He asked me if I'd go in this house and get his girl and tell her he wanted to see her. I said yes, so we drove up to this place, and I just walked into this house where a big old rough-looking guy was sitting at the kitchen table reading a newspaper. The guy looked at me in a strange way when I asked for the girl and where she was. He said she was upstairs, so I just walked right up to her room, knocked on the door, then told her about Leo being downstairs. She couldn't believe that I walked right into her father's house and came up to her bedroom. That damn Leo set me up because he was afraid to go in there because her old man was known for knocking the shit out of any guy that came after his daughter.

When I attended church services in Hutch on Sundays, the minister would shake uncontrollably while talking during the service. I listened intensely as he read this poem called "Invictus." I took it as my motto then and even have it hanging on my wall today.

INVICTUS
By William Earnest Henley, 1849-1903

Out of the night that covers me,
Black as the Pit from pole to pole,
I thank whatever Gods may be
For my unconquerable soul.

In the fell clutch of circumstance
I have not winced nor cried aloud,
Under the bludgeonings of chance
My head is bloody, but unbowed.

Beyond this place of wrath and tears
Looms but the horror of the shade,
And yet the menace of the years
Finds, and shall find me, unafraid.

It matters not how strait the gate,
How charged with punishment the scroll,
I am the master of my fate;
I am the captain of my soul.

I had a big-time lawyer in Kansas City who got my time cut short for a price. I was sentenced to Hutchinson reformatory for 10-21 years for highway robbery, and he was able to get me out in a couple of years. So when I was getting short, they gave me an easy job of taking food down to the guys in D-cell house.

I'd go into the kitchen and get food for the guys in the hole and walk past a guard who would check every tray I was carrying out to the guys on my way back out of the kitchen. This guard sat up behind a tall three-sided desk leading to the kitchen. I always carried a piece of string tied onto my shoe with a paper clip on the other end when I went by the guard into the kitchen. I'd drop the string in the kitchen and get the trays and walk back by the guard at the desk, leaving for the hole. The guys in the kitchen would hook the paper clip to a shoe box that they filled with some ham, cheese or whatever they could give me inside. After the guard checked the trays, I would step out of sight, then get on my knees and pull the string slowly toward me all along the floor in front of the guard's desk without him seeing it or seeing me.

When I was in Hutch, I showed the guys in the kitchen how to make cottage cheese from the fresh milk that they served you back in those days. I used to help my aunt and uncle on their farm in Lawson, Missouri make it all the time. You just take the milk that curdled off the top of the fresh milk and place it in a pillowcase. Hang the pillowcase up somewhere so it could drip dry. When it was dry, you just keep squeezing the pillowcase to break the cottage cheese up into smaller pieces. All of the guys I knew had fresh cottage cheese in the dining room at every meal if they wanted it. We kept it for ourselves and didn't share it with the general population.

They gave me a whole set of keys to open up all the doors to go down to feed all the guys in the hole, in D-cell house. That's when I found out one of the keys fit a lock to a door that led down below the cell house, and I went down there to look for a way to break out.

I stole the keys to the basement off the key ring and just looked around down there all the time for a way to get out of that place. Then I found out from my lawyer that I didn't have much more time to do, so I decided I was never going to use them. I showed the keys to two guys in the hole I was friends with and told them all they had to do was go down into the basement to a big round window leading to the outside to make their break. The bars on that window were so rusty, all you had to do was pull them back and forth to break them loose or bend them up to get out. I asked them to wait until I got out before they made their break since they could put two and two together and pin the missing keys on me. I read in the newspaper after I got out that two guys escaped from the place, and I knew it was them. They sneaked out during a movie one night and got away in the dark. They both got caught months later, and neither one snitched on me as the one who gave them the keys.

Well, with my time served' I was able to get out on parole back to my foster parents' house and back on the streets of Kansas City, Kansas.

4

After Hutch

WHEN I GOT back home, my gang was waiting for me to start casing places for us to rob, so I got right back to pulling scores like I had never left.

We went into a grocery store on Holmes Avenue in Kansas City, Missouri and walked right into the office with our guns drawn. They gave us the money from the safe, then handed us a folded newspaper, which ended up having $3,000 hidden inside it. They thought it was an inside job because they said we knew all about the money in the newspaper. We never did get any heat from that one because they blamed it on a black guy who worked there.

Willie at age 21.

We robbed a drugstore at 18th and Quindaro and got $9,000 and, boy, were we surprised! We found out later it must have been a drug house, so when we'd rob drugstores from then on we started getting morphine sulfate and codeine and traded it to a whore on Central Avenue at the Flat Iron Building for her services.

They called her Tralla or Loretta, and she was a beautiful woman then, and we could only imagine how beautiful she must have been when she was younger. When the cops would come to her asking about me, she told them she'd never tell them anything about me, and she'd hide me out any time I asked her to. Every time we found out that Tralla's pimp beat the shit outta her, we'd find him and beat the shit out of him.

One time I was with Tralla laying low because I had too much heat on me. Tralla heard some noise, and when she looked out the window, she said the cops were out front. She told me to go out the back way, so I ran to the back window, jumped out, and that first step was a doozey. I had no idea it was a six-foot drop, but when I jumped I fell and rolled on the ground. By the time I got up, the cops had come around back and started shooting at me, but I scaled the fence and luckily made my break in one piece.

I met my girlfriend, Alma, back in those days when I used to go to the movies, and she'd always be there with her brother. We went everywhere together and remained close for years, but when I was sent to the joint I told her to forget about me and we went our separate ways. She married and had a family, but later when I got out we still talked and remained friends until her death in 2003. We loved reminiscing about the old days and how it used to be and all of the places we went together. Her parents liked my foster parents and had hoped that someday we'd get married, but it wasn't meant to be. The Electric Theater had vaudeville acts on Saturday night, and we saw a lot of stars back then. I remember when Alma and I saw Brian Dennehy for a 10-cent ticket.

My girlfriend and I used to go to one joint on weekends at 92nd and Holmes that was wide open outside the city limits and had burlesque shows and great bands. There were other joints around 72nd Street, but that used to be the city limits and anything past that was a mud road.

A woman named Louise Boman, who worked at the pharmacy in Katz Drugstore, had a little brother who was known as "Little Jimmy Dickens," a country western singer.

I would go to strip clubs back then and see Fanny Brice dancing on stage.

A Croatian girl named Louise Sachen went to New York and became a burlesque dancer. She returned to Kansas City wearing a blonde wig and going by the name "Queen of Alaska." All the guys went to see her because "she was one of our own."

Andy Divine's parents had a little grocery store at Orchard and Reynolds on the triangle down on Sixth Street. They would tell you all about Andy being Gene Autry's sidekick when you walked in there.

It was Alan Alda's father who was a straight man back then at the Burlesque in Kansas City, Missouri. He was a tall, good-looking man. The Gaze Burlesque had a midnight show that would let the blacks in, but they had to sit up in the balcony. It was on 12th Street in Kansas City, Missouri, where they had five theaters all in one block. There was the Victory, Whirl in Motion, Newman, Pantages and the Regent all down the line door to door. Olson Johnson and his wife were African hunters, and they were down there all the time because they lived right in Kansas City. They would make movies about their safaris and how they captured the animals. They were there with a big lion in a cage out front and were saying, "Step right in for the main show."

I saw Harry Houdini once there at the Pantages. Everyone said that he was a big fake, and these other magicians would tell me how he would do his tricks and how he used twin sisters to saw a lady in half so one would be on one side and then you see her sister come out the other side. Right down on the corner from the Pantages was a bar on the corner, and we would all meet the stars in there for drinks and talk about the shows. The Schubert Theater was on Grand Avenue, and it was for the elite. They had curtains around the balcony seating and a huge lounge area where the people would gather during intermissions or before the show. It was the most luxurious theater to attend in those days, and they had the best shows that traveled throughout the United States.

There was Guy Kibby, the famous comedian, that we'd go to see whenever he was downtown. Ellen Burstyn was another one from this area who made it out in Hollywood; she was a schoolteacher before she became a star.

They'd come right off the stage and come into the bar, so we'd talk and drink with all of them. Alma and I and another couple saw the original "Our Gang" on stage back in the early '20s and wanted to meet them. Knowing they'd exit out the back stage door and not go to the bar, we were all waiting to say hello. Mary, Mickey, Farina, Porky and Joe came out, but they just kept their heads down and walked up the alley to the back door of the hotel where they were staying without saying a word to us when we said hello.

Mickey Rooney's dad used to work at the Burlesque also; his name was "Little Joe Yule." Mickey Rooney lived with his aunt and was raised in Kansas City, Missouri.

Jean Harlow was from Kansas City, Kansas, and her father owned the Brown Photography Studio right across the street from the Electric Theater at Sixth and Minnesota Avenue. Out front was a big square column that had her pictures on all four sides plus a huge picture in the window. She was a brunette back then when she first started out, and her dad took all the photos that were submitted to the studios. She attended Lowell Grade School in Kansas City, Kansas.

Even Joan Crawford used to strip in a burlesque show on 12th Street before she made it out in Hollywood. Her picture used to be on the column at Brown's Photography Studio back then, too.

William Powell worked at Palace Clothing at Ninth and Main selling clothes before he went to Hollywood.

Larry Parks, the guy who played Al Jolson in the first "talkie," was from Olathe, Kansas. I used to have lunch with all of them back then at the Hotel Muehlebach without giving it a second thought, before they got famous and just worked around town.

I knew this kid named Buddy Rodgers whose father was a big-time judge in town. That judge would marry anyone, even 15-year-old kids, and became notorious for it, and all the newspapers started printing negative stories about him. Buddy Rodgers was the guy from Olathe, Kansas who became the movie star who ended up marrying Mary Pickford out in Hollywood.

Alma and I used to go drinking at the Rendezvous Lounge at the Hotel Muehlebach several nights a week and on weekends. Sometimes I would meet and talk to Wallace Berry and his brother Noah Berry after they became movie stars. They lived up on Admiral Boulevard in Kansas City, Missouri. They were all-right guys, and we always had a good conversation about the old days when we were kids selling newspapers up on Eighth and Grand. Wally was a big tall man with rough-looking features, but an all-right guy and good guy to talk to.

My old partners, Alfie Kanton and Bud O'Dell, highjacked a ciga-rette truck in North Kansas City when they were kids. The truck was hauling a $30,000 load of cigarettes. They packed them in these big huge boxes about a hundred cases of cigarettes to a box, and you couldn't pick it up and carry it because your hands would just slide off the sides they were so big and awkward. So Alfie and Bud got these big hay hooks and dug one into each side to carry the boxes off, even knowing that some of the cigarettes were going to be torn apart inside. They drove the truck over to the north end of town to a garage and dumped out the boxes and then put the truck back out on the street. They went down to collect some money from a guy named Jack Tracy out on Troost Avenue, and they figured they had $3,000 coming from the score. When they asked Jack for their money, he just said, "Get the hell out of here, you punks." So they pulled a gun on him and shot him in the leg. Jack got up, saying, "You shot me, you son-of-bitches," as he reached to grab a shotgun in the corner of the room. They didn't know it, but they shot him in his wooden leg, so they shot him again and then took off. So Jack was wounded and needed help, so he went down to Dago town, thinking the Dagos would help him, but the Dagos didn't want any heat on themselves by helping him, so they found Jack's body later that day dumped on the street in North Kansas City. It was in the papers because I was in jail at the time and read about it.

The Mafia would always joke, "If you ever want to get rid of a dead body, take it over to the Kansas side and dump it. Hell, they haven't solved a murder in over 40 years."

I was on a train to Omaha and sat down next to a guy who said his name was Jon Voight. He said that he was going to New York City for a part in a picture. He told me that he was the son of a Czech American golf pro and wanted to become a movie star.

The Manor Baking Company used a messenger to walk to the bank to deposit their money. With masks on and guns drawn, we grabbed the messenger on Troost Avenue at two in the afternoon. Then we got away clean by running through the Isis Movie Theater that was owned by a Croatian just like us. I bought the tickets to the movie just before we did the score, knowing we would use his place for a clean exit. Still holding our pistols, we gave the guy our tickets and ran down the aisle, out the exit, over the back wall, up a fire escape, over a roof and down the alley. We threw the money in the back seat of our car and took off back to Kansas where we split a little over $2,000 on that job.

When Red Bever, my partner, worked at the Hotel Muehlebach as a bellboy, he was telling me about a salesmen selecting him for a special assignment to watch a certain black box. I asked him to describe the box, and he said it was a black box about two foot tall, 18 inches square, that contained small drawers top to bottom. Red didn't know it at the time, but what he had been assigned to watch was a box full of diamonds by a diamond salesman. We removed the salesman of his cache, but it drew so damn much heat we never repeated the score.

Red saw a guy walking toward us on Main Street with a real nice topcoat on. Red told him to take the coat off, which he did, and Red tried it on. He told him to take off his shoes, and Red tried them on and they fit, so Red beat the shit out of him and just walked off wearing his shoes and topcoat, leaving him lying on the sidewalk all beat up.

There was a Pontiac dealer at Eighth and Minnesota Avenue who kept a list out in the showroom of everyone's name and address who bought a new car. I'd come back when different guys were working and say my name was so and so and I lost my keys. They would make me another one, and then we'd go to the address and get the car.

We were going to hijack a truck coming down Minnesota Avenue one morning when he made one of his stops. We didn't wear masks, but Red put bandages on his face for a disguise. We were waiting at a light, and a woman came up to Red and asked him how he got hurt and felt so sorry for him and asked if he needed any help. We were glad she'd gone from the corner when we hijacked the full truckload of whiskey that day.

There was a warehouse down on James Street that we decided to blow the safe on. We didn't know anything about blowing safes, so we ran after we lit it, and when it blew all the windows busted out and it damn near blew up the building. We never tried to find the safe in all the rubble and just left and went home.

A gang from Armourdale went in to rob a place and one guy's shotgun accidentally went off, blowing his leg off.

Nobody in the neighborhood liked a cop named Steve Hajdina; he was always showing off his power with threats. Hajdina walked with a limp because his girlfriend shot him in the leg after he beat the shit out of her. Nobody liked him because he was always beating up on his girlfriend all the time. His buddy's name was Page, and he told me that this town wasn't big enough for all of us and told me to get out of town. He always targeted beating up my gang and me, but one time when we all met up at Seventh and Central Avenue we got the upper hand and beat the shit out of him and his partner. The streetcars stopped along the street, and everyone got out of their cars driving down the street to watch the fight. The guy, Hassig, who owned the drugstore on the corner of Seventh and Central, invited us in after the fight and said we could have anything we wanted from now on because he didn't like the son-of-a-bitch either.

We got lucky because we knew the judge who we were going before on these charges. His name was "Judge Judy," and we met him one day over in Kansas City, Missouri trying to find a whorehouse. My partner and I took him to a whorehouse, and I told the girls to take extra good care of him. They told us later that he didn't have anything down below, but all four girls made him happy that night, all night long. He was the judge we went in front of, and when he saw us, he just dropped all the charges and dismissed the case. The cops couldn't believe it when we just walked out of the courtroom.

There was a prosecutor in Kansas City back then that if you had any money you would never have to do any time, even if it was murder.

I was playing chess with a black guy in jail down at the City Market. One cop didn't like blacks, and when they locked the black guy in his cell, he poured gasoline and oil on him and set him on fire.

The old city jail just had a board in the corner you were supposed to sit on to shit or piss into. Whatever you did, you did not sit on it because guys would just squat over it and it was covered. There was water running toward the corner all the time, but the shit just floated around in circles and the place stunk like hell. They didn't have toilets in the jails back then, but if you paid a jailer you'd get better care and a chance to go out of the cell to a real toilet.

When we found out that all the gambling places in Covington, Kentucky were wide open, we went down there to case the joints. We drove around and around and couldn't find any of the joints anywhere. Then we saw a little black kid standing on a street corner who couldn't have been more than six years old. So we drove up alongside and I asked him if he knew any place where we could get a drink. He said, "No." Then we asked him if he knew any place where we could dance with some girls. He said: "No," but then he put his hands on his hips and cocked his head, looked me straight in the eye and said, "Are you looking for a whorehouse, mister?" We laughed so hard we had to sit there for a few minutes to regain our composure. Then we gave the cocky little shit a $10 bill and headed in the direction he pointed us to toward the whorehouses.

In those joints in Covington, Kentucky, you could sit down and have drinks with the entertainers, and that's how we met Billy Holliday and Alvino Ray who played the xylophone in the band back then. We sat around casing the place while we were having our drinks and watched as some guys would come there by taxicab. If they were high rollers and had big wins, the place would send them back home in a limousine. They did that so the limousine could go and get them the next day and bring them back to gamble some more, giving the house a chance to win all their money back.

We found out that all of the joints only closed down nine days a year and that's during Grand Jury investigations.

I met a guy, Kazie, who was out of Kansas City, and he was dealing cards in one joint. He told us about the peepholes all around the place and that they had a gun guard walking around a catwalk behind the wall. Kazie also told me to look at that guy over there at the bar. He was waiting for his wife to come and bring her paycheck and he would play it all and lose it just like he already did with his check, and then they'd give him $20 to get his ass out and go home; he did that every single week. After casing the places down there, we decided we couldn't rob them. They had too many gun guards on catwalks with peepholes all around the inside of these places.

Another time when I robbing this joint, I had a .45 automatic in my hand and the guy I had the gun on kept looking at me and then down on the floor. I looked down on the floor and my clip had fallen out. I guess I hit the damn thing and the clip fell out. I knew that it had one bullet in the chamber though, but after that I was leery to carry any automatic from then on. I got a gun that I could look down and see the slugs in the barrel. I got me a .357 Magnum, and that son-of-a-bitch was big.

I used to have lunch with B.G. (Benny Goodman), the bandleader, up in Buffalo, New York. You just dress well and go into the best places and you meet them and can sit and talk with them. Benny was a tall guy with wavy hair and enjoyed talking with his fans. He sure stood out in a crowd when he walked in a place, so erect, six feet tall or more, wearing a nice topcoat and carrying his clarinet case under his arm.

Also Clyde McCoy, the guy who played the trumpet and one of my favorites, "Sugar Blues," was there and I got his autograph. He signed his name with musical notes that looked very extraordinary. I also met Gene Krupa, the drummer, but he seemed to be on dope all of the time, and then I realized how he could play those drums so hard and so long like he did.

In Buffalo, New York when we were robbing all these gambling joints, Harry O'Dell and my other partner, Sam Ricketts, and I would set up all the scores. One guy, Charlie Sheck, was telling us about a gambling joint up there that was a good score. So later another guy named Sam came to us, telling us about the same joint that was a good score. I told him I already got that score from another guy and he was the one who would be in on the cut. Now this guy was mad that I found out about the score from the other guy and he wouldn't get a cut from it. You had to be real careful because when they got pissed off they might just squeal on all of us. So Charlie Sheck came back later to tell us that he talked to a street cop and it was all right to rob the joint up there if the cop could get a cut. In those days, all these Dagos up there wanted a cut from our scores, but we knew something was up because when Harry and I went in to check it out we could see a guy sitting in the corner with a riot gun on his lap. We knew this place cashed checks, and we saw the money box sitting on the counter out in the open, where before they always kept it under the counter. We knew right away that was a setup, so we blew the score and got the hell out of there and went to rob another gambling joint instead. We knew these places could only get $9,000 at a time to cash payroll checks because insurance companies would only allow so much money in their place at one time, so they had to keep going to the bank for more money and we'd catch 'em in the process. There were a lot of industries up there in Buffalo at that time, and we cased and robbed most of them because they had more money than the banks did back then.

One time in Buffalo I was walking down the street casing a gambling joint in a seedy part of town, and I walked by a woman walking down the street toward me. Just moments later, these cops nabbed me and also had hold of the woman who just walked by. She was telling them that she never said a word to me, and I told them the same thing — that she didn't say a word to me and just walked by, so they let me go. I had a gun in my sock, was wanted by the police, and I wouldn't have gone without a fight. Luckily, that prostitute just passed me by that time.

We were going to rob a gambling joint in Buffalo, New York, so before the gambling ever began we walked inside the joint and sat down, drank some coffee and read the newspaper. Then when the place opened and the gambling began, they closed and locked the front doors after frisking everyone to make sure they weren't packing any guns. Once everyone was starting the games, I walked toward the back to the restroom and opened the window, which was right alongside the outside fire escape. My partner handed me our guns through the bars of the window, and we went back in and robbed the place.

All the gambling joints had crooked dice back then. One corner shaved, one with a BB in a corner, one called shakedown with BB's inside and one with a magnet on the table. It was funny to see a guy throw the dice and see them just flip on their own, showing a seven. Guys were stupid to play against the house in those places. Others would throw the dice into a pitcher of water, and if they sank to the bottom showing a seven, they would know that they were loaded.

There was another speakeasy and gambling house in that area of Buffalo, New York that we wanted to hit. You couldn't just walk in; you had to be brought in by someone who was known in the place. I was standing outside of the joint when a cab pulled up and all these people got out of the cab and went up to the door. When the door opened for them to step in, I just walked in right alongside of them. You were watched when you were walking in up the steps, so I knew we couldn't bring in any weapons. We just did the same thing as before because just next door there was a theater that had a fire escape outside on the back of the building that also led up to the gambling joint. I went to the restroom in the gambling joint and opened up the window, and my partner was out on the fire escape and handed me the guns through the open window. As soon as we got all the money and ran out the front door, we took over a limo driver who was parked right in front, and he took us out of Buffalo and all the way to Ohio. When we hit the roadblocks the cops set up, they'd just let the limo pass through, thinking that couldn't have been the getaway car the robbers used. We thought for sure Otto Grecio, the chauffeur, who lived in Buffalo, was going to turn us in to the cops, but he never did. In fact, he set us up on a few more good scores in Buffalo that we got later.

We went over into Canada, and they just kept your driver's license at the border, and when you came back they'd return it to you. This is when we found out in Canada you get on a streetcar in the back and get off it in the front. Quite a bit of confusion at first before we figured this out with people pushing us and we didn't know why. They wanted us out of the way so they could go to the front to exit.

I remember driving by this runway, and we stopped to see a fighter plane take off and soar up into the air. It was only a few minutes before the cops were there wanting to know what we were doing and we had to talk our way out of that rather than for them to check our phony driver's licenses.

I used to go to a racetrack outside of Buffalo, New York to case for a potential score. It was a hackney race, and I didn't like that shit where they'd stop and start and have to go back and start all over. The horses would be pulling a little wagon around the track. I met a guy who made his living betting on the horses up there, and he would make lots of money from it and said he had a system.

They had all the sports clubs right on Niagara Falls at Lockport. Hell, they were better than banks, and the gambling was all wide open and they were just raking in all the money. The Dagos all ran the places up there in those days, and we robbed them all.

When we went into Covington, Kentucky, there was a big nightclub named Smitz Rendezvous it was a movie theater built into a nightclub. The floor was on an incline, and they had steps up to the stage where the entertainment would be. We were there one evening and saw Billy Bo Jangles, the famous tap dancer who danced with Shirley Temple in an old movie. When he tapped, you could see that his feet weren't a half-inch off of the floor the entire time, and it was a first-rate show to watch. It was something to see him dance with staccato steps like his feet would never hit the floor and were floating on air, truly remarkable.

Betty Hutton was even singing down there at the Cat and the Fiddle that was just a honky-tonk bar. The way she was discovered was the Vincent Lopes band was playing in one of the better nightclubs around town, and one of the guys from the band went down and listened to her sing. He came back and told Vincent Lopes that she should be listened to. So they got her to audition with his band and, as they say, the rest is history.

We robbed so many different places I can't remember for sure where it was, but one time a guy was in this cage looking down and smoking a short cigar when I yelled and told him to open up, and he told me, "You can't come in here." Now I had a .45 caliber pistol pointing at his head and he was telling me that I couldn't come in there. He looked like a big burly Danny Devito, and when he looked up and saw the .45 caliber gun cocked and pointing at him, he backed off and opened up the door, and we proceeded to rob the place.

One time we were ready to go in the door to rob a gambling joint, and Maxie, our driver, got scared and took off with our getaway car, so we decided to just leave without hitting the place. We found out later from a guy we knew who worked inside that the cops were behind the second door ready to shoot us when we walked in. So old Maxie saved our lives that time by not sticking around and keeping us from going into the place.

Another time we were going inside to rob one of these joints, and as I rushed in the door and pushed a .45 pistol in a guy's back, right away he hollered, "Quit hitting me, Goddamn it." Then he turned around and saw that big .45 with the hammer cocked back and said, "Oh, my God, oh, my God!"

Not one time in all the times that I was ever arrested throughout my entire life did I ever submit willingly to a pinch.

I remember when the old Wyandotte County jail was in a house. There was this big building that was a mansion at Seventh and State in Kansas City, Kansas that they turned into a jail. You could just smell the strong formaldehyde in that son-of-a-bitch all the time because that's how they tried to clean it up and disinfect it. It was a historical building even back in those days.

Then I was in the new county jail when they first opened it up on 7th Street in the courthouse building. The old Jackson County jail was in the City Market area, and that sure was a junky jail. When I was in that city Jail back then, you couldn't flush the stools. They would shut off all of the water, thinking that the dopeheads wouldn't hide their dope in the shitty water. They were mistaken, because even when it was filled to the top of the bowl they would put their hands in the shitty water that was used by 15 guys or more in the holding cell and stash their dope. They would put the dope in condoms to stay dry.

The cells in that old jail were made out of cold iron bars, and if you had the right tools you could bust through them without any problem. The cells weren't even attached to the ground and could be moved around to different parts of the room and would just take quite a few guys to move them.

Back then most of the bondsmen were Jews. When they would come in the jail to talk to the guys about getting out, most of the guys would tell them they didn't have any money or anything. The bonds-men would ask, "What kind of shoes do you have on?" They would take anything of value to them to get these guys out on bond. One Jew Bondsmen got me out and rode over to the Kansas side with me to a restaurant close to my house. The owner loaned me $50 to give to the bondsmen. Then the bondsmen told me that he'd get an appeal for me, but it would cost a few more bucks. I contacted my lawyer and told him what the bondsman said, and he said, "Appeal to what? You're out and there's nothing for him to appeal to." The guy was just trying to milk me for more money.

When the cops were rushing into the house to get me on March 5, 1934, I opened the window in the front room to look like I went out that way, but what I did was move an overstuffed chair and lifted up a grate on the floor that was nothing but a hole. I got down inside the hole, pulling the grate back over, when I heard a cop come into the room and yell to the others, "He made a clean getaway out the window."

Then I heard old man Radki coming home, and although I wanted to stay hidden where I was, I knew I had to get the hell out of there because the old man would shit his pants with all these cops looking for me. I would have stayed hidden right there if it hadn't been for the old man coming home, and he even said later that I should have stayed hidden out in the basement for a while. He knew the reason I left was I didn't want to draw any more heat on him there in the house. I sneaked out the back and went up the street and met a kid I went to school with named Bodie Simski. He told me that they were still driving all around looking for me. I told him I knew that because they were just down to the house trying to get me.

I wanted to get across the viaduct and down on James Street to hide out, but I just got to the top of Fifth Street hill by Barnett Avenue, and here they all appeared coming right at me. I tried to hide down behind this house, but they all started firing at me, and I was cut down with a riot gun. I slipped away and kept going past Armstrong Avenue. Even though I was bleeding badly, I knew I had to try to get away. I was shot with double-ott slugs, which are the size of .32 caliber shells, but still I staggered into a new car lot, Desoto Auto Agency at Fourth and Minnesota Avenue, and climbed into one of the new cars on the lot. Boston Daniels was one of the cops who saw me, and they all started shooting again. I got out of the car and slid down on the ground and got away, but they kept firing shells into that brand new car. It was riddled with shells and all torn apart when they got through, but I got away. I tried to turn around and go back toward home, but they caught me again on Armstrong Avenue. I was going blind and staggering from losing so much blood, so that's where they got me. They just threw me in a police car and took me to City Hall on Sixth and Ann Avenue where the jail was.

My younger brother, Frank, told me later that Mom came to school to get him, saying that Willie just got shot. We didn't have a phone back then, so a cop came to the door and told her that if she wanted to see me I was at city hall in the old jail, and they both came down to see me but I certainly didn't remember it.

They didn't call a doctor; they called the coroner, and I heard the coroner tell the cops that I lost a lot of blood and he didn't want to be responsible for me dying in the jail there. He said that I needed blood and to get me to the hospital right away. What they tried and wanted to do was just lock me up in a cell without any medical attention at all in hopes that I would die. They had me all chained up when they took me by ambulance over to the Missouri side to General Hospital. They never did give me any blood when I got there, but there was a young Dago kid named Tony Contrary who was in the hospital cell with me. He kept telling me that I lost a hell of a lot of blood, and he was feeding me oranges all the time, one right after the other. He told me that I needed the oranges because of all the blood I lost, and the guy was sure right because he saved my life. There were a few slugs in me right beneath the skin, and Tony was popping them out on my arms and legs. He kept telling me that I had to get out of there, and I told him, hell, I knew that. Tony was telling me that his brother's name was Nuncio and he was a cab driver and that someone shot him in the head.

The room we were in was a jail cell on the lower floor of the hospital, and they had an armed guard sitting right there by my cot watching me. A bunch of sirens went off, and the guard got up and opened the door and walked out into the hall to see what was going on. When he did that, I got up and went out the window. We were on the first floor, and the drop wasn't a big one, but it sure was rough all shot up like I was. All I had on was the gown from the hospital, and I could barely make it I was so weak from losing so much blood. I found out later that guard got fired or suspended or something for leaving my side in that room. I walked from the hospital down to the Terminal Cab Company and got into a cab, but the cab driver yelled and told me that I couldn't do that and to get the hell out of his cab. I didn't budge from the cab, and I told him to take me down to Dago Town, which he did. The guys told me that they'd help me get back over to the Kansas side so this Dago and I were in the back of the cab heading back to the Kansas side when we got stopped by the cops in one of the many roadblocks they had all over town trying to nab me.

What saved me was I had a hospital gown on and my hair was all disheveled and I had my head lying on the Dago's shoulder. They thought I was a broad sitting close to the guy in the back seat and just let us go right through the roadblock.

They took me down to a Dago friend of mine, Joe Brazen, who had a pool hall down on Kansas Avenue, and he took me to Topeka, Kansas. I was kept hidden by this bootlegger named Carl Ruben who I sold a lot of bootleg booze to back then. He had a farm along the river where he hid his still and all his booze and, man, was there a lot of whiskey stacked around out there. Carl brought a veterinarian out by the river to see me, and he showed me how to take a piece of cotton with Vaseline on it and put that down inside each bullet hole so it could drain and heal from the inside out without closing up and getting infected. I changed the cotton often until a Band-Aid was sufficient. Sulfur was the only drug or antibiotic available at that time.

The Kaw River was so narrow there where I was you could walk across it. The water kept pushing up the sand around there and, hell, you could walk across the river because it was only a few feet wide. I figured if anyone came I'd just take off across the river to the other side. I don't even know how long I stayed out there at that bootlegger's place, but it was for quite a while. A black man, his wife and son lived in the farmhouse owned by Carl Ruben, and they watched Carl's still and booze. While I was healing, they came to feed me every day, and it was my first time for eating "soul food," and I have to say it was delicious. They took good care of me and fed me real well, and I always had plenty of food to eat.

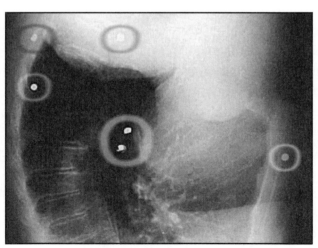

This X-ray was taken in 2003, and it shows the six slugs that Willie still carries around.

Then I made the mistake of thinking I was going to get out of there, so I walked to downtown Topeka and was going to steal a car to drive back home. I didn't notice the guy standing on the corner watching me. Well, he was a cop. Hell, I was still so weak I couldn't do anything to even try to get away from him when he grabbed me. I should have stayed by the river because I was weak, skinny and so white from all the blood that I lost. I couldn't even put up a fight, so they hauled my ass off to jail.

I got caught July 4th in Topeka, and on that same day Red Kurkindal broke out of the Kansas reform school, took hostages across the state line, got caught and was sentenced to life. Bonnie and Clyde were shot and killed on that day near Plain Dealing, Louisiana.

The old lady even tried to sue the cops who shot me, but the courts laughed at her back then because they all wanted me dead and off the streets. The court would not even file the charges and told her to go home and forget about it.

Dope fiends jacked everything up back then, and I hated them for it. I was brought back from Topeka to the brand new Jackson County jail. They had church services in there where they would take you out of your cell into a room to speak about yourself. We wanted to get some guns in that room and even had a hiding place right in the corner behind the door before you walk in. We knew that we could get a visitor to come in there and put the guns in there for us. So the next day we were coming out because they were going to have a little service when they stopped us, saying we couldn't come out for the service any more because the dope fiends got caught bringing dope in. The bastards stopped us from going to services, and I know I would have gotten out of there if it hadn't been for those rotten-ass dope fiends.

Later my lawyer got me out on bond, but us guys had to go back to the Jackson County jail to visit a guy we knew, Steve Stemski, who was there, and we wanted to find out where our Browning automatic rifle was, because he was the guy who hid it for us. When we visited him, there was a guard sitting right by the door, so we started talking in Polish, asking him where the gun was hid. He told us and we went down and got it for our next score. It was a Browning Automatic that was a gas-powered barrel over barrel. They were high-powered, and the Kansas City Police only had three of them back then, but we got one of them. They wouldn't pierce a concrete block, but they'd sure break it up. They used big bottle-necked bullets that were dangerous because we shot them off a couple of times and the shell would jam up and the bullets would get pressure inside and they wouldn't fire out. I didn't like those bottlenecks, but they were powerful slugs. Mike Kowalski ended up with it, and he kept it hidden down on Kansas Avenue.

After I got all shot up and escaped from the hospital, the cops came to my mother's home looking for me, thinking they had me hidden somewhere. They threw down the clothes I was wearing when I got shot for my mom to see. My foster father, old man Radki, lifted up the tan jacket with a belt in the back like all the gangsters wore back then, along with a blue shirt and matching tan pants that were full of bullet holes and covered with blood.

About a week before I got shot, the cops killed my partner, Charlie Yurcheck. I just left him one evening when he was walking down the street at Sixth and Tremont Avenue. The cops pulled up on him and shot him right there. The cop who killed him committed suicide later on. He was worried that someone would come after him. He had lost his daughter some time before and just went out to her grave and blew his head off. The cops would just pull up on you and shoot you in those days like they did me, but I made it.

I had so many partners in those days, I can't even remember their names. There was a dangerous gang out of Armourdale named the "Rock and Riley's." They were a bad-ass gang at that time. A guy in the gang asked me to help another guy named Red Lore who had just gotten out of prison and needed to make some money. I said, "Okay," and took the son-of-a-bitch with us. We stuck up this gambling joint down on Kansas Avenue. Hell, the guy was stir-crazy and his mind was all jacked up. He was supposed to be drawn down on the guy standing by the door and holding him and watching him while the robbery took place. The guy wanted to move over by these coats hanging up on the wall. I caught him trying to move closer and stopped him and found out when I went over to the coats he was trying to get close to his gun that was there. Red was just walking around like he didn't know what the hell was going on. I thought that poor son-of-a-bitch was going to get us killed in that robbery. Later on, Red and some other guy tried to rob a store with a candy pistol. In those days you could buy a toy pistol filled with candy. His mind was all jacked up and he didn't know what the hell he was doing, and they both got busted. Lucky they both didn't get their asses shot off.

Back in those days you would find at least one dead body on Central Avenue every week. Johnny Rocks and his brother, Riley, from the Armourdale gang hung out with us. One time we were on Central Avenue just bumming around and split up to go home. I was walking away and heard a round of shots. I found out later that the cops waited on them to come home and blew them away. That's what they wanted to do with my gang and me. We found out from the neighbors that a battery of detectives busted into the house they lived in, firing as they entered, and all the newspapers said that they shot five guys in self-defense.

Back then you wore your own clothes while you were in any of the jails, and some of the dirtiest, filthiest son-of-a-bitches would come in there. In the city jail the bars were back a little way away from the window, but the guys would just wait until it was clear and throw a piece of string out the window down to the bottom where they had someone waiting, and they would get all kinds of shit in there. There was more shit in that jail than you could imagine, but again it was the dope fiends who always screwed it up for all of us.

A black guy in jail for bootlegging was from Leavenworth. A lot of guys were doing time in jail for bootlegging back then. He yelled at his woman when she visited him, saying, "Hey, baby, you saving that pussy for me? You better be," he said, while he continued giving her hell for screwing around with other guys. Then she yelled back at him, "Hey, baby, just remember it's mine and I can haul coal in it if I want to."

One time I wanted to go into Fifth Street Hall just to tell this guy to come out of there because I wanted to talk to him. The guy at the door wouldn't let me just go in without paying first. I didn't want to pay because I wasn't going to stay. He gave me a hard time and refused to let me in, so I got bullheaded and got even with him. There was a friend of mine, a kid I went to school with — I don't know why, but he always needed to take a crap all the time. He had something wrong with his guts or something. I just asked him if he'd do it, and he put a pile right in the front seat of the guy's car. The Model-T Fords back then didn't have a door on the driver's side; they just had the door over on the passenger side. Harry climbed up in the car and squatted over the driver's seat; and the next thing you know he was wiping up and was finished, leaving a big pile of shit on the guy's front seat. He did this right in front of Fifth Street Hall with all the people walking around and going in and out of the dance hall. You just didn't mess with us guys back in those days. He should have never told me that I couldn't just walk in and out of the place.

There was another place called "Five Corners" that we were going to rob. Harry, my partner, got a guy to help us from Kansas City, Kansas — I think his name was Sam. He was sitting on the bed right before we were going to rob the joint, and he said, "You know what? If I get caught. I won't get to see my wife any more." I said right away, "Shit, I ain't going with this son-of-a-bitch with that kind of an attitude." I asked Harry where in the hell did he get this guy for the job that's worried about seeing his old lady. He sure screwed up that score because I wouldn't take him with us for the reason he thought he was getting caught before we even went into the place.

In the J.C. Penney's store on Minnesota Avenue the cashier sat up behind a high counter, which worked out well for us. Us guys would go into the store and just look around for stuff to steal. We would tie a string on whatever it was we wanted and place it on the floor, so then when we walked out of the store we would be releasing the roll of string in our pocket. Once we got outside and out of view of the cashier we'd pull on our strings, bringing out whatever it was we tied on to the other end right out of the front door of the store. We'd just tug on the string, pulling it right along the floor where it was out of view from the cashier. We did this in a lot of places and even got our bullets like this from this one store right under their noses or, should I say, under the counter.

I grew up in a way that the law never affected me in anything I did. Most of the girls used to fight over who was going out with me because I always took them to the best places in town. I always took them to the best restaurants and the best stage shows around. I belonged to a theatrical list on the Country Club Plaza, along with the Play Goers of Kansas City. The Play Goers league was an elite group in Kansas City. It only cost $100 a year to be a member. They would just mail you the tickets to the newest shows in town at the Newman, the Royal, plus a few other theaters around town. I would receive flyers in the mail on the shows coming up in all the theaters in Greater Kansas City, so that I could put in my reservation. At one theater I even had a private box right behind the orchestra that let me enjoy the show by peeking through a small section of the curtain to be reclusive or to just open the curtain completely to view the entire stage. We had private show boxes in the upper loges, but I never cared to be so far away from the stage and always waited for a vacancy right behind the orchestra.

I saw every stage play and act that came into town with many famous people, including a famous violinist named Rubanoff with his Stradivarius violin that was worth a fortune even back then. He was a Jewish guy with ivory white skin and black curly hair, and his music was exceptionally outstanding.

I saw "Guys and Dolls" over and over and can't tell you how many times I returned to see Gypsy Rose Lee. Gypsy Rose Lee was the most famous legendary stripper of all times, and she made her debut in Kansas City during the '30s. Her real name was Louise Hovick, and she was of Slovenian descent. She was known for telling the cops during a raid at the famous Minsky's Burlesque house in New York that she wasn't naked; she was completely covered with a blue spotlight.

She would begin her show by sticking her leg out from behind the purple velvet curtain. Then began moving it back and forth slowly, she'd say, "Well, boys?" Then when the music, "The Stripper," started, she proceeded to dance across the stage and down the runway with her big tits bouncing up and down along with each beat of the drum from the orchestra. She was heavyset and not skinny like you'd see all the women strippers today. During her show she would run around and around the stage with her big tits bouncing up and down and almost falling out of her bra, but not missing one beat of the music. It was sure a good show, and I enjoyed it the many times that I returned to see it.

At 103rd and Wornall Avenue in Kansas City, Missouri, there was a nightclub that was wide open because it was way outside the city limits. You couldn't get a parking place within a half-mile from the place on weekends when Gypsy Rose Lee would do her show downtown, then come out to this club and do another performance later that night.

There was a movie made in the 1960s starring Natalie Wood about Gypsy Rose Lee that was very good, and I saw that movie over and over in later years.

When we'd go to see Wallace Berry at 12th and Paseo where he lived back then, we'd drive my brand new cars down the streets, and all of the whores on the street corners would jump onto the running board and hang on riding with us trying to get our business.

During the dust bowl, you just got used to driving around in the dust and hoped your car would continue to run in it. There was one time we were going to Topeka, Kansas right in the middle of this dust storm and I could hear the carburetor starting to spit and crackle; then the car just died. The carburetor was full of dirt and had to be taken off and cleaned out before you could start to drive again. You'd go through that two or three times a day when the dust was really blowing, but you just did it if you wanted to drive.

One time we cased a big bakery and watched a guy walk out and take the money to the bank in a brown paper bag every day. When we were ready to do the score, we just pulled along side of him while sitting in the car, told him to throw the bag of money in the car. He threw the bag in the car, and we drove off as fast as we could just around the corner and immediately parked the car in this residential district and got out. We walked back to a place where we could look down and observe the area the robbery had taken place from the top of a hill, and we saw that there were cops all over the place stopping and searching every vehicle that came through from every direction. We just walked around the corner and went into this bar and sat there for a few hours having drinks until the heat was gone, then took off.

There was a Green Hills gambling joint in North Kansas City, and we went to rob the place, even seeing the four gun guards at the top of the stairs leading to the gaming tables. We got the money and ran to our car to make our getaway when they closed these big double iron gates in front of us on the driveway out. We hit that gate dead center at top speed with the big Buick, and it broke loose with such a force the gates swung open all the way, then swung back and collapsed, hanging there on their hinges. As soon as we got on the road, we knew they expected us to use the main highways and probably head back to the city and they'd have the highways covered looking for us. We headed in a different direction on a back road to Leavenworth where we just hung around there in a bar, lying low for a while until the heat was off, then went back to Kansas City.

Another place that we cased was the mafia's "Barley Duque's" in the City Market area of Kansas City, Missouri. You had to get upstairs by way of the luxuriously carpeted steps to the big gambling joint upstairs. Hell, they had gunmen all over the place in a specially built gun gallery above the main floor, plus four guards on the roof. We dismissed that job as a possibility because they had too many guns, so we just stayed to see the floor show. They had quite a floor show that was lively and very entertaining. The master of ceremonies was a guy just beginning his career named Skeets Gallagher who later would get into movies and star with legendary names like Jean Harlow out in California.

Two guys and I were getting away from a score in a big old Nash automobile and could hear the sirens of the cops in the distance. I turned into Swope Park and drove fast on the wet pavement, making all the sharp curves trying to hide from the cops. I was driving too fast when I tried to make one corner, and the car got out of control and started to skid and went around and around in circles a few times before it flipped over on its top and started twirling around, and all I could hear was four wheels spinning until it smashed into a tree stump. When we hit the tree stump, my skull smashed against the windshield and I got a big gash when I flew out through the jagged glass. Back then there was no safety glass on cars, and the glass in the windshield in most wrecks decapitated a lot of people. The car itself was so big and heavy it didn't crack up in that wreck like my head did. The other two guys took off to get away, leaving me on the ground bleeding and knocked unconscious. A Good Samaritan stopped to help me and put me in his car and took me to General Hospital. I gave them a fictitious name because I was wanted in Kansas at the time. I didn't know it at the time, but the guy who helped me was an off-duty cop, so when he got me to General Hospital he made a few calls, checking up on the name that I'd given him.

I was sitting in the waiting room bleeding all over the place, and two women watching me were getting sick from the sight of all the blood, so the hospital staff suggested that I be carried into a small room out of sight of all the others. They did me a favor because there was an open window in that room about five feet up the wall, so I climbed up and jumped out the window and was able to shimmy down a clay drain pipe alongside the building for the one-story drop. I had to steal a car; then I headed for Dr. Brathaway down on James Street where he sewed my head up. Even today I still have the six-inch scar across the top of my forehead. The doctor knew that he could've been picked up and charged by the police for helping me, but the money I paid him made him take the chance.

My sister Agnes had married John Uziel Sr., and they lived in a little gray house that sat back away from the street just south of Meyer's Milk Company on Fifth street. They just had their first baby, a girl named Jeane. Agnes walked up to Katz Drugstore and purchased bandages, gauze, tape, Mercurochrome and Band-Aids. I stayed in the closet after escaping from the hospital to rest and heal.

I was home one day back in March 1935 and could see all the cops pulling up in front of the house coming after me, so I sneaked out the back and climbed up on the roof between the house and the garage and laid low and out of sight until I thought they had all left. I took off running, but they were still watching for me and saw me running and came after me.

I found out later it was a guy named John Kowalski who snitched on me. You know that son-of-a-bitch couldn't even drive a car, and I didn't know that until he got behind the wheel. We robbed a jewelry store, Woodstock-Hoefer Company, down at 10th and Main in Kansas City, Missouri in the Perry building. So I was walking out of the store with all the jewelry cases stacked up high, heading for the car, and it wasn't there. I'd just looked out the window of the jewelry store and signaled at Mike by waving and letting him know everything was all right and to bring the car up in front so I could jump in with all these jewelry cases I had in my arms. This guy was Mike Lester, who we called "Snow" because he took cocaine all the time, and he'd accidentally killed his brother and was supposed to be a killer and wanted by the cops.

When my partner, Johnny Coutz, and I came outside of the store, the stupid son-of-a-bitch moved the car and couldn't remember where he moved it. As soon as we ran out of the place, the guy inside hit the alarm. Here I was going up and down 10th Street, then up and down Main Street, and the alarm was ringing and I got all these jewelry cases in my arms and can't find the getaway car. I kept screaming at him, asking where in the hell is the car, and he kept saying, "I don't know." We finally found it and got into the damn car and took off, but when the cops started chasing us, he jumped out of the car from behind the wheel, and the stupid son-of-a-bitch Kowalski got behind the wheel and couldn't even drive. So we're going down 23rd Street viaduct bouncing from one side of the bridge to the other because this guy couldn't control the car. John and I jumped out of the car and ran down under the bridge to the railroad tracks and started walking toward Kansas and I was still carrying all the jewelry cases. The cops were watching us from the top of the 23rd Street viaduct and watched as I headed for home. They started firing down at us and hit me with a riot gun that shot shells the size of .22 calibers. As I went down, I hurled all the jewelry cases filled with diamonds up into the air when I fell, and they all scattered there in the sand along the railroad tracks. I made it all the way back home, and when I saw the cops, I took off again, but they caught up with me and kept firing. I got away again, but I know they saw me trying to start a car sitting in a car lot.

The cops just left me for dead, but John found me and came back with Joe Bodner. They went down and picked up the diamonds, then took me to General Hospital over in Missouri. The doctor came in with Mercurochrome and Band-Aids and started popping out the shells that lay just under the skin. There was one shell that was between my legs that rubbed causing intense pain when I walked that was a lot deeper than any of the others, and the doctor had to dig that one out.

They had a guard sitting by my bed, and he got up and walked out of the room and came back in about five minutes with a cup of coffee. He looked at me with a surprising look and said, "Hell, what are you still doing here? I thought you'd be gone by now, Radkay." He was an all-right guy and didn't really cover me like he was supposed to. When I was feeling better, he told me to get up and go out into the hall to the nurse's desk to get my medication. I took that as a hint and just kept on walking by the nurse's station and right out the door and down to Armourdale where a Dago hid me out in the basement of his pool hall.

Kowalski was just walking down 23rd Street out in the open, and that's where he got pinched. They got him in jail, and he talked his ass off in there, telling them everything. Later I went and took his brother over to the Dagos, on the North End around Fifth and Independence Avenue where their neighborhood was and gave them some $3,000 to get him out on bond.

I was sitting at home about a week later when the cops came and surrounded the house, busted in and hauled my ass off to jail.

Both Mike and John got cut free of all charges, but since I was the guy fingered inside the place, I was facing time. They didn't do anything to help me when I got busted, and I gave them all those diamonds we had for $4,000, plus my cut of the $6,000 cash we got and they didn't do anything. They sentenced me to the Missouri State Prison in Jefferson City over this shit.

[AUTHOR'S NOTE: My uncle Willie told me about the jewelry store robbery and how it caused him to be sent to the Missouri Penitentiary. I was reviewing a sheet called "Summary of Offense," and in relation to the jewelry store robbery, it stated, "The police shot Willie." My uncle said he didn't remember being shot at that time. I decided to check the Kansas City Kansan newspaper microfilm dating back to March 4, 1935. It stated in the newspaper article that Willie was shot "12 times" in the arms, back and upper legs from Detective Joseph Schick of the motor theft squad. I printed the article and took it to my uncle at the nursing home where he now resides. I asked him how he could be shot 12 times and not remember it. He said that Joe Schick carried a riot gun which was a sawed-off shotgun and it "only" scat-

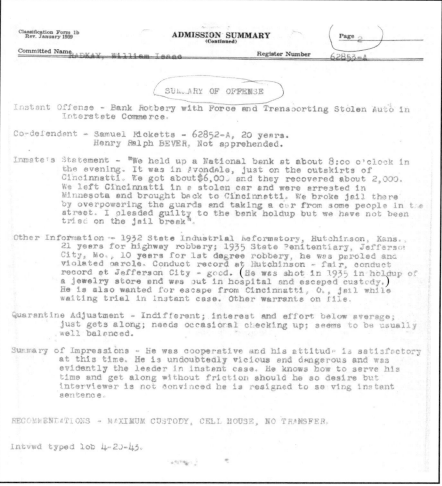

Classification Form 1b
Rev. January 1939

ADMISSION SUMMARY
(Continued)

Page 2

Committed Name RADKAY, William Isaac   Register Number 62853-A

SUMMARY OF OFFENSE

Instant Offense - Bank Robbery with Force and Transporting Stolen Auto in Interstate Commerce.

Co-defendant - Samuel Ricketts - 62852-A, 20 years.
                Henry Ralph BEVER, Not apprehended.

Inmate's Statement - "We held up a National bank at about 8:00 o'clock in the evening. It was in Avondale, just on the outskirts of Cincinnatti. We got about $6,000 and they recovered about 2,000. We left Cincinnatti in a stolen car and were arrested in Minnesota and brought back to Cincinnatti. We broke jail there by overpowering the guards and taking a car from some people in the street. I pleaded guilty to the bank holdup but we have not been tried on the jail break".

Other Information - 1932 State Industrial Reformatory, Hutchinson, Kans., 21 years for highway robbery; 1935 State Penitentiary, Jefferson City, Mo., 10 years for 1st degree robbery, he was paroled and violated parole. Conduct record at Hutchinson - fair, conduct record at Jefferson City - good. (He was shot in 1935 in holdup of a jewelry store and was out in hospital and escaped custody.) He is also wanted for escape from Cincinnatti, O., jail while waiting trial in Instant case. Other warrants on file.

Quarantine Adjustment - Indifferent; interest and effort below average; just gets along; needs occasional checking up; seems to be usually well balanced.

Summary of Impressions - He was cooperative and his attitude is satisfactory at this time. He is undoubtedly vicious and dangerous and was evidently the leader in instant case. He knows how to serve his time and get along without friction should he so desire but interviewer is not convinced he is resigned to serving instant sentence.

RECOMMENDATIONS - MAXIMUM CUSTODY, CELL HOUSE, NO TRANSFER.

Intvwd typed lob 4-20-43.

Willie's Admission Summary.

tered pellets the size of a .22 caliber shells.

Then Willie made the comment, "Tough skin, soft bullets, and they didn't hit anything important."

Willie's younger brother, Frank, said that whenever Joe Schick saw him in the neighborhood he always called him "Little Radkay" and would ask him if he was going to follow in his big brother's footsteps.]

Classification Form 1a
Rev. January 1939

UNITED STATES PENITENTIARY
ATLANTA, GEORGIA
ADMISSION SUMMARY

Committed Name **RADKAY, William Isaac**   Reg. No. **62853-A**   Classified **4-22-43**

True Name	**William Isaac Radkay**	Judicial District	**S-Ohio-Cincinnati**
Date of Birth	**9-24-11**	Offense **Bank Robbery with Force & Trans. Stolen**
Age	**31**	Sentence **20 Years**	Comm. Fine	Probation
Race	**White**	Sentence begins	**3-19-43**	* Auto In Inter-
Country of Birth	**U.S.A.**	Committed	**3-20-43**	state Commerce
Citizenship	**U.S.A.**	Eligible for Parole	**11-18-49**
Marital Status	**Single**	Conditional Release Date	**8-21-56**
Legal Residence	**Kansas City, Kans.**	Expires Full Term	**3-18-63**
		Detainers	

REPORTS REC'D FROM: F. B. I. **Yes**   U. S. ATTY. **Yes**   PROSECUTING AGENCY

1. PREVIOUS CRIMINAL RECORD:

Date	Place	Offense	Disposition	Source	Admit
1930	PD-Kansas City, Kans.	Disturbing the Peace	Pd. $5 Fine	Inmate	Yes
4-15-31	PD-Kansas City, Kans.	Highway Robbery	Dismissed	FBI	Yes
1-17-32	SR-Hutchinson, Kans.# 9950	Highway Robbery	10 to 21 Yrs. 10-8-34 Paroled	FBI	Yes
6-4-35	SP-Jefferson City,Mo.# 46497	Robbery	10 Years 10-30-40 Cond.Commutation	PBI	Yes
12-17-41	SO-Kansas City, Mo.	Robbery, 1st. Degree (4 charges)	Forfeited Bond	FBI	Yes

Wanted by SO-Kansas City,Mo. for Jumping Bond - No Warrant filed

Wanted by SP-Jefferson City,Mo. as Parole Violator No Warrant filed

Wabted by SO-Cincinnati,Ohio for 3 cases of Armed Robbery No Warrant filed

Subject escaped jail while awaiting trial but will not be wanted for escape

From the **K.C. KANSAN,** *March 4, 1935:*

TWO OTHERS SEIZED IN JEWELRY HOLDUP
William Radkay, Badly Wounded by Police, and Mike Lister Arrested

Two other men hunted by police in connection with the Woodstock-Hoefer Jewelry company robbery in Kansas City, Mo., yesterday morning, in which $15,000 in jewelry was stolen and most of it recovered, were arrested today by police within ten minutes of each other.

The first captured was William Isaac Radkay, 24 years old, 250 North Fifth Street. He was shot by Joseph Schick of the motor theft squad. Mike Lister, 29, 516 Ohio Avenue, was captured as the result of a ruse when he called James Cashin, city detective, who held him on the line while Cashin's partner, Harry Hartung, traced the call to a pool hall on Osage Avenue, and a police car was ordered to proceed there at once.

Radkay suffered twelve severe wounds in the arms, back and upper legs from shot from Schick's riot gun, which the officer fired at the ex-convict when he fled after spotting the police car at Fifth Street and Barnett Avenue.

A youth who was with Radkay when the cruising car passed them as they walked along the street, shouted "the cops!" to Radkay and ran. Radkay ducked between two houses, and the officers left their car to follow. Schick fired as Radkay turned to cut behind a coal shed. Altho wounded, the man kept on going. Boddington called police headquarters and asked for more cars. The police radio broadcast the call, and detectives and police cars in the vicinity were there in a matter of seconds.

Radkay finally was found at Fifth Street and Armstrong Avenue after he had made a desperate, tho unsuccessful, attempt to escape by using a motor car sitting in the Shaw Motor Company's used car lot at that corner. It was there he was arrested by officers in another car.

Radkay has a police record. He served time in the Hutchinson reformatory for participation in the Leader Clothing company holdup the night of November 28, 1931.

It was while police were bringing Radkay to police headquarters that Lister called Cashin on the telephone, explaining he wasn't in on yesterday morning's holdup and asking the detectives to make a date with him for 4 o'clock this afternoon "to talk the thing over."

Cashin said that he'd be glad to hear Lister's story, and went into great detail as to the time and place of meeting. Meanwhile Hartung was tracing the telephone call. The police department radioed one of its cars to the address from which the call came. There they found Lister, still talking on the phone. They arrested him.

He came in accompanied by two officers to be booked, as Radkay already had been booked, for vagrancy and highway robbery.

Lister also has a police record.

William White, who was arrested yesterday in connection with the theft, is being held by Kansas City, Mo., police.

Lister signed a waiver and was turned to officers from Kansas City, Mo. He was taken there for questioning. According to Jack Jenkins, head of the detective department, Lister denied he had any connection in yesterday morning's holdup.

5

Missouri State Prison

I DID TIME in the 65-acre State Penitentiary in Jefferson City, Missouri, that was built back in 1836 from 1935-1939.

In Jeff City all convicts had to walk with what they called "lock step." You had to put your right hand on the convict's shoulder who was in front of you and shuffle — normal walking was not permitted. Even if only two convicts were walking, they had to walk in lock step. After a few years of continuous shuffling, you did it just by habit even after you got out.

There was disciplinary silence in the dining room; you were not permitted to talk or make a sound. The food there was like garbage, and you'd hear a lot of guys complain after gagging and throwing up the food, breaking the silence. When they did that, all of us paid the price when we left to go out of the dining room. Every guard in the joint would be standing in a line with their billy clubs, cracking all of us on the head and shoulders. A lot of the guys just had to go straight to the hospital to get sewed up when they had their heads busted open. Later on you'd have to laugh when you saw all these guys who were lined up for outside detail with gauze and bandages all around their heads; we called them the "cotton top" crew.

You'd get breakfast only on Saturdays and Sundays, and the other two meals were frozen sandwiches and soup, and the sandwiches were frozen when you got them.

They took IQ tests on every convict when they first came in, but I found out that other convicts did all the tests and recording of the tests. I was told that if I paid off the convicts who gave the test I would receive a high IQ score, and if I didn't they'd give me a low score. I told them to go to hell because I sure didn't give a shit about what IQ score I got in prison.

My job was making shoes for the Brown Shoe Company in St. Louis, for which I was paid five cents a day, along with all the other guys working in the factory. The Brown Shoe Company sold the shoes to Sears Roebuck and Company and also Montgomery Ward stores all over the United States. Even then it seemed a bit ironic to me that the State was assisting those companies in making big money from the public who didn't know the origins of those shoes they were buying, and certainly paying a lot more then it actually cost to make them. The shoes had a logo on the bottom that to the naked eye looked like a bunch of flowers, but if you'd look at it eye level you could make out the printing saying: "Made in Missouri Penitentiary."

A number of guys worked outside the walls down in the coal mine. If you dug coal for 12 hours a day, you'd get extra days of good time and get out quicker if you lived through it and didn't pay later breathing the coal dust. The pit was 80 feet down, and the guys said that they thought about escaping, but hell, digging another hole to get out would have been impossible.

The guards in the towers each had their own whistle that they'd use in defining tones back and forth to one another all night long.

In any case, while in prison there I knew a number of inmates who were on death row, and I knew and saw a number of men who were hanged for their crimes. I always remember how these inmates accepted their fate like real men. In those days the hanging of an inmate was open to the public. Because of these public hangings, there was an unusual quirk that prison doctors performed before an inmate was executed: the doctor would stuff the prisoner's anal cavity firmly with cotton and also they would stretch a rubber band tightly around the prisoner's penis. The cotton and the rubber band were used to keep the prisoner from having a bowel movement and urinating on himself, which naturally and automatically happened when they were dropped through the scaffold trap door. This allowed the executed inmate a measure of dignity in front of all the onlookers who watched these public hangings. We'd hear the guys yell to all the cons the night before the execution, saying that he'd got his cotton and rubber band and he was ready to face them.

There were these two guys locked up on death row that was right by solitary confinement where I just happened to be for 30 days. They had killed a highway patrolman in Boone County, Missouri. One of the guys got the death penalty and was hung, and the other got life. The one who got life worked with me in the shoe factory for a while, but then he killed a guy out on the yard and they hung him, too.

There was this guy in Jeff City from Arkansas who was screwing his sister for years and got mad 'cause she got married and wouldn't let him screw her any more. He told me that he sat and waited by a tree with a shotgun in the moonlight and blew his brother-in-law away when he walked out of the house. He said that he didn't like the idea of him screwing his sister. He got a life sentence, but acted like he really didn't care. He was always chewing tobacco, which the state gives you, and it was always running down the side of his chin and down his neck. Then, instead of getting a haircut in the barber shop like most of the guys did, he'd come down to the shoe shop and take the knife we used to cut the leather with and just whack off clumps of his hair. He wasn't the only guy who did that, and we never could figure out why they just didn't go to the barber.

I was in Jeff City when the radio program "Gang Busters" came on with my story. We were robbing so many banks and gambling places that we were making the whole East Coast hot. They insinuated that I talked out of the side of my mouth and carried a machine gun on that program. Hell, I don't talk out of the side of my mouth, but that's what they made the people think about me. They did stories on all the wanted criminals during those days. The show came on Saturday nights at eight p.m., and when it began there were machine guns going off as the introduction to every story. I even wrote to the radio station to try to get a copy of the program, but couldn't. Some of the guys in Jeff City had their own radios in there, and they wouldn't censor radio programs back then, and they told me about it because they'd listened to it.

George Marune, one of my partners up in Buffalo, died while I was in Jeff City. He got away clean and didn't get caught, but ended up dying. What a shame! I used to go down to Dago town to visit with him and plan scores, not realizing the cops were watching me enter and exit his apartment, putting more heat on both of us.

I was in the hospital in Jeff City one time because of an injury to my knee jumping out of a window to get away from the cops. I noticed all the convicts who worked in the hospital were walking around with a pair of pliers in their back pockets. I found out later that a guy who had a gold tooth was dying in the hospital and they were all waiting for him to go. One guy said, "Damn that son-of-a-bitch, he'll probably die on someone else's shift."

One thing for certain that I found out back then was that the State joints do what they want to do, and the Federal joints go by the rules. For instance, when a rapist came into Jeff City while I was there, he was taken immediately to the prison hospital and castrated before putting him out into the prison population. That made him a marked man in front of all the other convicts, and they usually didn't live too long once the convicts found out that they were rapists. I remembered seeing this heavyset guy when I was in the hospital who had breasts that were big and hanging down just like a woman's, and everyone called him Big Momma. I saw him a few months later out in the yard, and he showed me the horrible zig-zag surgery scars and slits that went from one side of his chest to the other where they cut his breasts out.

Another time out on the yard, two convicts got into a fight, and one had a shiv, and there was a lot of blood. Two guards tried to break them up, but without success. All of a sudden, there was a loud whistle, and with that the two guards stepped back, and the guards up in the gun tower fired at the two convicts, killing them. Nothing was said about it because we knew we had to keep our mouths shut because it was just normal back then and their way of control and power over us guys.

Tom Scott, deputy warden, would walk out in the yard amongst us cons carrying a cane as a weapon and have two huge black guards behind him leading two bad-ass dogs on chains, growling and snarling, just wanting to break free. No one would try to make a move to get to the deputy warden under that kind of security.

I was there in 1938 when they built the gas chamber in the far corner of the yard where all the convicts could see it. The convicts built the entire place stone by stone, and we watched as they brought in the gas chamber along with the 40-foot tower to expel the cyanide gas out into the open air. The entire building was painted white on completion, and any guy going into the yard would have to see it and know it could be used on them. When there was an execution, number six and number seven towers were evacuated. All inmates working at the powerhouse would be kept inside until the execution was over. Officers were assigned outside with shotguns, and guards in the towers were doubled. I could watch the gas chamber and all the activity with a mirror I held out through the bars of my cell aimed out the window. I'd see the car drive up with the condemned man and watch them walk inside. They sealed the chamber with heavy coatings of Vaseline to prevent any leakage during the execution. Then they exhausted the cyanide gas out of the tower for two hours afterward before going inside with protective rubber suits to hose the cyanide residue off the dead man. I could watch as all the cars and the hearse with the body eventually drove away from the place.

I usually watched every execution with my mirror, but sat out on one who was a friend of mine who worked with me in the shoe factory. He got into an argument over stupid bullshit with another guy in the shoe shop, and the kid ended up dead. They executed him and it was just over bullshit, and I hated to even reflect on it.

James Earl Ray was there (who later was accused of assassinating Martin Luther King Jr.), and he was what you called a Gallery Boy in B-Cell House. You could pay him to clean your cell, do your laundry, and shine your shoes or other chores for you. He told me when I first came in that he'd have to charge me for toilet paper. I said, "You're going to charge me for free shit paper? Get the hell outta here and out of my sight, you little son-of-a-bitch." He was just trying to hustle a few bucks from any guy who didn't know better so he could survive.

Pretty Boy Floyd, whose real name was Lester Gillis, was in Jeff City when I was, and he sure had a lot of bum raps pinned on him. The guy was good to a lot of people, and that's why they protected him from the cops for so long down in Oklahoma and into the Ozarks. He made the mistake of going to Dago town in Kansas City, Missouri, trying to buy protection from the Mafia. Hell, they turned on him because they didn't want any of his heat on them, and he had to shoot his way out of the city. He told me over that incident he took a guy named Charlie into the woods that set him up and blew his brains out, plus messed his fingers up so they'd never know who it was. He told me that he rented a round concrete fireproof building in Buffalo, New York that didn't have any corners because they were scared and wanted to hide out there for a while. He told me don't help anybody in the city and that they'd turn you in, and to be careful of the ones you're good to in the city, that they'd hide you for a while, then turn you in.

Two guys from Kansas City, Kansas named John Colbrick and Joe Laincovich robbed the National Guard Armory up at the Memorial Hall building at 600 N. Seventh Street, and they got gunnysacks full of guns and stuff. They were selling those .45 caliber pistols for $5 each. I know that because when Pretty Boy Floyd got caught he even had one of those guns on him.

We all slept on mattresses that were filled with straw at Jeff City, and they all had fleas and bugs in them back then. It seemed like all the time we had to go through fumigation in the showers to get rid of all the bugs and shit on us. After a while you get used to it as just another day in the joint.

There was an old man named Higgins who got a life sentence for molesting all his daughters from the time they were babies until the time they were teenagers.

Another guy was caught screwing his pet pig and was sentenced to Jeff City. He did his time, got out, and only a few months later came back with another sentence for screwing his pet pig again. After I got out years later, I saw him on the streets of Kansas City, Missouri and asked him how he was. He told me that he'd stayed out longer this time than ever before — his pig died!

When Wallace Berry was already a movie star, he'd come there to Jeff City. His chauffeur was doing 40 years for manslaughter, supposedly on a bum charge, and his name was Larry Rush. Larry had a sister that was Wallace Berry's housemaid, plus they were a duo in private because she and Larry were both high yellow blacks and they had to keep it a secret in those days. Wally would visit Larry and tell him he got a good lawyer to work on getting him out. Wallace Berry flew his own plane that was made especially for him by a guy named Wally Howard. Wally Howard Speedster's made planes for the war, and he also made racers to fly faster than any other private plane out there. He'd fly the plane low over the yard, tipping his wings to let Larry know that he was in town to visit him. He'd land just north of the prison on a small landing strip and get a ride to the prison. Eventually he got all the charges dropped on Larry, and he got out a free man. I used to tell Larry to say my hellos to Wally when they visited to let him know I was there.

I knew of two escapes from Jeff City while I was there. One was a guy named Wilson we called the mole, who dug his way out of the place toward the river.

Another guy hid out in the factory where I was working behind a pile of bricks left over from demolishing a lot of the old buildings. There was a spot on the yard that the wall was only nine feet high on the other side. The guy tied a rope to one of the old buildings and swung like Tarzan up and over the wall out of sight and to freedom.

They always wondered how they got all the dope inside the joint at Jeff City, and we used to just watch it take place and laugh. The yard was built inside a hole with 62-foot walls on the inside and only five feet high in some places on the outside. The guys would be playing handball out in the yard and intentionally hit the ball over the wall where the wall was short on the other side. A cohort would be waiting to throw another ball back over the wall that was filled with dope. This could go on all afternoon or until the guards got suspicious. Those guys would be playing handball all afternoon if they could.

Prison guards in Jeff City only made a dollar a day back then, and they would readily chain you to the cell door as punishment. If you had to go to the bathroom, you did it right there where you stood, and if you complained, it wasn't unusual for the guards to crease the guy's skull.

I had an old man as a cell partner who slept on the top bunk, and he was always sick, coughing, choking and gagging. One time I noticed after lock-down he was awfully quiet without making a sound. I got out of my bunk to check on him, and the old son-of-a-bitch had cut his wrists, committing suicide. I yelled for the guard, yelling the old man was dead in here. He told me to shut up and go to sleep and they'd get him out of there when they opened up the doors in the morning at seven a.m. Then to make matters worse, he let his shit out 'cause he couldn't hold his mustard, and I had to put up with that all night.

6

After Jeff City

WHEN I CAME back home from Jeff City, two of my partners, Buddy O'Dell and Alfie Kanton, were waiting for me, and we got right back to casing joints to rob.

They used to have this Croatian Lodge that all the old-timers belonged to in those days. It was a must that you had to be in the Lodge if you lived on Strawberry Hill, and the one we had was named "All for one." I was in the Lodge for years, but this son-of-a-bitch kicked me outta there because of my police record. The guy who had me kicked out was named Sambol, and his son was convicted for embezzlement while he was working for some coal company, but that was all right and he was never kicked out of the lodge. Also, there used to be a little Croatian newspaper published on the hill, and in it they told how I got shot by the city police, and I think that's really why they kicked me out.

There were a husband and wife in the Lodge who also owned a grocery store across the street from Fifth Street Hall who voted to remove me from the Lodge. They cashed payroll checks for their customers at the grocery store, so they kept a lot of cash around at all times. I was sitting in their place one evening reading the newspaper and heard the husband ask his wife in Croatian if she put all the money away that was on hand to cash checks. She said, "Yes, I did," and he handed her a check to cash for a customer. When I heard that, I left the place and stood outside in the dark looking toward their building and could see through the window as she ascended the well-lit stairway to their apartment on the second floor. She kept turning on lights as she walked through the apartment, and when she entered her bedroom, she removed a tin box from under some clothes on the top shelf in the closet and removed money from it. She then turned all the lights out as she locked the apartment door behind her and returned downstairs with the cash for the customer's payroll check. I went to the walkway between the buildings to sum up how to get up to that second-floor apartment window. Then I actually had to crack a smile when I saw this tall ladder further down the walkway leaning up against an adjacent building. I maneuvered the wooden ladder by balancing it straight up and walking it down through the narrow passage right to the bedroom window. I climbed up the ladder, pushed up the unlocked window and entered their bedroom to retrieve the box from the closet that contained about $2,800. I positioned the ladder back exactly where it was before I left to go home. I returned the next day to listen to all the stories about the big robbery in their apartment building. They ended up thinking it was another tenant and fortified their apartment doors and fortified all the locks to prevent someone from ever coming in again, but they never did lock that upstairs window.

Alma and I used to go down to the Hotel Muehlebach in about 1941 and listen to Ann-Margret sing in the Rendezvous Lounge where she first started out before she went to Hollywood. We used to listen to a Polish guy named Liberace play the piano when he was in town performing at the Rendezvous Lounge, and that guy put on a good show even back then.

Alma and I, along with two other couples, were on our way home one Sunday morning after a night out on the town and heard the newspaper kids yelling, "Japs attack Pearl Harbor." No one knew where Pearl Harbor was, and we all thought it was the name of some woman who got attacked in the city somewhere. It wasn't until we got the paper and read all about it that we knew our soldiers had been attacked by the Japanese on an island out in the Pacific.

I went to park my car in a parking lot in Kansas City, Missouri, heading for the Rendezvous Lounge one time, and couldn't believe the guy parking my car was a guy I did time with in Jeff City for stealing cars. He told me that he could get me any keys for any car in the entire parking lot. Then he said that he could get me the names and address of all the guys who parked their cars there so when we took the cars we'd have all the necessary information with us in case we got stopped.

I remember one guy named Jimmy who had a lot of heat on him, and he was called in by the Dagos to meet at a place on 15th Street. When he got down there, they just shot and killed him because of all the heat that was on him, because they didn't want the heat to come back to them.

This kid, Jim Landry, from Kansas City, Kansas, got out of Leavenworth penitentiary, took a bus and rode it to the station at Seventh and State Avenue. There was a cop waiting for him to get off that bus, and before he was able to enter the terminal he shot him right between the eyes. Nothing was ever said in the newspapers about the shooting, only Jimmy's obituary.

Gasoline was tight back in 1941 during wartime, and you had to have an E-card to drive from 7 p.m to 7 a.m. I always stole the E-card from a doctor because he could drive at any time, and there was no limit to the amount of gasoline he could purchase. I had a gasoline station owner named Chet putting gas into my car and my girlfriend's car whenever we needed it. He eventually turned me in to the police. This guy made a lot of money off us guys because when we stole a car we'd drive it into his station, and Chet would break them down to resell the parts. I kept a bunch of hot cars in his garage in Kansas City, Kansas, and only drove the cheap cars to case places so as not to look suspicious, but then used the best and fastest cars for our getaways. This guy, Chet, who I was paying to watch over my cars, went out for a joy ride in one of my fast cars. The cops stopped the son-of-a-bitch, and they put so much heat and pressure on him because of us guys that he ratted on us.

During the war they went around the entire city and dug up all the streetcar tracks that they'd blacktopped over to reuse the iron.

There were two pool halls run by Sicilians and Dagos at Independence and Prospect that sold tires and hot cars during wartime when tires were impossible to get. You could go in and put 35 cents down on four brand new tires back then. I bought four tires and had them hanging up in the garage, and when I went to jail the old man sold them.

My brother, Frank, used to buy his tires at a salvage yard where they'd only cost 15 cents if you took them off the vehicle yourself.

I had a .32.20-gauge gun that required longer shells than a regular .32 caliber, and during the war shells were hard to get. This one guy who sold them told me that by law he could only sell enough bullets to fill up the barrel of my gun and no more. I stood there and had him fill the barrel up, then I'd empty the barrel, putting the bullets in my pocket, and hand the empty gun back for the guy to fill it up again. I did this repeatedly until I had at least a box of shells for my gun.

There used to be the Urban that ran from Kansas City to either Lansing or Leavenworth for a nickel. We guys would go up to the Lansing State Penitentiary to get on special tours to visit inside of the prison. We'd take a hell of a lot of cigarettes with us, and while we were walking with the crowd through the dining room, we'd lay these packs of cigarettes down on the tables, and as fast as we laid them down the convicts would be grabbing them up. They also had tours that went through Leavenworth prison, but they didn't go all over inside the prison like they did in Lansing. They even used to have those kinds of tours in Jeff City, but had to stop all of them because some guys started bringing dope inside to the convicts.

I used to sell whiskey to an all-black club at Third and Washington where they had a big dance hall. I remember delivering a load one time, and a little boy came out screaming over and over again, "I want to take a mess, I want to take a mess." We didn't know what he meant at first, but then he showed us what it was by dropping his drawers and taking a shit right there on the floor, and all we could do was just laugh like hell. Those blacks were good friends of mine and even hid me out a few times until it was safe for me to leave town.

At first, my gang and I would buy all our clothes at Leader's Clothing; then we started going to Woolf Brothers, and eventually we'd only wear tailor-made suits from Jack Henry's on the Country Club Plaza. If a guy joined our gang and didn't have a suit, we'd buy him one and everything to go with it.

There was a place on the corner of Michigan Avenue in Chicago named Finchly's that was just a door with a narrow window glass down one side that was the entire front of his store. Behind that door was one of the best tailors I ever did business with the entire time I was in Chicago.

Willie (right) by his 1941 Buick Century, with Pete Schutte.

We never wore spats back then because I always thought they should be worn with tuxedos, and I never wore a tuxedo. When you'd see a guy wearing spats with a suit back then, you could bet his shoes were worn out and he was covering them up.

We cased the armored cars for days that were driving in and out of an alley in Chicago. We watched them loading up money, but it wasn't until the third day that we saw all the gun guards who were just inside the building waiting for trouble, so we passed on that score.

We were lucky we didn't do the robbery at Loose Wiles Bakery either, because after casing that place we noticed all the gun guards who stood by the armored truck inside the garage while it was being loaded.

After a robbery in Kansas City, we headed for Leavenworth by the back roads until things cooled down. We pulled into a gas station to get gas and decided to get something to eat and clean up a little. We paid the guy to park our car in his garage while we took some rooms at a nearby hotel.

When we were walking back through the gas station to the car, I noticed the service attendant giving us a strange look like he was scared to death.

I asked Red if he said anything to the guy to scare him and he said no. Then Red said that all he did was have the guy remove the ball hitch from the back bumper and throw it in the trunk. I yelled, "You stupid son-of-a-bitch, we have all the shotguns, high-powered rifles and handguns in the damn trunk, and you just showed them to him." We had to snatch another car right away and dump that car because the attendant could identify us to the police. I told Sam I wanted to do a job in some town somewhere, split the money, and then just dump Red off at the closest bar. I wanted to take off leaving him behind to fend for himself because he was nothing but trouble, but then I was also afraid of the heat he might put on us if he started talking.

7

On the Lam

MY STEPMOTHER AND stepfather caused me to go on the lam, and I couldn't do anything about it. My girlfriend, Alma, could've told you she was right there with me at the time they said it happened, and it was just a bum rap. There were three of us couples who would stay out all night on the weekends and hit the joints to listen to the music and watch the floor shows. We were all together when I found out the police were looking for me for something I didn't do. I asked the old man if he thought that any of the three couples would lie when they said that I was with them, and he said no, he didn't think they would lie. I said, "Who do you believe then, the people with this phony charge or the couples you know who were with me and told the truth?" He said, "Those people said it was you," and I could have hit him in his mouth. I got a call from my lawyer, and he said that they already took my case before the Grand Jury. That means you're going right to trial right then, and that was it and I wasn't going to have a preliminary hearing so that I could try to defend myself. I had to go on the lam to get away from that bum rap. I could have gotten out of that rap. Hell, I beat some good raps back then, and even the cops said they knew it was a phony charge. The cops knew that rape wasn't my M-O and said they knew I got out of a couple of good raps and knew that this one was a phony rap that this gal was trying to pin on me.

It was a rape case and I didn't even know these people, but the gal picked me out of a lineup, saying it was me and she would've known me in the middle of the night if I was naked. I found out later that they were just after money because they told Bill Eder, a gambler and the husband to this gal I went to school with, that they just wanted money from me because they knew I had money back then. This gal who picked me out of the lineup was Bill Eder's wife, and he told me she wanted $400 not to prosecute on the rape charges. I told him I'd give her the $400 to drop that bum rap. My foster parents wouldn't believe me and kept saying that it must be you 'cause that woman said it was you. I named about eight people who told him where I was and couldn't have been where that gal said I was.

I had to take off and became a fugitive for two years over this shit. I had a Dago lawyer go up there and pay off the $400 later, but it was my foster folks who were the ones who screwed me around. If they would've given my $5,000 stash to the lawyer, I could have gotten out of that bum rap. Instead, they sold my Buick car and took all my money and didn't do anything to help me, the sons-of-bitches.

I called my girl and told her that I was going to take it on the lam. I told Alma because I knew she wouldn't say anything — she never did — and I kept in touch with her most of the time while I was on the road. I sent her $5,000 and more to give to my folks to fix that bond to keep the heat off me. I told Alma she was the best friend I ever had and the only one I could ever really trust.

My aunt died and left my Uncle Alec a widower on the farm in Lawson, Missouri, northeast of Kansas City. He decided to move into the city with my foster parents into their boarding house. When I first went on the lam, we hid our cars in his barn and lived in his old house on the farm to try to straighten things out on my warrants and figure out what we were going to do. Every time we traveled to the farm, we would go through Kearney, Missouri, which was on the way driving from the city. We always stopped to look at the cabin of Jesse James and his family, which was a tourist stop that was real popular in those days. We liked to walk through the cabin and listen to all the stories about the James Gang.

We read in the newspapers about another phony charge that the cops in Kansas City, Kansas were trying to put on us, and we wanted to get it straightened out by our lawyers right away. So we tried to drive back into the city by going through Bonner Springs, Kansas, but saw the cops had set up roadblocks for us guys. The stupid sons-of-bitches had the roadblocks set up to keep us from leaving the city and we weren't even in the city. We grabbed our heaviest firepower and started shooting and drove our way into the city through the roadblock. If you start firing first and don't let up, everyone ducks for cover and you can go right through, but you can't let up or stop shooting. We got to our lawyer's office and had him start to get these phony charges off us because we weren't even in town at the time.

Johnny, this ornery kid who was with us, said that he needed some cigarettes, and there was a place down in Armourdale that had the kind he wanted. I drove down to 10th and Kansas Avenue and pulled up in front of the place and told Johnny the place looked like it was closed. He said, "I know!" Then there was a loud bang, crash, and there went the front window, and Johnny was climbing inside and turned around and asked me what kind of cigars I wanted. Then we guys had to shoot our way back through another roadblock to get out of the city and head for St. Louis.

I did a few days in the St. Louis jail before bonding out one time, and every morning you'd carry your shit and piss bucket out to a water trough in the center of the room and dump it in. Then you'd rinse the bucket out and put some water in it to take back to your cell for another 24 hours.

They threw me in a lineup, and when they asked me my name I remained silent. They kept asking me to tell them my name and were getting more and more irritated each time. A real nice guard came up alongside of me and with great compassion and concern looked me in the eye and said, "You'd better give them your name because you might get into a lot of trouble." Here I was wanted for jumping bond, car thefts, numerous robberies, bank robberies, escapes and had detainers in Michigan and one in Ohio, and he was worried I'd get be getting into trouble for not giving them my name. I called my lawyer in Kansas City, and it didn't take long before they cut me loose and before they found out all about me. I high-tailed it out of there and went to a guy I knew who drove me back to Excelsior Springs, Missouri.

I knew someone who did time in the Eastern State Prison in Pennsylvania that was known for being one of the worst prisons around. He told me you wore a hood pulled over your head so you couldn't see any of the other convicts in their cells or on either side of the cell house when they took you out and you walked down the corridor. You stayed in your cell 24 hours a day, seven days a week, and had no visitors, books, letters or contact at all with the outside.

We were in Kankakee, Illinois casing the Bear's Supermarkets, and I went into one. While I was there, I noticed a motorcycle rider just walk up to the counter and pick up a collection jar that had a bunch of change in it and walk out. Then when I was casing the other Bear's market, I saw another motorcycle rider take another collection jar from the counter and walk out with it. We went to this bar to get a couple of drinks, and while we were there at least 25 or 30 motorcycle riders came in the place. One of them made the mistake of patting one of the girls with us on her ass. We waited until they left and were all riding down the highway, and we just drove by and peppered them with our .410 shotguns that had birdshot in it.

In Cicero, Illinois, you could buy a Stebins .351 rifle that was just like a machine gun that used clips at a hardware store.

It was a hot day in Peoria, Illinois when I was walking around casing places. I passed a woman who was sweeping her sidewalk, and she asked me if I wanted to come in for iced tea to cool down, and I went inside with her and took a break.

When I was locked up in a jail in Montana, the sheriff was the guy who fought Jack Dempsey. The sheriff was a real big guy, and Jack Dempsey was a little guy. I met and talked to Jack Dempsey in New York where he ran a bar because I knew the girl he was going with at the time.

When us guys wanted to go back to Kansas City, we were always afraid of any heat from the cops still looking for us. So we'd take a train to Excelsior Springs, Missouri, northeast of the city. Then we'd have my buddy Alfie drive up there to pick us up to drive back to the city, letting us know if the cops were still after us and what was going on. No one would notice a stranger in Excelsior Springs because they did such a business with the mineral baths and springs that people from all over would be going in and out of there. No one questioned you if you were a stranger, and the rooms were only $3 a night. They would have bands that did concerts in the park at night that drew huge crowds from all over.

Alfie set me up for a mud bath one time that I'd never done before, telling me how soft it would make my skin and complexion, and I fell for it and agreed to do it. First of all, I think they scraped the mud off the bottom of the river because it smelled like rotten, stinky, smelly fish. I felt like a fool lying there in the smelly mud while Alfie was taking a mineral bath, laughing his ass off at me and telling me what a sight I was.

We both did the mineral bath later on, and I found out you can hardly stand up because you can't sink in the mineral bath it's so thick, and when you try to put your feet down to stand they keep coming back up to the top. Now that bath I really did enjoy, and it actually did make my skin feel softer.

We saw Gene Autry, the "singing cowboy," and Gabby Hayes enjoying a mineral bath one time when we were there. It was a good place to hide out, plus the food was cheap and good. For a dime you could get three flapjacks and a cup of bottomless coffee.

We'd always take the train back to Chicago and enjoyed sitting in the parlor car having a drink to pass the time during the trip. We met and talked to quite a few young people wanting to begin their stardom in Chicago, and one was Marlon Brando who was from Omaha. He said he was heading for Chicago to become a star. Buddy Epson was a real tall guy in a good-looking suit who was also heading to Chicago to do a stage show where he'd tap dance and sing in the show.

Once Buddy and Sam, my partners, and I were riding in a parlor car on our way to Chicago from Kansas City. Buddy went to try to get some gals for us to have drinks with. He brought back three gals, and Sam and I started laughing because two of them were dykes, and they were eyeing every move we tried to make on the young cute girl in the middle.

While walking in front of Marshall Field's Store in Chicago one night I noticed that they had dogs running around the inside of the store as security so that was nice to know and nice to stay away from.

When you walked down Michigan Avenue back then, either the working girls would approach you or someone wanting money for food would line up to stop all of the passersby coming down the avenue. All of us guys got used to it after a while and began referring to certain stores on the street by saying that such and such store is just about "four mooches down the street."

In Chicago there were tunnels running under the streets all over the downtown area. I checked a few of them out and saw that there were doors leading up to every department store from the inside of those tunnels.

We'd check on grocery stores in any good-size town, and if a guy had a chain of them, I'd walk in and tell the manager that I was with the Acme Safe Deposit Company, and could I contract carrying his money to the bank for him? One owner said, "No, thank you, I have the sheriff's department come over and take the money to the bank for us." That's all we needed to know to have it cased for a potential score.

We eventually went to Joplin, Missouri and rented rooms in a building named Ridgeway Apartments. It was 1941, and during the war it wasn't easy to rent apartments as it was before the war because of all the fear people had about invasion of the enemy into our country. This ended up being one of our main hideouts for over a year. If we got separated anywhere along the way after our scores, we'd meet there. We'd pay the rent on it every six months and live just like an ordinary citizen in this corner three-room pad, Rooms 41, 42 and 43.

Now in Chicago I remember the old Cook County jail was the filthiest, dirtiest jail I'd ever been in, and they had bars that were about 15 feet from the front of your cell. You just stood up to the bars in your cell and talked to your visitors who were standing on the other side behind those bars 15 feet away. If you could imagine about eight guys on one side and eight visitors on the other side all talking at once, you didn't know who was talking to who. One black guy would yell out, "I'm standing on my stiff dick for you, Momma." Everything would be going on in their yelling shit back and forth, and it was damn near impossible to understand what was being said directly to you from your visitor. I remember when someone yelled out, "Is anybody getting out of here on Sunday morning?" Then you'd hear someone reply, "Yeah, if they died on Saturday night." When the visitors had to leave, the guys would all go toward the back of their cells where they were able to drop notes down on a string every night yelling back and forth to people standing below. I remember one gal told the guy that it would be easy for him to find her because she would be the one standing on the corner wearing an evening gown.

Something I didn't know was when I went down to Louisville, Kentucky Kate, Sam's girlfriend, and I were walking down the street, and there was a black guy coming toward us, and he jumped off of the curb. I said, "What's the matter with that guy?" Then I found out that they just got out of the way for white people walking down the street. Another time I was in Cincinnati and got on this bus to go to Newport, and the bus driver stopped the bus and said, "All right, you know better than that." I didn't know what it was, but a black guy was sitting toward the front of the bus and he made him go to the back. Then I noticed this sign that said, "Coloreds all to the back." Things were a lot different back then and in that part of the country. The Mason-Dixon line was the Ohio River in Newport, Kentucky.

Kate, Sam's girlfriend, always wanted to go to a fortune teller, and there were plenty of them wanting to tell you the future. So I guess the broad in there must have thought that we were married and referred to us as a loving couple. She'd talk about us together and gave us some good luck pieces to carry with us in the gambling joints. She wanted us to show her our money so she could bless it so it would double and triple in size. Newport was a big gambling town back then, and the streets were lined up with fortune teller shops with the big gold balls hanging over the entrance, and they all wanted to bless your money before you went to gamble.

Taking a train from New York to Florida back then, the train had to stop at the base of a mountain and hook up two extra engines, one on the front and one on the back of the train, to give it the boost it needed to make it up over the top. Sam, Kate and I took the train to Miami, Florida, to enjoy the warmer climate and look around.

I knew Kate for quite a while because I did time with her brother in Jeff City. He was in a bad-ass gang from Armourdale, and we both used to read about each other in the newspapers. Kate married Sam Ricketts, and she introduced me to him and shortly after that we became partners.

To blend in with the people in Florida, we bought light tailored suits, hat and shoes to adapt to the climate. I was walking around casing places, and the heat just went right through the thin soles of the white shoes, and I couldn't walk because my feet were burning so bad. I said to hell with that shit and got my other shoes that had thicker leather soles to walk around in.

We got a motel and stuck around for a week checking things out for potential scores. I fell asleep on the couch listening to Big Band music on the radio, and Sam got some fingernail polish out of Kay's makeup kit and painted my toenails a bright red.

I had Sam take a picture of Kate and me in front of this house with the address numbers in plain view in the photograph. When I got my phony driver's license using the alias Samuel Isaac Ruben, I put the photograph next to it so if a cop would see my driver's license he would see a picture of my wife and me in front of our house.

We didn't like planning any robberies in Florida because there's only one main road in and out of the state. I liked Chicago and lower Manhattan where you could just blend in and never be seen if you were on the lam. I had a partner who got into trouble with the police in Kansas City, Kansas, so he went on the lam to a hotel on Third Street in lower Manhattan. In those days you walked into a hotel and handed the guy at the desk $3, and he'd tell you to go upstairs and pick out your own room by choosing one with the door open. My partner hid out there for over two years until they got the charges fixed and he was told it was safe to return to Kansas City.

I made sure I brought back several boxes of the hand-rolled Cuban cigars that were rolled right in front of you in those little shops back then. I'd never tasted a good cigar since, even though those might have been from tobacco plants brought over from Cuba and grown in Florida.

Kate and Sam wanted to go on a boat ride out in the ocean, so we bought tickets for a trip around the Keys and back. During the boat ride down to the Keys, the captain told us we'd be passing Palm Island Palace where Al Capone lived. They told us that there were restrictions and no one was able to get close to his property along the shore. They supplied us with binoculars, and everyone was able to view the beachfront estate. Then we all saw Big Al himself sitting in a chair wearing a kimono, bare legs showing, wearing a big straw hat, holding a fishing pole. Also, you couldn't help but catch a glimpse of the big guy standing behind Big Al ,watching our boat and holding a rifle in clear sight.

Once out on the water, the captain came and told everyone that there was a chance we could be pulled over by the United States Coast Guard. I froze when I heard that the Coast Guard can stop all touring boats and they're subject to search for foreigners or Germans trying to enter the country since this was during wartime. We were both hot as hell and sweated out the entire trip all the way back to shore, thinking that we'd get busted.

After forgetting about Florida, we headed north again, picking up another guy to work with us named Red Bever who Sam said was okay. I found out fast that Red was a drunk, and I hated it when Sam would go drinking with him because he didn't know when to stop and always caused trouble. I told Sam that Red and his drinking would be our ticket back to the penitentiary.

My partners and I went to Buffalo, New York when we were hot and rented the round fireproof building on Rhode Island Avenue that Pretty Boy Floyd hid out in. It was solid concrete and fireproof, and I'd read about it in the newspapers because when you walked right outside on the corner that's where President McKinley was assassinated. We had to lay low for a while until we could get out of the city since we hit 'em with a bunch of scores and became too hot to move around.

I remember once in Norwood, Ohio, we were just sitting in a bar, and Red turned to me and said, "I bet I can shoot more bottles off the back bar than you can." I told him he was a crazy son-of-a-bitch and got up, turned around to leave, and I heard bang, bang and bang. Sure enough, he was shooting at all the bottles on the back bar. I hated him for drawing all this heat on us when we were already hot from the jobs we pulled.

I have always suffered from allergies, and one time I'd just gotten a shot of antihistamine from a doctor and it messed me up where I felt like I was walking on air. I was walking down Euclid Street in Cleveland, Ohio, and I accidentally bumped into three women walking toward me. They asked if I was all right and wanted to go into a restaurant and have a cup of coffee. I agreed, and once we got inside and I wiped my tearing eyes, I was surprised to be looking at the "Andrew Sisters," Patty, Maxine and Laverne, who were the top singers and movie stars of the 1940s. We had lunch together and just talked about music and events in the news. They all were wearing a heavy yellow-looking makeup on their faces that was unflattering, to say the least, but the conversation was great and I enjoyed their company and the time we spent together.

I was watching a Jew open up a jewelry store on a Monday. I watched how fast he had to go in and turn off the alarms; he had to turn off the night alarm to the day alarm. What I did was take my wristwatch in on a Friday and left it to be cleaned. Then when he opened the store early on Monday I was there and he let me in because he knew I was coming after my watch. We took him to a back room, secured the front door and back door, then proceeded to empty out the store. Now in Cleveland they didn't turn on any sirens on the police cars back then; they just turned on blue lights that didn't give us any problem, and we got away.

We found a hardware store that sold the extra firepower we needed, so we busted in the place a couple weeks before hitting the Cincinnati bank and cleaned out all the weapons.

One time we were robbing the Second National bank in Cincinnati on Rockdale Avenue in a Jewish neighborhood, and what we didn't know was when they turned on the bank alarm it turns all the traffic lights red on all four sides to stop the traffic. The guy we got as our driver named George Ballin was just sitting there and said, "What do you want me to do?" I said: "To hell with the red lights; let's get going." We jumped up on the curb around all the stopped traffic and got away. Here we'd just robbed a bank, and that stupid son-of-a-bitch wanted to wait for a red light because he didn't want to break a traffic violation. We had this all planned out because what we did was headed for a one-way street that was a dead end. We could see the cops following us down there, but what they didn't know was that we had another car over the hill. We jumped out of the car and over this fence and up the hill, then down another hill to our other car, and that's how we got away because they couldn't come after us.

Cincinnati was the city of seven hills, and I think I walked all of them. I met and dated a girl who was an usher in a movie theater in

Cincinnati named Jean Peters, and I read in the papers later on she married Howard Hughes.

Later in Cincinnati I walked into the post office to get some stamps and saw they had our pictures up on the wall "Wanted by the FBI." I knew we had to be cautious and lay low for a while until we could get out of town.

I'd always walk around town checking and casing things out for a future prospect. Down on Main Street in Cincinnati they had this little market area where lots of peddlers had things to sell. I fell for a young girl who worked at a juice stand. I really liked her, and several times a day I'd drop by just to see her and talk to her and buy some juice, in addition to giving her a nice tip every time. I drank so much juice it was coming out my ears, and I swear my skin even looked like it was changing color. I took her out to dinner and a show at one of the clubs one night, and afterward she took me home to meet the aunt that she lived with. I really liked her, but in actuality came to my senses, knowing I couldn't bring her into the kind of life I was living. It was hard to stop seeing her and I hated it, but I knew it was best for her in the long run. We were out walking around one Saturday afternoon and noticed that the streets were blocked with hundreds of people who were just waiting around in all directions. We found out later that Bob Hope and Bing Crosby were making an appearance in town that day.

We got an apartment in Cincinnati, and while sitting at the kitchen table reading the paper, I caught some movement out the corner of my eye. I went to investigate and didn't see a thing. About an hour later I saw something run across the floor, and I woke up Sam and Kate and told them that there's a dog in this apartment, but they just thought I was crazy and seeing things. One night we were listening to Gangbusters on the radio that did another story about us guys, when this little black dog walked into the front room and just sat and looked at us. I got up to go toward the dog, and it ran behind the icebox through a little hole in the wall and back out into the hall.

It was up in Minnesota at the Happy Hour Restaurant in Loring Park, where Red shot a soldier in the bar just because he was drunk and acting crazy like he did when he was drunk. We didn't know it, but Red was also making phone calls to his girlfriend back in Kansas City

WANTED BY THE FBI

SAMUEL RICKETTS, with aliases: George Mason, Sam Rickett, Sam Ricketts, Bob Roberts, George Roberts, Thomas Roberts, "Doc" Ricketts, George Thomas, George Wright, Robert Wright, "Shingle;" age, 28 years, (born December 30, 1914, Atchison, Kansas); height, 5 feet 11 1/8 inches; weight, 135 pounds; eyes, dark brown; hair, black; complexion, sallow; build, slender; race, white; nationality, American; education, 8th grade; occupation, baker; peculiarities, prominent lower jaw, sunken eyes, formerly inmate of insane asylum; FBI Number 1486260; Fingerprint Classification, 16 O 29 W 000 24.
I 20 W 10I

Photographs taken in 1942

Photographs taken in 1942

WILLIAM ISAAC RADKAY, with aliases: James Murphy, William Isaac Ratkay, Willie Batke, Bob Reene, Sammy Reuben, Samuel Isaac Reuben, Samuel Isaac Rowan, George E. Rowan, Sam Rubin; age, 31 years (born September 24, 1911, Kansas City, Kansas); height, 5 feet, 9 3/4 inches; weight, 153 pounds; eyes, brown; hair, dark brown, wavy; build, slender; complexion, sallow; race, white; nationality, American; education, 9th grade; occupation, shoe repairman, lathe operator, carpenter, packing plant worker, steel worker; scars and marks, small scar back left hand, large scar left thumb and palm, small pit scar above right eyebrow, scar middle forehead, 2 small scars right cheek, scar upper lip, bullet scar upper left arm; peculiarities, frequents night clubs; FBI Number 911699.
Fingerprint Classification, 2 O 1 R 100 6.
M 17 R III

HARRY RALPH BEVER, with aliases: Ralph Bever, Harry Ralph Beaver, Larry Dugan, L. J. Dugan, Larry James Dugan, Fred Matthews; age, 26 years (born September 13, 1916, at Millgrove, Missouri); height, 5 feet 9 3/8 inches; weight, 175 pounds; eyes, gray-green, wears rimless glasses; hair, red, wavy; build, medium stocky; complexion, ruddy; race, white; nationality, American; education, 2 years high school; occupation, cook, laborer, bell hop, porter; scars and marks, tattoo, double heart, initials "RB" right arm, 4 small scars right wrist, vaccination left arm, small scar right upper lip, scar left side neck and left earlobe; peculiarities, bushy, red eyebrows, 1 gold crown tooth upper right; FBI Number 2413512.
Fingerprint Classification, 18 L 1 R 100 5.
M 1 U 0I0

Photographs taken in 1942

CLARENCE ALBERT PARSONS, with aliases: Woodrow Holbrook, Clarence Wells; age, 23 years (born at Vanceburg, Kentucky, July 3, 1919); height, 5 feet 10 inches; weight, 150 pounds; eyes, brown; hair, brown; complexion, fair; build, medium; race, white; nationality, American; scars, scar on middle finger of left hand, moles on left and right side of face, vaccination scar on left arm; FBI Number 2135406; Fingerprint Classification, 27 L 25 W 100 16.
L 1 U 000

Photograph taken in 1942

ARTHUR RAYMOND PARSONS, with aliases: Arthur Wells, "Arch," "Bill;" age, 24 years (born at Ravenswood, West Virginia, May 11, 1918); height, 5 feet 9 inches; weight, 170 pounds; eyes, blue; hair, blond, wavy; complexion, ruddy; build, medium; race, white; nationality, American; occupation, cook; scars, 1/2 inch scar left thumb, 3 moles on face, mole on back of neck, vaccination scar on left arm; peculiarities, reported to be mentally deficient; FBI Number 1759011; Fingerprint Classification, 17 O 29 W M00 14.
I 18 U 00I

Photograph taken in 1942

SAMUEL RICKETTS, WILLIAM ISAAC RADKAY, HARRY RALPH BEVER, CLARENCE ALBERT PARSONS, and ARTHUR RAYMOND PARSONS, Federal prisoners who escaped from the Hamilton County Jail, Cincinnati, Ohio, on February 12, 1943, are five of the most desperate and dangerous criminals at large today. RICKETTS, RADKAY, and BEVER were being held for prosecution in connection with the armed robbery the Second National Bank, Avondale Branch, Cincinnati, Ohio, which occurred on October 31, 1942. CLARENCE and ARTHUR PARS... were sentenced on November 23, 1942, in Federal Court at Cincinnati, Ohio, to serve seventy-five years each for kidnaping. Federal complaints were filed against each of these five subjects on February 13, 1943, at Cincinnati, Ohio, charging them with violation of the Federal Escape Act.

If you are in possession of any information concerning the location of any of these subjects, please communicate by telephone or telegraph collect with the undersigned, or with the nearest Division of the Federal Bureau of Investigation, United States Department of Justice, the local addresses and telephone numbers of which are set forth on the reverse side of this notice.

JOHN EDGAR HOOVER, DIRECTOR
FEDERAL BUREAU OF INVESTIGATION
UNITED STATES DEPARTMENT OF JUSTICE
WASHINGTON, D. C.
TELEPHONE, NATIONAL 7117

February 15, 1943

"The picture on this FBI poster was taken about a year earlier when I was in their custody (my picture is next to the arrow, top left). They beat the shit out of me, then tossed me in a cell. A couple of hours later they handcuffed and shackled me and dragged me out for the picture."

and the lines were tapped, so they were able to keep a trace on us. The girls that we were seeing from the Happy Hour Restaurant also told the FBI, after the shooting of the soldier, where we were staying at the apartment there in Minnesota.

When I came back to the apartment with the girl I'd picked up in a bar, we walked in the apartment and it was filled with FBI men. I carried identification on me saying my name was Samuel Isaac Ruben, with a phony picture of my wife and me, and I figured it looked real good and would give me some cover.

All the FBI had their guns drawn, and when the girl I was with saw that, she fainted and peed on herself when she hit the floor. I started taking off my coat, saying, "Man, what is this? I'm a married man with four kids, and I can't be getting into trouble with this girl." They relaxed and lowered their guns while listening to my story, and when they did that, I swirled my coat at them and hit the window, making my escape. Outside the window was a tree, and I was heading right through the glass for a branch of it, but what I didn't know was in Minnesota the windows are double-paned because of the cold winters. When I hit the double-pane glass window, I broke through it, but I just slid down the side of the building two stories, hitting the tree branches all the way down.

That was all I remembered until I woke up three days later in a bed and tried to move, but couldn't. I was shackled and strapped down to the bed by my hands, feet and midsection. A good-looking young nurse came in with a newspaper to show me the big headlines of my capture, and in a sexy voice said, "Sammy, you've been a bad boy." She said that I'd been unconscious for three days and wasn't expected to live in the beginning. She'd bring me coffee several times during the day and even tried to loosen up my cuffs to make it easier to drink. She'd sit and talk to me, and we'd laugh as she complimented me on the color of my red toenail polish which was half-gone by now.

They had a guard sitting in the room 24 hours a day watching me, and in three or four days he had the cute nurse transferred to another department because he thought she was getting too friendly with me. When they got rid of her, they got this old hag who even put another strap across my belly and sure kept the straps a lot tighter all over me than the other nurse.

When they took me to the jail in St. Paul, Minnesota, I still refused to give them my right name and insisted that I was Samuel Isaac Ruben.

When I was going into the jail, that damn Red yelled out to me, saying: "Hi, Willie!"

Later the FBI came up to me and said, "Radkay, let's cut this shit out; we know who you are by your fingerprints that we took from you when you were in a coma for three days." I just said: "Well, well, imagine that!"

So here I was in the St. Paul jail, heading back to face bank robbery charges in Cincinnati. They transferred us to the jail by automobile with U.S. marshals who had guns drawn the entire trip.

From **THE KANSAS CITY STAR,** *February 27, 1943:*

William I. Radkay, Who Called Himself "Little Al Capone," Leads Group, Which was Widely Sought

Minneapolis police yesterday stopped the operations of a gang described as "one of the toughest in the country" when they arrested three Kansas Citizens following a shooting in a Minneapolis bar. All three have criminal records here, and one is still wanted by Kansas City police. He is William Radkay, 31 years old, alias Sam Radke and Sam Rubin, who called himself the "Little Al Capone of Kansas City, Kansas," in 1931 and who engineered the $9,000 Woodstock Hoefer Watch and Jewelry Company holdup March 4, 1935. He was injured yesterday trying to escape from Minneapolis police by jumping out of a second-story hotel room and was taken to the Minneapolis General hospital where he was chained to his bed.

The other two guys are George (Sam) Ricketts, alias George Wright, wanted with Radkay for holdups in the East, and Harry Ralph Bever, 26, alias Harry Dugan, a former cook and bellhop in a hotel here. Radkay gave Kansas City police his address as 250 North Fifth street, Kansas City, Kansas. Wright told Minneapolis police he lived at 3023 Montgall avenue, Kansas City, the home of his mother, and Bever said he lived at 115 East Thirty-third street, Kansas City.

Firearms in Their Car.

Bever is a deserter from the army and is wanted by the Federal Bureau of Investigation on several counts, Minneapolis police said. They added Bever admitted shooting Cpl. Harold Bartholomew, 34, in the Minneapolis bar Monday night, and was in possession of a stolen car, in which numerous firearms and license plates from eight states were found.

Bartholomew was wounded in the jaw. He is expected to recover. Radkay has a long record with Kansas City police. He was sentenced to the Kansas reformatory at Hutchinson, December 1935, for holding up Max Fox Jewelry store November 2, 1931. For his part in the jewelry holdup, Radkay was sentenced to serve ten years in the Missouri penitentiary. Radkay received a parole from that prison. He was arrested after a holdup here last December 16, and released on $10,000 bond later in December.

In Niagara Falls Holdup

Nothing more was heard of "Little Al Capone" until August, when the Niagara Falls, NY., police department asked police here to check on Missouri license plates of a car which was used in holding up a tavern at Niagara Falls by four men. The plates had been issued to Ricketts. Pictures of the three men now held and Harry O'Dell, who was thought to be in the car, were identified by the Niagara Falls victims. Similar holdups followed in Cincinnati, Cleveland and Milwaukee, with only three men participating in the robberies specializing in gambling joints, nightclubs and taverns.

From **THE KANSAS CITY STAR**, *February 27, 1943:*

After Escape from Police Here in Revolver Battle, Men Steal a Car and Flee Eastward.

A lucky break in finding a parked car with motor running gave the three desperadoes who escaped a hail of bullets here last night an opportunity to flee the city and reach St. Louis early this morning, Lester W. Kircher, superintendent of the police burglary and robbery unit, believed today.

Reports gathered by the detectives and FBI agents who are directing the search indicate that William I. Radkay, 31 years old, and Harry R. Bever, 26, both of Kansas City, and Samuel Ricketts, 28, of St. Paul, stole a maroon Pontiac coach within two hours of the shooting and escaped.

Meet after Their Escape.

Police believe the men had a prearranged plan to meet after they had separated in escaping from the trap in the 1800 block on Pendleton avenue early last night. Bever ran in a southwesterly direction from the scene, and the others dodged away toward the southeast. The trap was sprung shortly after 6 o'clock. A few minutes after 8 o'clock, police learned a Pontiac coupe owned by Floyd South, 621 Woodland avenue, was stolen from in front of the South home. South had left his machine parked at the curb with motor running and gasoline ration book in the glove compartment. He parked at 8:05 o'clock, was in his home ten minutes, and found the car gone when he returned.

At 6 o'clock this morning police received a radio message from St. Louis that a maroon Pontiac coupe had dashed at top speed through Kirkwood, just outside of St. Louis. Two patrolmen there attempted to stop the car, firing two shots, but it never slackened speed.

Three Men in a Car.

The Kirkwood officers said three men were in the coupe, but were unable to obtain the license number. When taken from here the Pontiac carried 1942 Missouri plates 716-908. Highway police of Missouri and bordering states have been notified to keep a close lookout for the machine.

The three men escaped from the Hamilton County jail in Cincinnati while awaiting trial on bank robbery charges. Information they were in Kansas City was received by Willis early yesterday and the trap was prepared. The tip the trio was in Kansas City came from a traffic patrolman at Independence and Woodland avenues who saw the car Friday.

Radkay has a long list of arrests in police records of Kansas City, Kansas. No specific charge is pending against Bever here, but police records show pick-up orders from St. Joseph on a highway robbery charge, and from Ft. Benning, GA.

From **THE KANSAS CITY STAR**, *March 1, 1943:*

KILLERS 'HOLE UP' HERE

FBI Believes Radkay, Bever and Ricketts Are in City. All Citizens Are Asked to Be on Lookout for the Desperadoes Who Escaped Trap Last Friday Night.

Lookout for the Desperadoes Who Escaped Trap Last Friday Night.

Three bandits described by the FBI as the most vicious and dangerous criminals at large in this country, and made more desperate by minor injuries and shortage of funds are believed by FBI agents to be "holed up" in Kansas City, a potential menace to all citizens.

Since their escape from a police and FBI net in a pistol battle in the 1800 block on Pendleton avenue Friday night, the Federal Bureau of Investigation has extended its search over a wide area. It found evidence today, Dwight Brantley, agent in charge, said, that the men still are here, ready for a new outbreak.

Long String of Crimes.

The FBI today asked that every citizen be on the lookout for William Isaac Radkay, Ralph Bever and Samuel Ricketts, all with aliases, all with criminal records. They are wanted for the armed robbery of a bank at Cincinnati, November 23, and bureau agents list a long series of other crimes for which the government is prepared to prosecute them.

The men have friends in Kansas City, and the FBI believes they have had help in keeping under cover.

"They can't stay hidden long," an agent said today. "They are about out of money, they have injuries to be treated, and unless they are captured they may be expected to stage any kind of a crime to get away."

Radkay is described as the leader of the mob. He was born thirty-one years ago in Kansas City, Kansas. To illustrate his desperate character, an agent for the bureau described an escape recently from agents at Minneapolis.

Out Window to Freedom.

Radkay was cornered in his second-story room in a hotel and ostensibly was ready to surrender. When he removed his coat and the agent reached for it, Radkay plunged through a window to the street below. He suffered a broken arm and an injured head. He still has a limp in the right foot, the FBI said.

Bever is described as a cold-blooded killer. After the bank robbery in Cincinnati, FBI agents were told Bever was in a restroom in a Cincinnati tavern when he dropped his pistol. As he stooped to pick it up, he remarked to a soldier in uniform, "I'm a tough guy."

The soldier replied. "If you are so tough, why aren't you in the army?" Bever, agents assert, whirled at the soldier, saying: "I'll show you how tough I am," and shot him in the head. The soldier is recovering from dangerous injuries, according to the information.

Bever is described as using the aliases Larry Dugan, L.J. Dugan and Fred Matthews. He is 26 years old and was born at Millgrove, Missouri.

His Nickname Tattooed.

He is 5 feet 9-1/2 inches tall, weight 175 pounds, has gray-green eyes, hair red, wavy hair and a ruddy complexion. He has been a cook, bell-boy, porter and laborer, has a double heart and the letters, Red, tattooed on the right arm.

Radkay is know also as James Murphy, William Isaac Ratkay, Willie Ratke, Bob Breese, Sammy Reubmen and George E. Rowan. He is 5 feet 9 inches tall, weighs 150 pounds, has brown eyes and hair and has worked as a shoe repairman, lathe operator, carpenter, packing plant worker and steelworker. He has scars on the back of the left hand, on the left thumb and palm, above the right eyebrow, on the middle forearm, upper lip and a bullet scar on the upper left arm. He is a persistent night club frequenter, the FBI said.

8

Cincinnati Jail Break

WHEN THE U.S. marshals led me into the Cincinnati jail, I was walking ahead of an old marshal coming down the steps behind me. He kicked me in the kidneys as hard as he could, and I dropped to my knees and he kicked me again, telling me to get up and keep on moving.

Here we were locked up in the Cincinnati jail — Sam Ricketts, Red Bever and me. The jail itself was boasted to be "escape proof," and we were put into a special unit that was high maximum security. We were watched and checked by a guard hourly walking outside the cells. Otherwise this guard just sat there in a bulletproof cage.

Kate came to visit me with my foster mother when I was locked up in Cincinnati. I told her not to say anything to the old lady because she didn't know anything, and the only reason she came to see me was to find out if I had any money hidden away back at the house.

A black trustee gave us the information that most of the guards would be off duty from the jail on Valentine's Day working traffic out on the roads. He said that they'd only have a skeleton crew on duty in the jail. After the trustee told us this information and knew we'd make our escape, he said that he'd go back to his cell and pray for us. We gave him all our extra suits and clothes because we weren't taking them with us. Then he went on to tell us not to go all the way down to the basement on the elevator because there was a guard down there in a gun cage.

We were hoping that a nice guard or one that was good to us wasn't on duty during the escape. There were two good guards that would even go to the store for us, and we sure hoped that they were out of the building when we made our break because we didn't want any confrontation with a guard that was good to us. This one guard we liked told me that they had to go in and raid a hotel, and when they were hauling a whore out the door, she started yelling so loud for all the people who were standing around watching to hear, "Look at him, he just screwed me, and now he wants to haul my ass off to jail."

It was Friday, Valentine's Day, February 12, 1943, when I made a shiv out of a shower handle that I bent straight and hid in the cast I had on my arm from my exit out of the window in Minnesota. I spilled the water from a mop bucket on the floor, and it flooded the entire cell with water. I pleaded for help from the guard, showing him the cast on my arm and telling him I couldn't get it cleaned up. That's when the guard came inside the cell to help me, and when he did, "he was ours."

Red had the metal rollers off a mop bucket, and he and Sam were hiding behind the door to the mop closet. One guard saw us out of our cells and said, "What the fuck are you doing?" That's when Red hit him with the metal rollers and made his head look like it had liver coming out of it. Red was a big guy weighing around 220 pounds, and he hit that guard so hard that we read in the papers later his mind was messed up and he couldn't return to work. None of the good guards were on duty that day in the jail, so it was easier for us to make our escape.

We told everyone in the jail that they could escape along with us. I asked a guy named Tony Treat who raped and murdered a nine-year-old girl and was still wearing these bloody overalls with a blood slick dried on the front of them if he wanted to escape. He put his index finger to his chin and pondered for a moment and then said, "No, I better not." I read in the newspapers later on that he was executed for his crime. He just sat around in his cell crying all day and night because he knew he was facing execution for what he'd done.

When we got off the elevator on the second floor, we met some guy in the corridor and told him we wanted to get out of the building. He said that he would tell us how to get out and leave us alone, and we told him: "No, you're going to go with us." We walked him down the hallway, which led us right out of the building.

It was five o'clock in the afternoon, and at the street light right in front of the jailhouse cars were stopped waiting for the light to change. Hell, you could take your choice of cars, so we grabbed the first car we got to, and I threw out the driver while Sam and Red got into the back seat. It was then we noticed a woman still sitting in the passenger seat, so we had to stop the car and push her out to continue on.

Two rape fiends tried to get into the car that we were in, and we told them hell no and booted them out. I read in the newspapers soon after that they were both later caught down by the river with two young girls that they had grabbed off the street and raped.

We were listening to the radio as we made our getaway in the stolen car and the reports of the jail break and how they described the car we were driving, saying it had white wall tires with red wire wheels, and it damn sure did. We pulled into an open garage somewhere along the street and just closed the door behind us. We figured the guy would come home and open up his garage and see the car and turn it in to the police, and we wanted to get as far away as possible from that garage. We were ready though; if anyone had opened up the garage before we got away, we were ready to grab them.

We kept walking away from the garage looking for anybody's house that we could take over. We noticed one house that looked like it didn't have anyone home, so we broke a window and got in. There was snow on the ground, and we made sure we didn't leave any footprints.

When we got inside the house, we noticed that all of the furniture was covered with white cloths and the pantry was loaded with canned goods. We thought we'd wait for someone to come home and just take them over.

We started small fires on the wood floor to heat up the canned food, and when we burned the floor too much just moved to a different spot.

Then I remembered that there was a murder mystery about this house that I'd read about in a detective magazine a few years before that this guy was a fire captain and was murdered in that house. It was in all the newspapers how the house was now abandoned, and a woman came in now and then and checked on it, and that's why all of the furniture was covered and the pantry was filled with canned goods.

Not far from this house was a hospital named St. Augustine's. At

From the **CINCINNATI ENQUIRER,** *February 13, 1943:*

FIVE PRISONERS ESCAPE FROM JAIL
Freedom Refused by 287. Federal Felons Subdue Guards and Matron, Then Grab Auto on Street — Soldier Brothers, Alleged Bank Robbers, Flee.

Five prisoners, two under 75-year sentences for kidnapping and three awaiting trial for bank robbery, which carries a possible life sentence, made a daring escape from Hamilton County Jail at 5:55 o'clock last night.

The break was executed with such cunning that for at least 30 minutes before they fled the five desperadoes were in complete charge of the jail, having overpowered the entire night crew of three jail guards, a dispatcher, and the chief matron. One guard was beaten.

As the prisoners held control of the jail they offered freedom to the 270 male prisoners and 17 women. None except the ringleaders accepted the opportunity. Among those refusing was Anthony (Tony) Treat, under death sentence for murder, and four women awaiting trial for murder.

Five Make Escape.

Those who escaped:

Arthur Parsons, 24 years old, and his brother, Clarence, 23, formerly of North Bend, who are under sentence for conviction under the Lindbergh law for kidnapping a 15-year-old Manchester, Ohio, girl.

Harry Bever, 27, Kansas City, Mo.; William C. Radkay, 27, Kansas City, Kan.; and Samuel Ricketts, 28, St. Paul, Minn. under Federal and state indictments for the robbery of the Second National Bank, Avondale. They were named also in robbery charges involving hold-ups at several suburban places last fall.

Familiar with the routine of jail life, the prisoners executed the delivery with the smoothness of a motion picture thriller,. Included in the details of the plot was the time that the outer guard ate his supper, which customarily is delivered to him at the main jail gate.

Wait for Third.

Upon leaving the sixth floor jail and failing to steal an automobile from a man and his wife on Central Parkway near Main Street, the five felons ran to the middle of the street, stopping a flow of evening traffic, to steal an automobile from another couple.

Less than two hours later this machine was abandoned in Avondale and another one stolen. The second car was abandoned after it was wrecked in a skid on the main drive in Eden Park, near the greenhouse.

Two of the suspects were reported to have fled from the wrecked machine. Almost immediately hundreds of police and sheriff's deputies blocked all foot and motor traffic at the entrances in the big park.

Just before this blockade was established, a stolen car in which the suspects were fleeing was chased and shot at by Patrolman Alvin Grahencamp.

After an hour's search over the grassy and wounded hills, made slippery by rain, the blockade was lifted when it became evident that the suspects had escaped.

Sheriff C. Taylor Handman, who took charge of the search, also launched an investigation into the jail delivery. Although stating that he would not fix the blame until his investigation was com-

(Continued next page)

pleted, he said that jail rules would be tightened.

"There'll be rules and orders here that nobody can misunderstand," the Sheriff said. "There will be drill and examination every week for every guard and employee. The slightest violation will bring summary dismissal."

Virtually every Sheriff's office employee of all shifts reported for duty as soon as the word of the break was broadcast.

Sheriff Handman said it was evident that ringleaders had figured out everything and timed the break to the smallest detail. He said it was possible they had outside assistance.

Details of the escape, assembled by Handman, his Chief Deputy, John Behle, Captain William Wiggerington, and Elmer Jansen and William Holtke, special investigators, showed that the quintet worked with precision. One of them even tarried long enough to change clothing, which was bloodied during the assault upon Ryan.

The delivery started, Handman and Behle said, when Albert Kneuven, an inner guard on the south block, answered an urgent call from prisoners in E Range that the cells and kitchen were being flooded by stopped-up plumbing. The two convicted kidnappers and the suspected bank robbers called out that they needed a mop and a bucket. A Negro trusty is said to have given them a mop, while the call for a bucket was repeated.

Kneuven, seeing that cell blocks were being flooded by water which, it was learned later, came from plumbing plugged by the prisoners. Kneuven, threatened with a roller from a mop bucket, a dirk fashioned to a dull point from a bath shower lever, and a piece of heavy wire shaped into a dagger, was held captive while two of the men went into the north block, where they overpowered the other inner guard, John Goermiller.

Goermiller said he was not aware that the prisoners were loose until they seized him. Throughout their operations the men were without shoes.

With Kneuven and Goermiller locked in cells, two or three of the armed men went to the kitchen, where they started to prepare a meal for Guard Ryan. Goermiller said he was asked what time Ryan usually ate. When he said he didn't know, he was told he was to take Ryan's meal to the main gate. This gate had to be opened from the outside before anyone could leave the jail.

Instead of cooking meat which they started to fry, the felons changed their plans. Two of them guarded Kneuven and Goermiller. The three others went to the sides of the main door to wait for Ryan to inquire for his supper.

Before doing this, however, the men called out to Treat, who is under death sentence for the sex slaying of 10-year-old Helen Sellers, telling him he could come along. Treat and other prisoners declined the opportunity, as did another prisoner whose first name is Tony.

When Ryan opened the main jail gate leading to safety, he was overwhelmed by the three men, one being one of the Parson brothers. He was robbed of his keys, which gave the five prisoners access to the elevators leading outdoors.

While Ryan was kept under guard, two of the thugs rushed into the jail office, seizing Clem Noll, dispatcher.

When he tried to get to a telephone, the two were upon him before he moved three feet, he said. Threatened with the dirk and a small knife, which the quintet did not abandon as they did some of their hand-fashioned weapons, Noll was taken into a small "isolation cell," just

(Continued next page)

within the main jail gate. He was kept there while two of the prisoners went to the seventh-floor quarters where women prisoners are kept. Telling Mrs. Margaret Stephens, Chief Matron, who was on duty alone, that "you better come along without any trouble," the pair led her to the isolation room and made her a prisoner with Noll.

During their stay in the women's quarters, the two men told the 17 women prisoners that "you all can come out." None, including four women awaiting trail for murder, left.

In fact, it was one of the women prisoners, Helen Ann (Buddy Hudson, awaiting trial on a forgery charge, who telephoned the alarm to Station X after they heard the convicts flee. One Negro woman, who pulled the automatic alarm in the jail office, refused to tell her name or to pose for a picture.

Released by other prisoners as soon as it became evident that the escapees had fled, the victims of the delivery made an immediate check of the cells which contained 270 male prisoners. Ryan, although bloody and painfully injured on the head, remained untreated until he had given information regarding the delivery. Later Patrolmen Charles Kathman and Charles Frick took him to General Hospital.

Before the five convicts left the jail office, one of the Parsons brothers forced one of the prisoners, who remained behind, to trade his trousers and shirt for clothing bloodied during the assault.

The quintet also took time to replace their shoes before they used the jail elevator to take them to the fourth-floor level.

Apparently not wishing to leave the Courthouse by one of the main doors, and not knowing which doors were open, the five pushed into the County Planning Commission Office, where they found William W. Kelly, a draftman.

One of them rabbit-punched Kelly on the back of the neck, telling him, "You're going to lead us out of this place!" When Kelly answered, "I can't do that," he said they forced him to accompany them through the corridors.

Jump from Window.

Kelly said he was told to "go ahead and see if the way is clear." He said that when the thugs reached the first-floor corridor, they saw an open window leading to the courtyard and stopped. Jumping from the window, which is only a few feet from the top of a garage roof, the five prisoners hung from the garage roof, then dropped 25 feet into the courtyard.

Running from the automobile driveway to Sycamore Street, they tried to take an automobile away from Mr. and Mrs. Raymond L. Schacdler, 533 East Thirteenth Street.

that time gasoline was being rationed, and you couldn't get any gas before seven in the morning or after seven in the evening. We knew that all doctors could get gas at any time because they had this "E" in their windshield, which meant that they were exempt from any restrictions. We waited there in the parking lot, and here comes this guy out of the hospital, so we grabbed him and took his car, which lucky for us was one with an "E" on the windshield, plus he had lots of gas coupons so we could get gas in the car.

We took him back to his house and tied him up and left him in his basement. We hid out in his house for a short while, then took off in his car. We put some letters in the mailbox to his house in case he had other family members living there, plus one to the police in Cincinnati telling them he was there in the basement. We found out later in the papers that he got loose by himself, but by that time we were on the highway heading for Louisville.

We got into Louisville and realized we were in another area that had a hospital close by. I went in to rent a room and told the guy at the desk the room was for my wife, my daughter and me. I gave him a story that I was getting treatment at the hospital and I wanted a room close by where my wife and daughter would be joining me shortly. We knew that three guys couldn't rent a room without suspicion after the jailbreak, but the guy bought my story, and I slipped Sam and Red into the room later.

The FBI was all over the town searching for us, and I could hear them walking the corridor of the hotel we were in knocking on doors and asking questions. They knocked on our door, and I could hear the desk clerk say, "No, there is just a Mr. Sullivan with his wife and his daughter in there." I was lucky he took my word for it and believed the story I gave him.

We had to lay low for a while because out the window of this room we rented we could see guys in suits walking up to all the houses on the block, and we knew it was the FBI, and they were questioning all the residents in the area looking for us.

When we were ready to leave, we walked to a nearby garage that had valet parking. All the keys were hung up on a board ready to be chosen for our latest vehicle to freedom. We got into a car, and I could hear the guy behind me holler, "Stop that car." We got out of there all right and drove through St. Louis and on to Kansas City, Missouri, making our getaway.

We ended up at this hotel up on Troost Avenue, and again I was the one who rented the rooms and sneaked Sam and Red in later when I thought it was safe.

We had a lot of heat on us and knew that if we contacted any of our friends and family we had to be extra careful because they were watching for us. We knew this guy that had a lot of heat on himself just like we did, and he contacted a friend and asked for help, but the friend came and shot him in the head because he didn't want to put the heat or problems on himself by helping his friend.

Sam wanted to contact some of the Italians he knew in Kansas City, but I told him "No!" The Costa Nostra wanted to help you for a price, but they didn't want any heat on themselves and would just bump you off instead. The Costa Nostra wanted in on all the scores to get their cut of the profits, but didn't want in on anything else, especially the heat from guys who were wanted and being hunted like us.

I was walking back to the hotel room one afternoon and noticed the newspaper headline on a paper stand on the corner. It was a *Kansas City Star* Extra edition, and the headline read, "Get Rid of this Menace," and it had all three of our pictures printed on the bottom of the page.

When I walked back into the hotel lobby, I knew that the guy at the desk recognized me because he looked up at me and then down at the newspaper he had on the counter. I ran to the rooms and told the guys about our pictures in the paper and told them we had to get out of there fast.

Sam and I knew that the FBI would tap all our family's phones, so we knew better than to make any calls home. Now Red messed up by calling someone, a girlfriend, and her lines were tapped, and they traced it right to the hotel and to us.

We were going out the side entrance to the hotel, but it was too late because the desk clerk had called the FBI and they had the entire neighborhood surrounded. I walked outside, and right away the FBI spotted me and grabbed me on the street in front of the hotel. Red got away, and a truck driver took him out of town. Sam got a taxicab and got away from the hotel, but the FBI found out later where the cabdriver dropped him off. They went there surrounding the place and busted in and grabbed him and hauled him off.

We had a meeting place in Joplin, Missouri where we'd always meet if we got separated on any score. We just paid the rent at the Ridgeway Apartments for six months so it would always be ready for us. When Red went to Joplin and Sam and I didn't show up, he knew that the FBI had busted us. We found out later that Red went to a gas station on Central Avenue where this guy Chet was holding some money for all of us, plus had a few cars of ours parked and hidden. Red got all of the money and a car and went down to Texas.

Soon afterward Red murdered a deputy sheriff in Texas and was caught later by the Army for AWOL and murder. When they caught Red in Texas for murder, boy, did he start singing about everything we'd ever done together, but I understood that, knowing he was singing to try to save his own life from execution. He was executed for those crimes by a firing squad in Texas, and I'm just thankful that I wasn't with him because they probably would've executed me, too.

When we got busted in Kansas City later, the FBI asked us if we heard about the bogus story they had printed about us in the St. Louis paper. The story was about a shoot-out and capture of Red, Sam and me. They wanted us to think that the Kansas City police thought we were captured in St. Louis and we'd come out of the hole we were hiding in within the city.

We were transferred back to Cincinnati and sentenced for the bank robbery plus the escape.

The United States marshal told the Cincinnati jail authorities later, "That guy (talking about me) took pictures of the whole place when you first brought him in, and he was already planning his escape the first day you locked him up."

If they'd just put us in the general population part of the jail, we couldn't have escaped because there were too many "stool pigeons" but they put us in the maximum-security part of the jail instead.

From **THE KANSAS CITY STAR,** *March 2, 1943:*

FBI GETS TWO GANGSTERS

William Radkay, Leader of Desperate Criminal Band, and Samuel Ricketts Captured Here Without Any Gunplay or Resistance

—

Seek Third Man
Ralph Bever, Last of the Mob, Still Is Believed Hiding in Kansas City.
GIVES CREDIT TO THE STAR
**Dwight Brantley, Chief Here, Says Telephone "Tips" Came in From Readers.
An All-Night Search by Agents and Policemen for One of Desperadoes.**
BOTH ARE TAKEN EASILY
One Arrested Near Linwood and Troost, Another at 721 West Eleventh

MANACLED AND COWED, two prisoners, William Radkay (left) and Samuel Ricketts, are shown when they were arraigned before Charles H. Thompson, United States commissioner, at the federal building today. A heavy leather belt (visible on Radkay) around the waist of each man is linked to steel handcuffs by chains, permitting only limited movement of the criminals' hands. Radkay, the leader of the gang broken up here by the FBI, was dressed in a leather-paneled felt jacket, bright plaid shirt without tie, and gray trousers. He was hatless when captured. Ricketts wore an all-leather jacket, conventional shirt and tie and carried a gray felt hat. Both pleaded not guilty, and each was held under $50,000 bond for return to Cincinnati for trial on the bank robbery charges. (Kansas City Star photo). (Continued next page)

Two of the nation's top-ranking criminals, sought here by the government and police since they eluded arrest in a gun battle last Friday, were captured by FBI agents last night and early today without resistance.

William Isaac Radkay was picked up on Troost avenue about 5:30 o'clock yesterday afternoon by two special agents, and Samuel Ricketts was captured about 5:45 o'clock this morning cowering behind a basement door in a rooming house.

Ralph Bever, the third member of the mob, eluded the net set for them and is being sought in an intensive manhunt.

An Aid in the Capture.

Dwight Brantley, FBI special agent in charge, said the arrests were made on leads supplied by readers of The Star, following publication yesterday of photographs of the bandits and the story of their criminal exploits.

The hoodlums are described by Brantley as the most vicious and dangerous criminals in the nation, rating with such desperadoes as the former Touhy gang, the Dillinger mob and the Barker-Karpis outfit which once spread terror.

Bever, the bandit still eluding captors, will continue as a threat in the community until he is a prisoner, agents said. He is described as a cold-blooded, heartless criminal. He is the gunman who, when taunted by a soldier because he was not in uniform, shot the soldier through the head. Brantley asked today for further co-operation by citizens with information that may disclose Bever's hiding place.

Soon after The Star appeared on the streets last night with the pictures of the three desperadoes and the story of their being "holed up" here, the FBI office began to receive telephone calls from persons who believed they had seen men answering to the descriptions given.

On an Anonymous "Tip."

Among the first was a person who said: "I think the men are at 1106 East Thirty-third street."

This person gave no name and immediately broke the connection. Within a few minutes two motor cars carrying FBI agents were approaching the Amidor hotel at the address given.

Meanwhile, two other agents who were in the neighborhood on the city-wide search for the gangsters recognized and took Radkay on the street.

These agents, who had studied and memorized the features of the three convicts, were walking south on the east side of Troost avenue between Linwood boulevard and Thirty-third street. They passed Radkay going in the opposite direction.

"That's our man," one of the agents said, and the two whirled and pinned Radkay's arms behind him, taking him by complete surprise. The desperado was handcuffed and taken to the car of the agents near by and then to the office of the FBI on the seventh floor of the United States courthouse.

Radkay was unarmed and was believed to be fleeing from the quarters at the nearby hotel after having seen his own photograph on the front page of The Star. Agents learned later he had bought a copy of the newspaper a short time before he was captured.

No letup on Calls.

The calls continued to reach FBI headquarters through the night, Brantley said, and between 5 and 6 o'clock this morning another tip produced results. It was to the effect that two of the bandits could be found at a rooming house at 721 West Eleventh street.

Four FBI agents in one car and four patrolmen in another went quietly to the West Eleventh Street address and were admitted by the manager. Room by room, the place was searched. Lodgers were routed out and questioned, but the men sought apparently were not there. Officers remained outside to see that no one slipped away.

When all the remainder of the building had been combed, the agents went to

(Continued next page)

the basement searching for hiding places. Near the coal bin an officer closed a door that had been standing open, and behind it, cowering and knees shaking, was Ricketts. He offered no resistance. His hands went up when the moving door revealed him, Brantley, who was present, said.

His Comment Brief.

"Well, you've got me," he said, and that was his only spoken word immediately following his capture.

In moving on Rickett's hideout, the FBI verified the fact he was at the address through a taxicab driver.

At 5:25 this morning a Yellow cab was called to the Eleventh Street address. The driver, Fred Jewett, picked up a man at the entrance.

"I was to get another man here," the passenger said, "but I don't see him. Drive around the block and maybe we can spot him." The round trip was made without finding the other man. "Well, I guess someone else picked him up this morning," said the man as he discharged the taxi and returned to the rooming house.

Recognizes the Convict.

Back at his starting point Jewett was met by an FBI agent, who questioned him about the call, showing him a picture of one of the bandits. Jewett recognized Ricketts as the passenger.

Incidentally, Jewett said he has known Bever, the third member of the gang, for several years; that he used to be a hotel porter here.

"When sober, Bever is the mildest kind of a man," Jewett said, "but with a few drinks inside he goes clean crazy."

Agents investigating at the Amidor hotel said they learned the three bandits registered there at 12:25 o'clock last Thursday morning. It was Friday night that the bandits shot it out with FBI agents and police in the 1800 block on Pendleton avenue. The entrance is on Thirty-third street. A small lobby with a few chairs is on the ground floor. The desk is at the head of the stairs. The hotel is occupied mostly by war workers, Mrs. Maude Daly, manager, said.

Following Radkay's capture, police and FBI agents threw a guard over the whole neighborhood on Thirty-third street and Troost avenue. Men still were on duty there today.

No Money, No Baggage.

Search of the quarters the gangsters occupied indicated they had no baggage. Agents found only some shaving creams and a safety razor.

Brantley said the men had little money and he believed they were handicapped in their movements by a lack of funds. It was evident he said, they were dressed to appear as war workers, wearing leather jackets and dark trousers. They left no clothing in their quarters and neither man captured appeared to possess extra clothing.

Brantley said he learned Radkay had gone out to purchase a copy of The Star yesterday afternoon, then returned to his room. It was believed the men, seeing the "heat was on," had left the hotel one at a time. Radkay apparently was the last to leave.

In Chains and Handcuffs.

After questioning, the captured men were charged as fugitives from the Cincinnati bank robbery. Then, chained and handcuffed, they were taken before Charles H. Thompson, United States commissioner, for arraignment. Both men waived a removal hearing and were ordered to the Jackson County jail under $50,000 bonds each.

Henry L. Dillingham, United States marshal, said Radkay and Ricketts would be returned to Cincinnati "at a day and time not to be disclosed." Agents of the FBI said both prisoners had boasted previously they could break out of any jail."

The action, filed by Maurice M. Milligan, United States district attorney, was based upon a complaint now pending against Radkay, Ricketts and Bever

(Continued next page)

at Cincinnati, charging them with the bank robbery and escaping from the Hamilton County jail there.

Brantley and Dillingham took no chances when Radkay and Ricketts were taken from the FBI headquarters, on the seventh floor, to the marshal's office, two floors below. The hands of each prisoner were handcuffed and chained. As Radkay and Ricketts were taken from the finger-printing room of the marshal's office to Thompson's courtroom, safety belts were adjusted around the waist of each, with the handcuffs and chains clamped to steel rings on the belt. The men were unable to raise their arms over a few inches.

Give Data to FBI.

Radkay gave his age on his fingerprint card as 31, and his address as 250 North Fifth street, Kansas City, Kansas. He is slender, weighing 160 pounds, and standing 5 feet 9 inches tall. His complexion is fair.

Ricketts gave his home address as 3023 Montgall avenue, and his age as 28. He also is slender. He is 5 feet 11 inches tall, weighs 140 pounds and has brown hair.

Radkay and Ricketts appeared in court in the same clothing they wore when captured. Radkay had on a combination leather and felt jacket and wore blue trousers. He had no hat. The latter wore a new leather jacket and striped work trousers similar to those worn by factory and war workers. Ricketts' hat was of a light green shade.

When Thompson asked each how they pleaded to the complaint, both Radkay and Ricketts answered with a "Not guilty." In answer to Thompson's question whether they desired a hearing or would waive it, both spoke up at the same time, saying: "We waive a hearing."

THREE BAD MEN OF CRIME.

Gangsters Have Long Police Records in This Area.

A trail of criminal activities involving the three men extends back more than a decade in police and prison records.

William Radkay was a parolee from the Missouri penitentiary. He has a long list of arrests in both Kansas Citys. Almost every entry charges him with highway robbery. In 1935 he was shot by police with a riot gun following the daylight hold-up of the Woodstock-Hoefer Jewelry company. The loot was valued at $3,000. He was sentenced to the Missouri prison and was paroled in 1940. After his capture in 1935 he escaped from the General hospital and was caught again when he attempted to hold up a filling station at Topeka.

Radkay in 1931 called himself the "Little Al Capone." That was his boast when he was arrested in the holdup of the Leader Clothing company while 30 shoppers looked on. FBI officials said Radkay had been wounded at least eight times during his captures for various crimes. He boasted he was the leader of a gang of young Kansas City hoodlums more than ten years ago and made his start as a bootlegger.

Ralph Bever is an army deserter. He admitted shooting an army corporal in a Minneapolis bar last November, according to Minneapolis police. He was in possession of a stolen motor car with a set of licenses from eight states when arrested by police in the Minnesota city. The army corporal is expected to recover. Bever gave police two Kansas City addresses, 3026 Walnut street and 115 East Thirty-third street.

Samuel Ricketts, who claimed Minneapolis as his home, apparently teamed up with Bever and Radkay some months ago. Last August the police here were asked by the Niagara Falls, N.Y., department to check on Missouri license plates used on a car in the holdup of a tavern there. The plates were issued to Ricketts and pictures of the three men were identified by the victims of the Niagara Falls tavern robbery.

Similar holdups followed in Cincinnati, Cleveland and Milwaukee with three men participating.

[AUTHOR'S NOTE: When I showed Willie the news article from The Kansas City Star, March 2, 1943, he commented: "Look how young Sam and I were in that picture." Then he went on to say, "The way I met Sam Ricketts was he was married to Arlene, the wife of my ex-partner, the snitch John Alkes. Alkes couldn't do anything right. When I'd send him to case a job, he'd be back in 30 minutes. I'd tell him you couldn't case anything in 30 minutes, and I usually had to go do it myself to get it done right.

"That picture was taken inside a small office right next to the main courtroom and judge's chamber. They just pulled us out of our cells and into that room where all the newspaper reporters snapped the pictures.

"Sam was one of the top bakers at Manor Bakery in Kansas City, Missouri, and he worked the night shift. Arlene was keeping him straight working every day, but then I showed up and things changed. That's when Sam told me he watches this guy load up the money into the back of this step van every night, pull down the back door and drive off to make a nightly deposit at the bank.

"That was so damn easy I almost forgot about it. We followed the step van or bread truck when it left Manor Bakery, and the stupid son-of-a-bitch pulls up to the traffic light and stops with the driver's side door open. I jumped out from behind the wheel, ran up and jumped into the truck right alongside of him with my gun drawn. I told him to drive around the corner and park. That only took about a minute, and we got over $3,000, and back then that was a pretty good score. They never knew that we had inside information on that job, so they never suspected Sam.

"Sam and I were both sent to Atlanta Federal Penitentiary after being captured in Kansas City, Missouri, from the Cincinnati jailbreak, but they put Sam out in the general population where he went to work in the bakery right away. I was the one they kept in the segregation unit because I was considered a high escape risk."]

From **THE KANSAS CITY STAR,** *March 2, 1943:*

ARREST TWO SOUGHT IN ROBBERY
FBI Takes Wm. Radkay and Samuel Ricketts
Into Custody in K.C., Mo.; Bever at Large.

Two of the three desperate criminals who are wanted in Cincinnati, O., on bank robbery charges were taken into custody here last night. It was announced today by the federal bureau of investigation in Kansas City, Mo.

They are William Isaac Radkay, 31, and Samuel Ricketts, 28. The third man, Harry Ralph Bever, 26, still is being sought here.

Radkay, FBI officials said, was arrested while walking along Troost between Thirty-third and Linwood, last night. He offered no resistance.

This morning Ricketts also was taken without resistance when agents surrounded and entered a rooming house at 621 West Eleventh.

Acting on what they described as an anonymous tip, the agents entered the basement of the rooming house and pulled Ricketts out of a dark corner in which he was hiding. Dwight Brantley, FBI chief, said the man apparently had just entered the place.

Brantley expressed belief that the men had stuck together since their escape in a stolen car thru a hail of gunfire here last Friday night, and that Bever probably still is in the Kansas City area.

The men are wanted in Cincinnati for armed robbery of a bank on November 23. They were apprehended once, but escaped shortly afterward. They later turned up in numerous midwestern cities and finally a trap was set here last week when the FBI and police learned they were in town.

Agents set up a road block on a suburban street, but the fugitives crashed their stolen car over a curb and fled on foot when the machine overturned. They later were fortunate enough to find a car parked nearby with the motor running and continued their flight.

The bandits' wrecked car had been perforated by bullets, and agents were convinced at least one of the men had been wounded in the exchange of gunfire.

Early the next day reports were received that St. Louis police engaged in a futile pursuit of a car described as similar to the one which the men found with the motor running. Believing the men were short of funds and possibly wounded, however, agents discounted the St. Louis reports and tightened vigilance here.

9

Atlanta Federal Penitentiary

THEY PUT ABOUT 16 of us in a private railroad car in what they called a parlor car back in those days. It was a luxurious car with a fancy wood interior and the best furniture of the day, and the food was great, which we appreciated after the jail food we had up in Cincinnati. Of course, the car was also filled with armed U.S. marshals with guns drawn and at the ready at all times.

When we got to the Atlanta prison, we were all surprised that they put us right out into the main population of the prison. I remember also the warden put out the word that he wanted me to clip my fingernails before I had an interview with him because he didn't like 'em long.

It wasn't long before they yanked me out of the main population and threw me in STU (Special Treatment Unit). One guard told me later that they put us guys out into the main population to see if we would try to escape.

One of the first things they did to you in Atlanta was to cut off all your hair, so if you did escape you would be identifiable.

Clyde Tolson, J. Edgar Hoover's right-hand man, took me to Atlanta Prison personally, and rumors affectionately called him

Willie's Atlanta mugshot, 1943.

"J. Edgar's daddy." When Hoover died, the newspapers read: "Who is going to fill Hoover's shoes?" and the cartoons in all of the papers had a picture of women's high-heeled shoes. Tolson wasn't a bad-looking guy, and you usually saw him by Hoover's side in news clips back then.

When we got to the Atlanta Prison, Tolson told the authorities to put me in Segregation with no privileges at all because I was such a high risk to escape. The guard on duty was a good guy named Jackson who I liked immediately, and we really hit it off. Three days later after Tolson left and told Jackson that he was now in charge of the two tiers of Segregation, Jackson came to me and said, "I make the rules here, and I'm not going to let no Yankee from up North come down here to tell me what to do in my own jail." He'd say, "Ra-a-d-key," in a deep Southern Georgia accent, "I'm gonna put you upstairs where you won't be locked up all the time." He took me up to the third tier and left my door open so I'd have access to the recreation room where they had a radio, newspapers, magazines and coffee.

A fag tried to commit suicide when his lover left him for another man, and the authorities came to me and told me that the guy needed a blood transfusion and my blood was a match. I told them, "Hell, no, why should I save the life of a fag that is just going to get better and hang off some guy's joint again?" The authorities told me that this would be a bad mark on my report if I didn't comply. I told them, "What the shit do I care about what you write about me on some prison report?"

While I was up there by myself on third tier, a punk-ass kid came up to me acting real cocky and smarting off to me about something. I told him to go screw himself and get the hell away from me and I didn't want to hear his bullshit. He left, but it wasn't but a few minutes later that he came back with his big Jocker (lover) to protect him and wanting to start a fight with me. I knew we were going to fight, and he was a lot bigger than me, so I swung first and kept hitting both of them with my fists over and over again. There were more coming up the steps after me, but I just kept on swinging. A guy from Chicago that was also up there walked in and saw what was happening and hollered, "Willie," and threw me a fire extinguisher that was hanging up on the wall. I used that fire extinguisher on everybody coming at me, and I cleaned the stairwell with it, knocking out all the guys who were trying to jump me.

Jackson, the guard, heard about what I did and told me he liked it and really got a kick out of the fact that I whipped all those smart-ass punks. He said that he was sorry that he had to lock me up and write a report, but one of the guys had his skull gashed open pretty good. He said if it weren't for that he wouldn't even have written me up.

My nasal passage was all messed up, and it was hard for me to breathe at times. I guess I messed it up by fighting or falling or something. They took me to the hospital in Atlanta in chains and chained me down to the bed. The nurse asked the guards why I was chained down like I was, and no one answered her. While in the hospital, another nurse asked why I wasn't wearing any underpants under the hospital gown, and the guard told her that they didn't want to give me any clothes of any kind. She went on to ask where my clothes were, and the guard said that I didn't own any and they wanted me just like I was. The surgery opened my nasal passage, and I was able to breathe a lot better afterward.

While I was there in Segregation, I was locked up with Waxey Gordon, whose real name was Wexall. He later died in Alcatraz of a massive heart attack. He got the nickname "Waxey" from his friends who said he could slip a billfold out of a man's pocket like it was coated with wax. Waxey told me that the cops were always trying to capture him at the Lincoln Hotel he owned, but they finally had to set him up to do it. He had a guy who was supposed to be a friend named Max Stapler in the back of a cab, and he thought he was just buying information from him. Then with what the cops said was a drug deal, exchanging money in view of several policemen, it set up the charges and got him arrested on a phony rap of buying dope. He found out later that Max was a dopehead and was now working with the cops.

Colonel Louis De Compo was brought from Cuba and was there with me in jail. He had two bodyguards at his side all the time, and the United States had him in there for his own protection. He graduated from Harvard and was an educated and sensible guy to talk to.

There was a guy named Jerry Myles, and we used to call him "Five by Five" because of his size. Someone in the dining room was talking about me, and Jerry stood up and yelled, "Willie is a smart-ass loud mouth asshole, but he isn't a snitch." Later we were sitting around a bench, and Jerry had a clarinet in his hands. I reached for the clarinet, and he grabbed my hand and said, "You know I'm a fag, don't you?" Well, I didn't, but I sure respected the guy after that for telling me. From then on, we called him either "Heads and Tails" or "Tops and Bottoms."

Later on I heard that he went up to Montana Prison to do some time. He and a young kid started a riot and tried to escape, which left the deputy warden dead. After the National Guard and a team of men burst in, they found Jerry and the kid dead of an apparent murder-suicide at the top of a tower.

When I was in Segregation, there was another guy I knew out of Kansas City, who worked at Cudahay Packinghouse when I did, and he was a spy from Germany.

Max Stephen was there in Atlanta, and he was sentenced to death because he hid out spies in his restaurant at Windsor and Detroit, Michigan during the war, and he was given the death sentence.

Truman didn't believe in the death penalty, and his sentence, along with two other guys named Dasch and Bergen, was overturned.

I became friends with George John Dasch who was a Nazi saboteur. He used to tell me how they brought a German submarine right up into Long Island Sound, New York, in 1942, and rowed to shore in a small rowboat. When they got to shore, they met two Marines, and they made a deal with them and gave them a lot of money and told them if they wanted to see their parents alive again that they better take the money. Every German who came ashore there and in Florida had $200,000 cash on them for bribery and survival purposes. He told me that when travelers from the United States would visit Germany, Hitler would keep and stash all the American currency just for this purpose. He went on to say how in Germany they built small towns and cities in perfect replica of United States with stores and shops like they would have if they lived in America. Hell, Dasch knew all about Kansas City and other cities around the United States, but the one thing that they couldn't do was speak without talking in broken English. If they went to Chicago or an ethnic neighborhood, they might get away with that. If you go to certain places in Kansas, they'd spot you in a minute saying, "Hey, this guy's a foreigner and speaks broken English," and during wartime it was dangerous.

One of them went to the electric chair in Washington D.C. I can't remember who it was, but Dasch was telling me it was a young guy with them and a woman also went to the electric chair. They kept it all hush-hush, and they are buried where no one knows where they are. Dasch was telling me that they came after them one at a time and took them up in a secluded cell for interrogation, and he thought he was the only one in there, but he heard a cough and it was Peter Bergen.

Some convict called me a Yankee from up North, and I cussed him out and told him that the Civil War was over a long time ago, so shut the hell up. He went and snitched me off to the guards, and they moved me down to the first floor where there were 10 other guys who were being watched by the guards as troublemakers.

I was in jail there with a guy named George Gunn, and I have to laugh every time I remember him. He'd steal cars in other states and then steal license plates in Atlanta for all of these cars. He started his own taxicab service for the city of Atlanta and had quite a fleet of cabs, making a good income until someone ratted on him.

When I was down in Atlanta, the FBI came in and tried to pin all kinds of shit on me. They told me that they'd be there in the morning to take me to New York to pin a murder charge on me. I couldn't sleep and waited and waited all night wondering what the hell I was getting into, but luckily they never showed up the next morning or any other morning, and they just wanted me to sweat. Believe me, I sure did.

I was in the Segregation building down there, and it was a nice spot and the best spot to make an escape from inside. One guy, Vlasic, had nails he stole from the factory, and we knew we could take the wooden dining room tables apart, which were "one by sixes," and make us a ladder to go over the wall. Looking further out the window across the street, you could also see a mechanic's garage with cars coming in for repair and cars going out after pickup. That was the perfect place for us to head so we could get a car for our getaway. We grabbed some guards down there who were taking us out to the yard, and then we started making the ladder to go over the wall, but before we got too far, some guy inside called the front desk to tell them we were holding guards hostage. The guy just wanted commissaries and crap in there, and hell, we wanted to go over the wall. There was a blind spot that we knew they couldn't see us, and that's where we wanted to go over. The turret was out over the wall, and from the guard's tower he could not look straight down so there was the blind spot where he couldn't see us at all. We tried to go over the fence in the yard, but the guards, thanks to this guy who just wanted commissaries and crap, called up the National Guard and they had us surrounded.

They took me and locked me up in a cell in a different area, and I didn't ask any questions why even though they stood 24-hour guard over me. Then they called me out, and the FBI was there to ask me questions, and I told them that I didn't know what happened, and if I did I wouldn't tell them anyway. One FBI guy said, "By God, we appreciate that answer instead of sitting here giving us a cock and bull story." They said we got one guy who we are calling back for the fifth time and his entire story is cock and bull. They put me in a cell in D-block that was a punishment cell like a strip search cell, and there was no bed or anything in there.

George John Dasch and I became good friends and would walk out on the yard all the time. When I was leaving for Alcatraz and Dasch was leaving for Louisburg Prison in North Carolina, he said, "Well, friend, I'm going, but I wanted to say good-bye to a friend." After they were transferred to Louisburg Prison, they were deported back to Germany. Peter Bergen, who came with Dasch, was hardheaded and bullheaded and told Dasch not to associate with me because I looked like a Jew. We both ignored him and ended up becoming good friends.

There was another guy locked up in there named Jim Gin, and he was a pretty sharp car thief, and we talked about escaping from there. He was in the main population, and I was in segregation, so we'd communicate by writing notes in library books and sending them back and forth. He had a lot of class, and I figured he was going to help me get out of there. He had a little girlfriend who was also writing to me to keep in contact about upcoming plans to get out of there. The girlfriend was sharp and knew how to write her letters in code where we could understand what was being said and the authorities couldn't. She had already gotten a few guys together to help on the outside to get us away from the place, but they transferred me to Alcatraz too quickly to get anything going.

I met a New York gang, Oley and Geary, and they were telling me how they used a two-wheeled cart in an armored car robbery. They had ice in the cart and would be out front of the building every day so they didn't draw any suspicion. Under the ice was hidden the machine guns that they used in the robbery. After they robbed the armored car, they drove a trash truck a half-mile to Brooklyn and took a boat to Long Island Sound. Jack Geary said he was riding on the subway with a brown paper bag on his lap with $150,000 in it. Jack's dad lived in poverty and was kicked out of an apartment every three or four days in the seedy part of town, but wouldn't take a penny of stolen money his son ever tried to give him. Jack Geary slumped over one day, falling beneath a truck, and died in the Atlanta penitentiary.

Another guy I met was George Sylvester Varrick who wrote propaganda, and J. Edgar Hoover called him a poison pen writer. He was the bastard son of Wilhelm Kaiser and wrote the book *Salome* and *Wandering Jew*.

After that, Jackson and I became good friends and would have friendly conversations every time he was on duty. It was Jackson who came up to say good-bye to me one night when he was getting off work, and that was when I knew that I was headed for Alcatraz in the morning.

They came in and got me up one morning at 5 a.m. and walked me out and put me on a bus. I asked them where we were going and no one answered, but in actuality I knew. They took us to a train car that was inside the penitentiary, then pushed it outside and hooked us up to a train right behind the locomotive. I remember the jerking and bumping when they'd bump against us to hook us up. We sure did eat well on the train because it was all good food from the Harvey House Restaurant. Then we got off at Union Station in Kansas City and they put us on a bus out in the railroad yards away from the main terminal and took us on to Leavenworth.

The bus had to travel across the intercity viaduct into Kansas on its way to the Federal Penitentiary in Leavenworth, Kansas. While on the viaduct heading west, I could clearly see St. John's Church, St.

John's Orphanage and all the homes of my neighborhood from up on the bridge. My thoughts upon seeing the orphanage were that my sister, Agnes, had separated from her husband, John Uziel Sr., and their three children — Jeane, John Jr. and Patty — were living in the orphanage at that time.

When the bus got off the viaduct and on to Minnesota Avenue, at the corner of Fourth street I saw a kid that I went to school with. I yelled and screamed to him from the bus, but he didn't hear me and we just drove right by.

When they put us in our cells in Leavenworth, a guy I knew from Missouri penitentiary came to give us our food, and he said that we were going out to the West Coast. I knew for sure now after having a hunch all along that I was headed for Alcatraz.

10

Alcatraz

WE WERE TRANSPORTED to Union Station in Kansas City, Missouri by bus from Leavenworth Penitentiary, then loaded up in a boxcar away from the main terminal. Everyone had heavy steel shackles that would squeeze your wrist and ankles tightly. We were all shackled to each other and wore only cloth house slippers. We had a good meal from the famous Harvey's Restaurant (noted for the "Harvey Girls" as portrayed in a movie starring Judy Garland). The boxcar was then pushed out into the railroad yard and hooked to an engine with more bumping and jerking when we were hooked up.

We were on a private train with bars and dark screens that you couldn't even see through and there was a gun gallery and guards on each end of the train.

There were 16 guys transferred from Leavenworth to Alcatraz on that train, and every town where we slowed down or stopped had the National Guard holding rifles along the pathway by the prison car keeping spectators away by telling them to move on.

The National Guard was also keeping anyone from getting too close to the train and trying to look through the windows with the screen that was about one-fourth-inch squares, plus the bars that you couldn't see through anyway. There were no cushions or pads to sit on, just a hard wooden bench all the way. When the train stopped at various towns along the route pulling the prison car, we could hear people standing by the tracks commenting, "What kind of a car is this?"

Damn near the entire trip there was one guy who had to take a crap every 15 minutes or so, and the poor son-of-a-bitch he was chained to had to go with him and stand close to him while he was on the pot. He stunk up the entire car, but we were satisfied that the pot was close to one gun guard, and you could tell by his face he was suffering from the stench. I was lucky enough to sit by a window and got a slight breath of fresh air through the screen and bars.

The train stopped at Richmond, California, and if the tide had been up, they would have just put the prison car on a barge for the trip over to Alcatraz. The tide was down, so they backed the train car up to the dock and loaded us out onto a prison launch. The name on the side of the launch was "SS JOHNSTON," the warden on Alcatraz at that time.

When I was going to Alcatraz, George John Dasch and Peter Bergen were on the same train with us, but they were separated along the way and didn't come to Alcatraz, thinking they'd get killed by some convicts. Things like that happened in New York all the time where a patriot would kill a suspected communist during wartime. So Dasch didn't go to Alcatraz, but I never knew where they shipped him during that trip, but possibly towards Washington, D.C. because I think he ended up on Riker's island, but I don't know for sure.

It was a dreary, foggy Sunday afternoon, and the waters were real rough on the ride from Richmond to Alcatraz. That boat was rocking and rolling in the rough waters. The swells would lift the boat up; then it'd go back down again, and all you saw were walls of water on both sides before it was ready to take you back up again.

Each man was given a bucket just in case they got seasick. All of the men were handcuffed and shackled together with leg irons, so no one had the thought of jumping into the water unless he wanted to drag everyone with him.

All of us guys on the launch who rode over to Alcatraz had on only pants and a shirt, no underwear or shoes, and we were wearing thin cloth slippers.

When we got off the launch on Alcatraz Island, us guys were still kept chained from ankle to waist irons and on to the other convicts. Together we were able to manipulate with about a 12-inch shuffle as we started us up a steep hill past a guard yelling out numbers for each prisoner. As I passed by, the guard yelled out the following number for me, "666," and I continued following the others in a line to the top of the hill.

On arrival they issued me a sheet, blanket, coveralls, a bar of soap

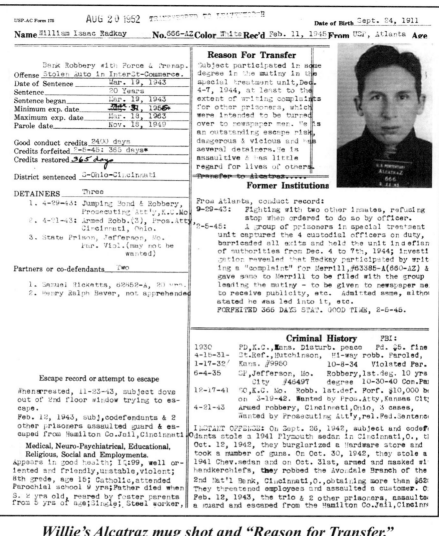

Willie's Alcatraz mug shot and "Reason for Transfer."

and toothpaste that was a gritty powder and could have been used to polish silver.

The bar of soap they gave us was good soap that was also used by the military. The cleaning soap they gave us was a large bar that you'd just throw down on the floor splattering the liquid inside when it broke, and then you'd just mop it up cleaning the floor.

Some of the guards worked on Alcatraz with the Army, and when it was transferred over into a federal prison, they stayed to get a big pay increase for the extra security.

When I first arrived, there were only 19 blacks, and the other 119 guys were the "cream of the criminal crop." When I was walked to my cell right after I arrived without an orientation phase, the first cell I passed I immediately recognized Alvin "Creepy" Karpis. He was a Slovak, and his real name was Karpavicz. I knew him from Hutch along with some other guys, and a lot of the guys I knew from Jeff City penitentiary.

The guys yelled out from their cells as they walked me by, saying, "Hey! Look who's here," "What the hell took you so long?" "We heard you were coming."

They said that they got the word that I was on my way out there from some guy who arrived earlier. Out on the yard everyone just stood around me listening to all the news, like who's in what joint for what, and who died or got killed, and who's on the lam, etc. because newspapers, radios and magazines were not allowed inside Alcatraz.

You wore snug, tight-fitting coveralls so if you tried to hide anything inside of them it would be obvious. Your number was on the breast pocket and on the back for easy identification. You could pass through the snitch box on the way to work and not have the buzzer go off unless you were carrying contraband in your coveralls. On weekends you wore a heavy blue denim shirt, pants and belt that also had your number on it (example: 666AZ) on the pocket of the shirt and on the back. This is when you stayed in the cell or went to church. When you'd go out to the yard, you had to change back into the coveralls.

There were no clocks or watches inside of Alcatraz, and when a guy would ask a guard what time it was he'd tell him, "Why do you want to know, you're not going anywhere."

I was put into the main population right after I arrived and was in cell 222 next to Cecil Snow whose number was 222 on the second gallery. The cells were five feet by nine feet, and you could stand in the middle and extend your arms out and touch both sides of the wall.

Cecil Snow made himself a guitar out of strings and a paper box and would always be strumming the melody "Little Joe." You could hardly hear it, just little dull sounds of plunk-plunks. Cecil had a laugh that was more like a cackle, and when you heard it, you just had to bust out laughing at him.

When the FBI was looking for Pretty Boy Floyd, Machine Gun Kelly and all those big-time bandits, they were running around down through Oklahoma trying to capture them. Anyway, the newspapers said the FBI and the National Guard were going to have a "big swoop" to get all these bank robbers captured within this "big swoop." They were stopping all the cars, and when they stopped Cecil Snow, he said, "Boy, what did I do?" and, "Damn, I didn't know that I had all this heat on me." He was in a Model-T with a little Indian girl who was in the car playing a ukulele with her pet rabbit on her lap. They spotted some checks in the car with him and found out that he'd burglarized a post office, plus he also had some mail in his car that he stolen from someone's mailbox, so they gave him federal time for that and sent him to Alcatraz. He's the only one that all those FBI and National Guard captured during that entire "big swoop," and the big-time bank robbers all got away, but they captured poor Cecil Snow, his girlfriend and her rabbit.

When you went to shower, all the guys on the tier had to stand outside their cells naked with just a towel waiting for the guard to tell them to go, and all of us would quickstep down the steps of the tier, then down the steps to the basement shower. They figured no one would try to make a break or cause trouble if they were naked and cold since there was no heat at all in the cell house, but luckily we did have hot water for the showers.

When you'd go to the showers, you could always tell the guys that did time in joints like Texas or in the south because they had huge scars on their backs from being lashed and whipped. I'm glad I didn't get caught down there because they were cruel, and I would've been a Yankee from the North.

One guy used to say the guards called out to you, "Hey, Yankee, where yah from?" This guy was telling me that he made the mistake of telling them he was from St. Louis, and they yelled out to the other guards, "We got us another Yank and we're gonna whip his ass for sure."

In the dining room we had long tables that seated five guys on one side and five on the other side with a long bench as a seat on each side. The guys in the kitchen put our food on metal trays, and we carried them to the assigned table where the silverware was already sitting at each spot. When we sat in the dining room, we used to say,

"Bring on the swill." When we were through eating before we could get up and leave, the guard had to come to the table to count the silverware. Everyone just forwarded it up to one end for the count when you were through, and after the count by the guard we were allowed to get up and leave. You couldn't talk in the dining room at all back then; everyone had to be silent. For security the dining room not only had the tear gas canisters in the ceiling to use on us if we rioted, but they had a gun guard walking the catwalk right outside the dining room window with a machine gun during every meal.

I had to laugh when at the dining room table I overheard some black guys whispering to each other, with one saying that so-and-so was the guy to see, and the other guy replied, "Hell, I don't know which one he is, all them white boys look alike to me." When we went on strike, the blacks went right along with us and turned the tables.

We had one guy named Scandel down in the kitchen who was the steward, and the son-of-a-bitch wouldn't dare send his laundry down for us to wash because it would end up in the bay because no one liked the prick. They were stealing the food out of the kitchen, and this little Charlie Forebush came and told me and Kelly that the guys would give them the meat to cook for all of us, and they would give it to their punk friends, and the rest of us guys would do without. They would give it to their jockers first; then they would give it to their other punk friends. One punk worked in the kitchen at night, and when he came out he would have this big ball of cheese rolled up under his shirt, and the punk would give it to his punk kid and punk friends. We hated it 'cause all the punks and punk suckers were eating the best food out of the kitchen and we'd get shit.

We heard after the war that they had a "meatless Tuesday" for us guys for the war effort, but hell, we wouldn't have known it because they didn't tell us shit about what we were going to eat, and if you didn't eat what they put in front of you, you starved.

Slim Pickens and I would always try to think of a way to escape from Alcatraz and worked hard at finding a way out. One time we had a guy named Hoskins jigger for us while we went to the basement looking around for a way out. We broke the padlock on a door to get down to the basement that was near the kitchen, so we had Hoskins sitting in a chair playing his guitar as a cover, and he was supposed to signal us if a guard was coming. The stupid son-of-a-bitch just got up and started walking away when a guy came running out of the kitchen saying, "You son-of-a-bitch, you are supposed to be sitting there jiggering for the guys in the basement," and he said that he just forgot all about it. It didn't take Slim and me too much longer to find out that Alcatraz was escape-proof.

By the kitchen they had these suggestion boxes, but they were really snitch boxes, and snitches could put the notes in there and not be suspected like they would if they walked up to a guard and started talking or slipped him a note. We found out one guy who wanted to make a name for himself would put notes in the boxes saying that so-and-so, writing his own name, was trying to make an escape. Then when the word would get around about so-and-so trying to make an escape, he would feel important and thought he was a bad son-of-a-bitch, when in reality he was only snitching on himself.

The buoys in the bay continuously clanged for 24 hours a day without stopping, and when it was foggy the foghorn went constantly, but eventually you just got used to the noise and blocked it out. The guards and their families had to listen to the same thing we did, and in some ways they were prisoners on that Island as well.

They had counts every 20 minutes and shakedowns every day, and some were worse than others. A black guy bought and played a saxophone and had it in his cell. When he saw there was a shakedown in his cell, he asked, "Who shook down my cell walking all over my sheet and stepping on my sax?" The guard said, "I did," as he was rocking back and forth from his toes to his heels acting cocky and then added, "What about it?" When he rocked back on his heels, the black guy picked up his sax, hit him on the head and wrapped the damn thing around his neck.

The guys in Alcatraz knew everything there was to know about the law, and Warden "Saltwater" Johnston was scared to death when they had filed copious charges on him, so he didn't screw with them and just left them alone.

It was a guy named Courtney Taylor on Alcatraz who wrote up the Supreme Court law about self-incrimination and pleading the Fifth Amendment when he was there. After he did that, Supreme Court Chief

Justice Warren got up and said, "It is time for the law authorities to know the law."

There was a friend of mine out of Detroit named Ray Stevens who knew everything about the law, and they never bothered Ray and let him read his books because they were afraid he would take them to court. They even gave him a cell in A-Block just for his law books, and they were stacked up to the ceiling. Every month he would get these law books from St. Paul, Minnesosta, and all of them were close to two inches thick. They had all these cases that were heard all over the country, and different sections in these books even came from California, and we would just read them like stories.

Of course, since the courts say that you are a layman, they had to appoint you a lawyer, and they would get them from San Francisco. All of the lawyers in San Francisco said that they were glad to work the cases of any guys on Alcatraz because they would do all of their own research, and all the lawyers had to do was present it in court. They found out not to screw with the guys on the rock because they knew more about the law than the local lawyers, and Chief Justice Warren even told them so.

There was another German who came to Alcatraz named Frolich that I read about previously in magazines, and he was classified as a major spy. He came over on the German ship Bremin, and this ship was hauling books to the American libraries, and nobody would pay attention to the pages in these books. When they would get the books in America, they would open them up and they would have all these special codes written in them. The magazine article I read had portrayed him as one of the most important spies ever captured. One day we were walking up the steps, and I couldn't believe this guy. He was screaming at us about stepping on cockroaches along the stairway, saying, "Don't kill dat cockroach, he didn't do nutting to you." All of the Germans would get together out on the yard and play soccer.

Another German spy was Kurt Breman, who had all these code books that he was just mailing back and forth to Germany using the United States Postal Service. Then when he got to Alcatraz, he said, "Perhaps I should've shot it out with them rather than this."

Homer (Whitey) Benkly and Burton Phillips were locked up in D-block for hitting Warden Johnston in the dining room. Whitey was a rough-ass kid and worked down in the laundry with Phillips and me. Phillips wanted to go on strike down in the laundry, and I told Whitey not go on the strike with him. Phillips did five or six years in D-block and is doing life, but Whitey he has a chance to get out, but he's not supposed to be in on any strike. I told him not to do it, and if they said anything to tell them that I stopped you from going on strike with those guys.

Later when Homer (Whitey) Binkley was leaving Alcatraz, he asked to have his cell, which was next to George Kelly, given to me, and Kelly approved it since you just didn't move next to someone unless they wanted you to. I moved next to Kelly and remained there all those seven years, and we became close friends. I was in cell #240, and George was in cell #238 of B-block just left of the cutoff.

George was a light sleeper, and if someone woke him up snoring, he'd take a rolled newspaper and slap me on the head by reaching around the wall that divided us, asking me who in the hell was snoring. You had to sleep with your head toward the bars for count, so I had to make an effort to borrow all his magazines and papers before we went to sleep each night.

When Kelly first came in, he weighed around 230 pounds, but after a few years he got down to 150 pounds, which was what I weighed. George liked to have his coveralls starched and pressed with nice creases in the legs, so I would wear his coveralls down to the laundry, wash, starch and press them and wear them back to the cell house. As I walked through the snitch box or past a guard, they just gave me a look, letting me know they knew those clothes weren't mine with number 117AZ on them, but also knew better than to say anything or argue with me.

George had a great sense of humor and was always smiling and never had a bad day that he wasn't friendly and happy. He talked modestly about his family and growing up with his sister, Ida, who he said he was very close to.

Kelly and I hit it off and enjoyed each other's company, becoming great friends who were able to make each other laugh while facing another day on Alcatraz. George and I enjoyed talking about such a variety of things like where we met back in Kansas City during the '20s. He'd always wake up with a smile on his face ready to pass an-

George Kelly's Alcatraz mug shot.

other day on Alcatraz.

George had handsome features and striking blue eyes for a man, but talked in a quiet tone of voice, not loud or boisterous like some articles printed about him said. I lived next to George, ate with George, worked with George, and sat and walked in the yard with George. Never once did I ever hear him brag about any of his scores or tell tall stories about things that he'd done like they printed. We always talked about what was going on around us and what we were going to do when we got out.

George wrote letters to Kathryn all the time, and when she got all her teeth pulled out, she sent him two photographs of herself, one with her teeth in and one without her teeth. George showed me the one without her teeth and commented, "What the hell would she send me this hideous son-of-a-bitch for?" In her letters Kathryn surreptitiously let George know she was having relationships with other female inmates.

Kelly knew that Kathryn shot and killed one of her husbands after he beat her when she back-talked him. He told me laughingly he always kept one eye open watching her so she wouldn't repeat the process. He said she had a bad mouth that would get her into trouble since she couldn't keep it shut and could be a bitch at times. Cleo Shannon was Kathryn Kelly's real name.

George "Machine Gun" Kelly.

[AUTHOR'S NOTE:

1. I asked my uncle if he ever heard that Kathryn gave away shells from Kelly's machine gun as souvenirs.

2. I asked if she bought him the machine gun.

3. I asked him if he ever boasted about being out of prison and home by Christmas.

He replied: "She never was around him when he used the machine gun and never had access to spent shells.

"She never gave him the machine gun because he told me he went down to the Dagos in Kansas City, Missouri to get it. You had to know someone or do time with someone in Dago town to get it because they just didn't sell them to anybody. He got a machine gun with a 50-shell drum and kept it locked up in a suitcase the entire time he had it when it wasn't in use.

"I never heard George boast about anything he ever did or intended to do the entire time we worked together and celled next to one another. He wasn't that type of guy. In fact, he was quiet and soft-spoken, so again most of that stuff you read about him was just to sell papers. He used to tell me that I led a more exciting life of crime and did a lot more scores than he did, but he just ended up with all the notoriety."]

George Kelly served a few months in a New Mexico prison for creasing a guy's skull and not just bootlegging.

CR-conditional release and not parole is how Kelly got out of Leavenworth in 1930. In 1932 Kelly, with his partner, Eddie Dahl, planned and kidnapped a banker's son in South Bend, Indiana.

I asked him what he thought about himself being a number one criminal, and he said he thought it was ridiculous, but he had to live with it.

Eventually he enjoyed the attention he would get when they brought in celebrities through the cell house coming right to his cell and introducing him as "Machine Gun Kelly" and saying hello to me right next door.

Cary Grant was a short guy who wore elevated shoes, and when he walked into the cell house, which was always musty smelling, his aftershave was so overwhelming the smell reeked in the cell house for hours. Kelly said to him when he approached, "I know you, you're Barbara Hutton's old man." He didn't come to close to the bars like some others did. Joe E. Brown, John Barrymore "The Profile," Tyrone Power and George Raft shook hands with a lot of us guys in the cell house, but Joe E. Brown entertained us with a whole act that had us all laughing. John Barrymore always wore this large-brimmed hat cocked to one side and a cape for instant recognition. I'd read in the papers where women would follow him from town to town when he traveled throughout the states, but always figured it was just a publicity stunt to let everyone know he was in town.

When senators and the governor came to visit, they always ended up at Kelly's cell introducing themselves to "Machine Gun Kelly!" I used to tease him all the time when they'd walked into the cell house, and I'd say, "Smile, George, you're on camera."

They didn't have the cells locked down for the movie stars, but when J. Edgar Hoover came in, they had to lock us down because everyone was calling him a fag, along with other choice words defining what queers did. When he came over to my cell, I started cussing him out like everyone else, and he told me that I was nothing but "a Chicago hoodlum and a bum."

General Joseph "Vinegar Joe" Stillwell toured through Alcatraz wearing loose-fitting clothes, telling us the story of living in a Jap concentration camp, starving and losing weight. General Frank Merrill, whose troops that were known as Merrill's Marauders, was with General Stillwell when he visited.

I asked George if he'd ever been shot, and he said yes, just once in the upper left arm, and the bullet had to be taken out. We both wondered if that wasn't what caused the serious bursitis in his shoulder later on.

Kelly was just like me; he loved to go out to the top nightclubs, best floor shows, and wear the finest clothes because money was no object. We'd listen to the bands and enjoy all the music, even though neither one of us could dance a step. My girlfriend, Alma, was even a dancing teacher back then, and she gave up trying to teach me after a short while.

Kelly did time with a guy named Anderson in Leavenworth, and when he met him again on the outside in Oklahoma, he was going with Kathryn. Kathryn and George began spending time together and eventually became a couple and got married in 1927.

Keating and Holden didn't like Kathryn at all, but put up with her because of their partnership with George. Someone wrote that Kathryn dressed as a man and participated in some of George's robberies. She never had anything to do with any of the robberies because all the guys that worked with Kelly didn't like her, so they didn't want her to know anything about what they were doing.

When George was doing time for bootlegging, he helped Keating and Holden escape from Kansas State Prison in Lansing. George worked in the office and was able to get phony I-D badges with their picture on it, and they walked right out the front gate. They told George to look them up after he got out, so George contacted them through a lawyer in Minnesota, and they ended up getting together and robbing banks. Working with them and doing a kidnapping gave George the idea of the Urschel kidnapping later on.

George robbed banks with Eddie Benz, who was known as the grandfather of bank robbers. George always used to tease Benz about one bank they wanted to rob in Washington state. Benz cased the place for a week, and it always had a bunch of people working inside, so they thought it was a busy bank. Then when they went back to rob the place, they found out that all the people in the bank were taking inventory because the bank was going out of business and getting ready to close. Kelly always ribbed Benz about that bank job while we were in Alcatraz, and it always made everyone laugh just talking about it.

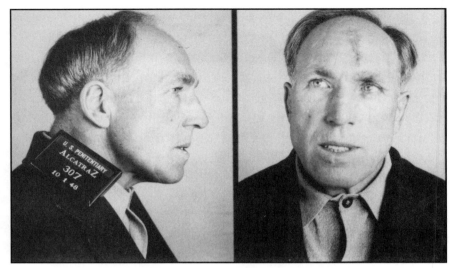

Alcatraz mug shot of Eddie Benz.

Benz wrote poetry to his mom, dad and grandmother when he was in Alcatraz, and Kelly used to tease him for doing it. He'd ask him, "Why would you write poetry to your grandmother? Here you are the biggest and most famous bank robber in the country and you're writing poetry to your family." Benz had a large red birthmark on his forehead and would always cover it up with makeup for his robberies, and later when he got out he had something surgically done to hide it. Benz celled on the same gallery down on the end with George and me, so we talked all the time.

Benz's style was to casually walk into a bank with a briefcase which he handed over the top of the cage to the cashier and asked her to fill it up.

Kelly never smoked, and I only smoked cigars, but I remember both of us rolling cigarettes for Alvin Bates, another bank robber who was Kelly's partner, while he was in the hospital. Alvin died in there, and they took his body to a San Francisco cemetery where they buried the prisoners.

All your newspapers, books and even the FBI information today about George R. Kelly's capture on the Herschel kidnapping case refer to the comment that George was supposed to have made. According to the FBI and the Memphis police, George was caught without a weapon, and George Kelly cried out, "Don't shoot, G-Men, don't shoot, G-

Men," as he surrendered to FBI agents. The saying became synonymous with the FBI agents, but Kelly told me that he didn't have a weapon because he couldn't get to it fast enough when they surprised him and Kathryn during the raid. He said that he never said a thing when he was captured, much less anything about any G-Men. He always figured that the FBI wanted the handle "G-Men" themselves, so they made up this story to the press about him making that comment, and once it hit the papers it was history.

Kelly found out later that an old partner snitched him off to the FBI for the reward money on them down in Memphis.

In the newspapers they said that Kelly picked up the Herschel ransom money, but it was his partner, George (Alvin) Bates, who picked up the money in Kansas City, Missouri on Armour Boulevard. We called him George Bates, but his real name is Alvin Bates, and he told Kirkpatrick who came down there with the money to face west and keep walking in the direction of the sun toward him and he would take the suitcase from him. When Alvin Bates brought George the ransom money in the suitcase, George said that the $200,000 was in five bundles and slid all around the suitcase when you carried it.

George said that they were driving south down 69 Highway out of Kansas City, and that's where they got stuck somewhere on some railroad tracks when they turned off onto a mud road. They gave some farmer a hundred dollars to pull them out with his tractor, and that farmer never saw that much money in his life. Anyway, they got all the money and split it up, and Tom Banks gave some of the money to "Kid Cann," whose real name was Isaac Bloomberg, a big mobster out of Minneapolis.

The FBI tried to arrest a lot of guys who had the marked money from the Herschel kidnapping ransom. Guys who ran gambling joints were arrested until their lawyers proved that it was just "legal tender" and used for services that they supplied the carriers of the marked bills, so they cut them loose.

I asked George if he was ever in World War I like some of the stories said, and his answer was, "No, I always started a war of my own."

Stories claimed that George and Kathryn had a bulldog that rode around with them in their Cadillac. It wasn't a bulldog, it was a Pekinese, and George called him a pussy-eating dog whose nose ran all the time and he'd slurp at it with his tongue.

George really felt bad that Kathryn and Kathryn's mother got time over the Urschel kidnapping and would mention this often and how it bothered him and made him feel remorseful.

Forget about the story saying the plane flew overhead on the Urschel kidnapping and that helped locate the place they were holding him. There were two U.S. marshals from Dallas who were sharp and on the ball, and they broke the case by just figuring it out. When Urschel told authorities that he remembered running his hand down a big car with wheel mounts on the sides when blindfolded and led inside of this building, they just had a hunch. They knew the only person in the area who had fancy cars like that was Boss Shannon's son-in-law, George R. Kelly. They dressed in bib overalls, walked up to Boss Shannon's house, and claimed they were checking the land for oil, which wasn't unusual in those days with all the oil wells in Oklahoma back then. Boss Shannon let them onto his property, and when they were walking around, they saw the big car with the wheel mounts and just put two and two together.

I remember the day when Bruce (Robert) Barnes, Kelly's son, visited him on Alcatraz. To get to visit a convict on Alcatraz, you had to write a letter to your congressman and receive a letter back for permission. Then if you were accepted, you were told the day of your visit, and an armed guard would meet you at the dock and ride over on the boat to Alcatraz and stay with you the entire time you were there until you got back off the boat on the dock.

I can only remember him visiting his dad just that one time, and when he came he was with a guy named Chris, and Warden Madigan let Chris walk around through the cell house while George was visiting his son. They walked right by me when Madigan showed him the cell next door, saying that Kelly stayed there.

When George came back, he was talking about his visit, and later that evening he hesitated for a moment and said, "I think my son is a punk." He said, "What the hell am I supposed to think when he tells me that he lives with this guy named Chris and they both sell women's shoes?"

George told me that he never wrote anything bad to the Urschels like they claimed in the newspapers. The newspapers said that in the courtroom he took his finger, moving it across his throat like he was going to slit their throats. He told me that the only thing he said in the courtroom was to the Indian prosecutor named Hyde, which was, "There used to be a bounty on your kind." George was wearing a thick leather belt around his waist with manacles chained to it, and he couldn't get his finger up to his throat for that kind of a motion even if he wanted to.

I never saw anything written on the wall of his cell either, so most of the stuff written in the newspapers about him was just to sell more papers.

George had a serious sinus problem that whenever they were infected and he blew his nose, you could smell the stink of the infected mucous in my cell.

George loved blondes and would talk about all the blondes he was going to get when he got out, but he was infatuated with a silent movie star named Fi-Fi Dor'se who looked just like Liza Minelli in *Cabaret,* with the same hairstyle that was pasted down on the side of her face in a big round curl. I'd ask George why he liked that old silent movie star, and he'd answer, "When you've seen those legs, you don't forget them."

I liked the silent movie stars, Billy Dove and Norma Tallmadge, and it gave us something to think about and talk about in there. We never thought that we would meet again and become such great friends on Alcatraz.

There was a Mafia guy named Charlie Corolla out on the Island, and he always used to call me a maverick or renegade since I never ran with the crowd and always kept to myself. It was a lot safer back then because he didn't like me and I didn't like him, and I survived being a maverick where a lot of other guys didn't.

Warden James A. "Saltwater" Johnston was a decent man, and you could talk to him about anything, as well as just walk up to him and start talking when he came to the dining room for every meal. He got his nickname because he was a warden at San Quentin, Fulton and now Alcatraz, and they were all by salt water.

I asked Warden Johnston if he remembered his visit to the Missouri penitentiary and went on to tell him I was in the cell in back of him staring at his back, not knowing that some day he would be my boss on Alcatraz. Saltwater was in the dining room at every meal, and you could talk to him or ask him any question that you wanted to.

I walked up to the warden in the dining room one day and asked him why I was sent to Alcatraz, and he just looked at me as though to say, "Are you for real?" Then he reminded me that I had detainers in Michigan and one in Ohio, plus charged with several bank robberies and numerous escapes, and that's when I just smiled, turned around and walked away.

Kelly used to tease me, saying, "There's the warden, go cuss him out." That's because one time I went up to ask for something, and he chewed my ass out for shit that I did in the laundry and told me to go sit down, but the very next day he came up to me and asked me what it was that I wanted from him. I remember another time in the dining room I walked right up to him to talk to him, and a guard walked up behind me and grabbed me, and Warden Johnston flagged the guard and told him to get away and leave me alone. You could talk to these guys like normal guys and they would listen to you, and that's why we were close in a lot of ways and all became good friends in the end.

I asked the warden one day in the dining room if he could get us some books from the San Francisco library about the early settling and building of the missionaries around California. He told me to just let him know what I wanted and he would try to get them. He had to pay $45 to rent these big old books about the early missionaries from the library. They came wrapped up in leather cases, and the pages in the books were made of onion paper and so thin you really had to be careful when turning pages in them. George and I enjoyed reading about all the history of the early missionaries and read all the books they sent us.

Saltwater Johnston would let some of us guys go out to the yard to watch the Third Fleet come in, and it was an incredible sight to see when all those ships came around to Alcatraz and over to Hunters Point; then the tug boats would take over. Airplanes flew under the Golden Gate Bridge, and last under the bridge were the subs, cruisers and destroyers. Many times we saw them tow in ships that were shot up during the war. The aircraft carrier, U.S.S. Lexington, that carried the A-bomb out into the ocean, passed under the Golden Gate Bridge.

The mat shop on Alcatraz made the nets that were used during wartime that were placed in the water under the Golden Gate Bridge to prevent enemy submarines from coming into the Bay.

The Blue Angels shot around like bullets and came in under the Golden Gate Bridge, then went straight up in the air before shooting back down again.

When the Third Fleet came into the bay, Admiral "Bull" Halsey came to visit the island. They piped him aboard and sounded his comings all around the island. Kelly and I were in the hospital at the time where I had surgery on my knee and Kelly had surgery on his shoulder. The doctor on Alcatraz named Yocum told Kelly and me that we were his two favorite patients. They really took good care of us and gave us the best Marine surgeons in San Francisco. Kelly had bursitis on his left shoulder that was pretty bad, and he had to wear his arm in a sling because of all the pain and couldn't lift or move his arm. The doctors pulled the socket right out of the shoulder and scraped it clean, and after that he healed back to normal and didn't have all that intense pain. They sure fixed my knee that I injured when I jumped out that second story window trying to escape in Minnesota by scraping it the same way.

Only women that ever came to Alcatraz were the two nurses who took care of a military guy who never should have been sent there in the first place.

There was this guy named Tommy Robinson that I used to sit across from in the dining room. He wasn't a thief or anything, but his case was a famous one in Louisville, Kentucky. This girl implicated was a socialite; her last name was Speedstol, and her family was well known in the community. He was going with this girl for quite a while down in Kentucky, and when they found out, the family had to say that he had kidnapped her to spare the embarrassment for her and her family of an involvement with a person of lower class. When he got caught, he had $50,000 cash on him that she'd given him to evade from authorities. In Kentucky you never slander or lambast a woman, but when he got up on the stand in court and did all his talking, he actually told the truth, and the papers came out with the headline: "He's talking himself to death." He was sentenced to die in the electric chair, but fortunately Truman commuted his sentence and he didn't get executed. When he eventually got out of Alcatraz, he didn't know what the hell to do with himself and got in trouble and got locked up again.

We used to make our own hair tonic on Alcatraz, and it was a mixture of Vaseline and kerosene, and it not only got rid of dandruff; it made your scalp and hair silky soft.

A little guy named Jimmy Lee was one of the black prison barbers. He came and told me he had a beef with a big black guy who wanted to make him his punk. He said just because he was a little guy he wanted us all to know he wasn't afraid of anyone. One day the big guy sat down in the barber chair, and Jimmy asked him how he wanted his hair cut. The big guy said cut it high, and with that Jimmy took a pair of barber shears and cut his throat.

One day while sitting at the dining room table, a famous safecracker named Fred Stefler was sitting across from me, and the guy was legendary for being able to open any safe that was around in those days. He was beating up on a small box of cereal, jabbing and jabbing at it with his fork, saying, "How in the hell do you open these son-of-a-bitches?"

Ghirardelli, the famous chocolate company that sits on the dock in San Francisco right across from Alcatraz, wanted to send over some chocolates over to the guys at Christmas. The government said, "No! They are being punished over here and they can't have anything." A couple of years later the government wanted to pass out Christmas candy to us guys, and we said, "No!" We threw it all back at them and told them to stick it up their ass.

A fag named Courtney Tailor could make duplications of company checks that were perfect and undetectable using slick pictures out of magazines and tape. He cashed these checks all across the United States while being driven around in a chauffeured limousine with his punk kid that he passed off as his son in the back seat with him.

There was a guy from Washington, D.C. who made it to Alcatraz because he started shooting every black he saw walking down the street.

All the blacks on Alcatraz had a white chalky look to their skin that was caused by the salt in the air from the water out in the bay.

Kelly told me about the first escape attempt from Alcatraz when Joseph Bowers was shot and killed by the guard in the tower. It was a tragic mistake because Joe was mentally challenged and just acted like a big kid. He stole a few bucks from a grocery store that happened to have the town's post office inside, making it a federal offense that sent him to Alcatraz. He was happy with the responsibility of keeping the place clean, and when he climbed the fence to get the trash, the guard unsuspectingly thought he was trying to escape.

There were some real whackos on Alcatraz, and at night you would hear one guy screaming and yelling all night, catching monkeys in his cell. Another guy would pray all night, praising God as loud as he could, and when it thundered, he would yell, "Come and get me, Jesus." Some of them would have to be put in straight jackets to keep them still at night. With a few of the other whackos, the guards would have to throw a bucket of water on their feet, and it would scare them so bad they'd run for the corner of the cell and stay there. Some of these guys thought doing this would get them out of Alcatraz and it did; it sent them right to the bughouse.

A black guy from St. Joseph, Missouri named Jimmy Grove got into a beef with a big black guy named Ben McMiller and ended up sticking him with a 20-penny nail that he flattened out. It sounded just like popping a balloon when he stuck him, and when they dragged him by my cell, beans were falling out of his stomach all the way to the hospital where he died of gangrene a short time later.

Whales would come into the bay almost every night. You'd see five or six of them swimming out there with their babies following along-side them, and all of them would have seagulls riding all along the tops of them. They'd come in with boats and sometimes even helicopters to shoo them back out under the bridge and into the ocean.

I read a newspaper article once that they put shark fins in the bay for the guys to see so they would stay out of the water and not try to escape. The guards told us they never did that because the live sharks were mainly on the east side of Alcatraz where all the garbage was dumped into the bay.

Clyde Tolson, J. Edgar Hoover's live-in companion, wanted to get on my writing and visitor's list when I was transferred to Alcatraz, but I wouldn't do it, because what the hell did I want to write to or have visits from him for? I figured he just wanted to be a phony friend so he could try to get information out of me, and I was wise to that shit and said no.

You could see just the tip of San Quentin from out the laundry window when the tide was out. Baby Face Nelson's real name was Lester Gillis, and his partner's name was Johnny Chase, and he lived in Sausalito, California. Here was Alcatraz, here was the Golden Gate Bridge, and here was Sausalito just a few miles apart. When the tide was down, Johnny could actually see where he lived. That was real funny that when the clouds would be all around every place else you'd see the sunlight open up right over Sausalito. They had this saying that the sun shines on Sausalito all of the time, and damn if it didn't!

The guard they called "Punch Drunk Pepper" was kept in the tower away from us guys because he was punch drunk. He was an ex-boxer, and up in the tower he would shadow box the whole shift he was up there. He had big cauliflower ears, and you could tell mentally he wasn't all there. They were afraid to put him around the convicts because he could easily start a riot, so they kept him up in the tower.

The guy they called "The terror of the Southwest," Floyd Hamilton, was a bonafide cleaning freak in the laundry on Alcatraz. His brother, Ray Hamilton, gave him the nickname on the outside when they were linked with Bonnie and Clyde and drove their getaway cars.

If a guard would shake down the cells, I'd ship his laundry out into the bay, but Warden Johnston always had his laundry done in the prison laundry without any problems. It wasn't unusual for a guard to come up to me and ask, "Are you still working in the laundry?" I knew he was thinking what would happen to his shit if he did something I didn't like.

I was notoriously famous for sending stuff out into the bay, and when a guard or any authority would start some shit and I got the word, his laundry went shooting out the drainpipes into the bay.

There was be an article in the San Francisco paper saying that the warden went into the cells every night to check on the heat from the radiators. That was a big joke because there was no heat in the cells at all or anywhere in the entire cell house — period.

When I was there, we only had cold water coming into our cells, and the water in the toilet bowl was a blue fluorescent with bubbles left by the diesel fuel from the ships in the bay.

When we'd get hosed down for being rowdy with the water coming from the bay, we'd be slick from head to toe with bubbles from the blue florescent water. Every time you'd go on strikes, you'd get locked up in D-Block and get hosed down with water. To cool us off, I guess? When they hit us with the water hose, I used to yell out, "Hey, boss, you missed me."

The fire hoses used the salt water from the Bay, and the pressure was so strong you couldn't walk towards it or come out of your cell when they hosed you down. Sometimes after they hosed us down, they'd throw us in the cells down in the dungeon. They were completely bare, smelled dank and musty, and the floors were always wet, but hell, you just got used to it like anything else in prison.

We did all the Maritime laundry and would steal percale sheets, blankets and other good stuff, sneaking it back into the cells under our tight coveralls. The guard knew, and he knew if he said anything when we went through the snitch box all his laundry would be out in the bay.

Once while I was eating in the dining room, I noticed this guard Martin was staring at me. I said to the guys at the table, "What the hell is he looking at?" They all laughed and told me it was probably the T-shirt I was wearing that said: "Welcome to Hawaii" along with the white sox that weren't prison issue. He didn't want to say anything to me because he knew he'd get his ass chewed out and his laundry sent out into the bay.

We would do about 3,000 pounds of Maritime laundry a month, and I would be the guy who billed the Navy for the service. I handled a lot of money on those transfers, but it was all on paper and not cash. They always had Naval officers coming over to the Island saying they wanted to see where the laundry was done, but we knew it was just to see guys like Machine Gun Kelly.

Once the Maritime sent in all these raincoats to be washed and cleaned, and all 65 guys who worked in the laundry walked out back to their cells wearing black raincoats. The guards commented, "What's this, a funeral procession?" But they let us go through the snitch box and on to our cells. Later when we all went to the dining room, they went in our cells and took all the raincoats back.

A good guard named Mannery who worked with us in the laundry used to bring us a newspaper to read even though it was illegal so we could keep up on the news of the day. A guy named Stinky Davis took the newspaper from Mannery and told him he wouldn't give it back until he brought him a carton of cigarettes. Mannery came to me and was worried about getting into trouble, so I went up to Stinky Davis and told him if he didn't give Mannery that newspaper back right away

I'd smash his head in, and the newspaper was returned in minutes. Old Mannery was a good-hearted guy and eventually got fired for being too nice to the cons that were really pricks who took advantage of him. He would tell us guys that there was going to be a shakedown so we wouldn't be caught with any contraband in our cells or on us, and you couldn't help but have respect for a good guard like that.

A guy named Dick Bales was an ex-Navy man and an excellent swimmer. When he tried to escape, he came back telling all of us that he couldn't even get away from the shore and it would be impossible to escape in the water.

Rufus McCain, the guy that Henri Young killed on Alcatraz, was a shotgun guard in an Arkansas prison. They made guards out of convicts back then, and a woman convict named Helen Stevens was on a chain gang and tried to get away, and Rufus shot her. They made a movie about these guys, *Murder in the First,* starring Kevin Bacon, but it wasn't accurate.

The guards could open individual cell doors using a clutch device located at the end of each row of cells.

Jimmy Quillen and Red brought me a snitch note written to Captain Tehash, saying we were gambling in the laundry, that was dropped in between the cells by a fag, Mainhurst. He used to fight for the job to pass out razor blades in the hospital so he could get on a guy's joint while he was up in the hospital. I went up to him and told him he better go to D-block and get locked up right now because I was holding back from doing something to him that would cause me to get a life sentence. Everyone knew from me right away that he was a snitch and an asshole, so he knew he'd better go to lockup for his own protection. When I told him he better check in, he did and then later was transferred out of the prison.

George told me that a guard befriended Al Capone and took a message out for him and got $45,000 cash which he spent on a piece of property, saying, "Where would I get that kind of money on my salary?"

Al Capone's brother, Ralph, used to say to him, "What are you trying to do, support all the guards?"

Al Capone always pushed a steel lawn roller around the baseball field for exercise on Alcatraz, plus he was a big guy and solid muscle.

In the shower with a guy once, he was heard saying to him, "I heard that you were talking about me? I like you and I'd hate to have to crush your skull, so I would appreciate it if you kept your mouth shut." He never heard another word out of that guy after that because he checked himself in the hole to get away from Al.

When Al was in Chicago, he was a powerful man who took care of the little guy by opening up soup kitchens so no one went hungry during the depression. At Christmas time he went all over the city with food and presents for all the kids. He was a top mob boss with unscrupulous actions, but it made him acceptable to the public because he was a charitably compassionate leader that city hall hated him for and had to get rid of him.

The exact location of Al's cell was #132 on the bottom floor, and they called him "The Wop with the Mop" because his detail was mopping the cell floors.

When Al Capone's mother came to visit him, she was wearing a corset with steel staves and garters that set off the snitch box. They made his mother take off her corset and garters and walk through the snitch box again. We were all told later that they were real lucky Capone didn't have those guards killed for treating his mother like that.

There was a guy named Jimmy Lucas who just wanted to make a name for himself by being known as the guy who stabbed Al Capone. He pricked Big Al down in the barbershop with a little blade only five inches long that didn't do much more than put a few nicks on him. When Big Al was jabbed, he automatically turned around and hit Jimmy so hard he actually stuck to the wall for several seconds before sliding down to the floor.

After the stabbing, Big Al had some big Italian cons as his bodyguards to go every place he went. The cons were just hoping someone would start some shit so they could protect Big Al and get paid generously for it, plus get the recognition.

They only put the whackos in the hospital for any length of time, and eventually Big Al went there when his mind started slipping from the syphilis and he couldn't remain out in the general population anymore. The symptoms were almost like Alzheimer's disease, not remembering things or people, plus doing crazy stuff like wiping shit on

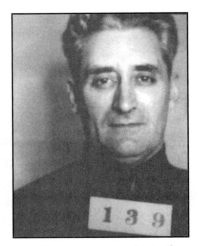

*Alcatraz mug shot of
Harvey Bailey.*

the walls or on himself. Capone stayed in the hospital close to four years before transferring out.

There was a bad son-of-a-bitch named Louie from Chicago who made seven witnesses and two congressmen disappear. He was bitching about how some stupid sons-a-bitch just left bodies lying around in the street for the cops to find. I asked him: "What do you do with the bodies, Louie?" He went on to tell George and me of the big furnace he had in the basement of this pool hall and how only one woman gave them the most difficulty, fighting back incessantly when they went to shove her in. He went on to say the furnace was cleaned out immediately afterward without leaving any trace. I told him, "Damn, Louie, I'd fight like hell, too, if you were trying to shove me in a burning furnace." Then Louie also went on to tell us that you had to shoot 'em in the lungs so they don't float when you throw them in the river.

Harvey Bailey was not involved with Kelly in the Urschel kidnapping and just got caught with some of the marked ransom money that George gave him paying back an old debt. Harvey was one of the greatest and best known bank robbers of the 1920s because of the enormous amounts he got away with back then. I know he hit a bank in Fort Scott, Kansas at Wall and Main Street and got over $30,000 in cash, plus that or more in "Lib," Liberty Bonds, that he spent buying a huge farm in Missouri. I know he robbed the Denver Mint and another bank in Lincoln, Nebraska and got an enormous haul.

I know how they got the guns into Lansing Prison when Harvey Bailey and those five guys made their escape back in 1933. One guy would have his brother come and visit him, and when they distracted the guard, he slipped him a gun wrapped inside a rubber glove up over the partition that separated the prisoner from his visitor in the middle of the table. Then this trustee would just casually come by with his mop and bucket, and the guns were dropped inside the mop water, then wheeled inside the cell house.

He used to send money to his brother, Voss, who lived in Kansas City, and the guy bought a nice piece of land with a big farmhouse on it, but wouldn't live there. He lived in this dinky apartment at 23rd and Paseo instead, and Harvey never could understand why.

I never called Bailey "Harvey"; I called him Tom, even though his real name was John, and most of the guys who were close to him called him Tom.

He worked in a different department than we did; he built and re-conditioned furniture. I went to watch him once down in the model shop and was surprised at the detailed precision used in the measurements on the manufacture of the furniture down there.

Bailey wasn't in on the Union Station massacre either; they just said it to try to pin a charge on a guy they really wanted to capture. It was LaCapra, a.k.a. Jimmie Needles, a junkie who opened up and snitched about the Kansas City Massacre. He had some heat on him, and when he turned himself in at Excelsior Springs, Missouri, he started talking, so they took him to see J. Edgar Hoover in Washington, D.C.

Adam Rochetti was the one who went to the gas chamber, and the guy was completely innocent of all charges. They were all at Adam's sister's place in Oklahoma, and they were talking about what they were going to do in Kansas City at the Union Station. Rochetti wasn't even in on it; he was just sitting there with the guys and his sister drinking beer and getting drunk. When the cops went to the room after LaCapra snitched, they found fingerprints on some beer bottles, and one set was Rochetti's, and that's when an innocent man went to the gas chamber.

Also, they always said that there were three people in the car when they opened fire at Union Station, but I know there were only two inside that car. It was a warm day in Kansas City, and they had a coat and hat up in the back window that made them think there were three guys in on it.

Tom Bailey liked to play cards out on the yard and wanted to teach George and me how to play bridge. He gambled on everything he played, whether it was dominoes, checkers or cards, and won most of the time.

I remember reading the headline in the newspapers after Bailey got caught that said: "He was more talkative than Charlie McCarthy

Willie and George on the yard.

without Edgar Bergen."

The picture above that was taken of us guys out on the yard shows me as the only guy looking up and spotting the two guards on the wall with a camera partially hidden behind the guard standing in front. I told Kelly sitting next to me to smile, they're taking our picture, so he took his cap off and combed his hair. Tom Bailey was sitting at the end of the table with his back to the camera, and all the guys were wrapped up in a serious game of poker with wooden dominoes for money. The guy wearing the sun visor cap is part Indian, John McDowell, and he was one of the dealers for the money games on the yard.

The old lady came to visit me on Alcatraz, and all she wanted to know was if I had any money stashed anywhere at the house or in the garage. My stepmother was ailing with emphysema, and they had her sitting there with this interpreter, two guards and a tape recorder. The visiting through this four-by-four-inch-thick blue bulletproof glass didn't make for a comforting visit anyway. I told her through this phone we used for communication that I had no money hidden or stashed anywhere and she got all the money I had when she took my stash of $5,000 plus my car.

I was there in Alcatraz when both of my foster parents died and couldn't attend their funeral. I thought that they'd leave me the house when they died, but found out later after the old man died the old woman was screwing around with a married neighbor man and left the house to him and his wife, and I didn't get shit.

There was one guard named Hanson who always looked for me to do shit so he could write me up when I caused trouble. He was a Swede and talked with an accent, and I didn't like him. I spent most of my day tearing up his laundry and shipping it out into the bay. As fast as it came in, I was shipping it out.

Some guy found a $20 bill in the Maritime laundry and was walking by the guard, Hanson, when he dropped it right in front of him. I jumped up right away and stepped in front of the guard, putting my foot on the 20. Hanson jumped when I did this and turned around and walked away so I had a chance to pick up the 20 and take off.

What I found many times in the pockets of the clothes from the Maritime laundry were cigar butts. When we'd get locked down at night and the guards walked away, sending the keys up front until morning, I would light up and smoke them. I knew the guards could smell them and knew what I was doing but also knew that they better not say anything to me about it or their laundry would be floating out in the bay.

You could cuss a guard out, but don't have a mirror or you'd go to the hole. I was always getting notes in my cell that my bed wasn't made right. Then after not getting one, I went up to ask the guard if he was mad at me or just missed me 'cause Wednesday I didn't get a note.

They had real thin mattresses on Alcatraz that weren't worth a shit, so I'd go into an unused cell and grab two or three more to make my bed more comfortable. One thing I appreciated was the fact that these mattresses didn't contain any fleas or bedbugs. When I was there, you had nothing on the shelf in your cell but three books: Bible, dictionary and one library book. I found a ping-pong ball down in the laundry once and brought it back up to my cell and hung it from the light fixture. It only lasted about four hours, and some guard took it out of there.

Miller, the associate warden, used to say, "Why do you do shit like that right in front of Hanson all the time?" At the moment I was tearing up my mattress because I was pissed off at him again and didn't give a shit about any write-up.

Now this guard, Shuttleworth, was an asshole who was transferred from a joint in Minnesota. He was taking Miller's place while he went

Record Form No. 8 (July, 1936)	CONDUCT RECORD		

DEPARTMENT OF JUSTICE
Penal and Correctional Institutions

USP.   ALCATRAZ, CALIF.
(Institution)   (Location)

Record of RADKAY, William I.   No. 666-AZ

FPI—LK—4-7-43—5M—588-5

Date	Prison Violations	Days Lost
4-27-45	SLOWING DOWN WORK BY HINDERING PRODUCTION IN THE LAUNDRY.#39388 by E. J. Miller, Assoc. Warden. ACTION: 4-27-45. Stated he had to live here with other inmates.(joined in with others in slowing down work at laundry). Solitary confinement, rest. diet, forfeit all privileges until further orders. A-Block. Sol. 5-1-45, removed from solitary to work, privileges restored.	
9-23-46	DESTRUCTION OF GOV. PROPERTY. Radkay inexecusably tore a mattress cover from top to bottom with his hands in order to empty it of its contents. This was absolutely uncalled for since he could have obtained a knife to cut the string by asking for it. W. Hansen, Instructor. ACTION: 9-24-46. Inmate admitted he was wrong, that this was a quick way of getting material out and in the wash. and that he just hadn't thought. Stated he absolutely would not to this again. Reprimanded and warned. Solitary suspended, pending future behavior	
10-30-46	INSOLENCE. Several times this inmate has called me vile names as I passed his cell. This morning I am sure it was him. A. E. Long, Sr. Officer ACTION: Solitary confinement, rest.diet until further orders. Inmate denied charge but officer Long was positive of not only this report but that he had done it previously on several occasions, also some other employees said he had done the same to him, although he would wait till just after they passed before he would make the remark. Last month, this inmate was given a suspended solitary sentence for destruction of Gov't property. 10-31-46. C.J.Shuttleworth, Acting Assoc.Warden 11-7-46, removed from solitary to idle in main cellhouse, until 11-12-46, when ret'd to work.	

Willie's Alcatraz conduct record, 1945-46.

on vacation, and Miller would've just cussed me out and let me go, but Shuttleworth wanted to pick on me because I was usually always the one raising all the hell anyway. I got a bum rap for cussing out Shuttleworth. Hell, I was always cussing out guards, but Miller was on vacation, and Shuttleworth put me in the hole for 10 days.

The hole wasn't totally pitch dark; some light would come in through the cracks in the door, which was just enough light to see with. They had a bunch of cells they used when you were thrown in the hole that had troughs built along the backside of the wall with an opening on both sides to the adjoining cell. This is where you'd piss and shit since there wasn't any toilet in the cell. When all of us guys would use them, we'd holler to the guard to turn on the water and he'd throw a bucket of water in the trough and all the shit would float by through all our cells until it went down the main sewer pipe out into the bay.

This guard named Mannery was the guard on duty while I was in the hole, and instead of just the bread and water he took care of us guys to make sure we had something special from the kitchen once a day and didn't go hungry.

Another guard said he was going to let me out early so I could go down and get something to eat, but what he didn't know was I had two sandwiches in my back pockets at the time. They made you wear your coveralls when you were thrown in the hole back then, and I always kept a string in my pocket. I dropped the string out the back of the cell, which led down to the kitchen right below. The guys in the kitchen would tie food and rolls to the string, and I could pull it back up into the cell and have a good meal instead of just the bread and water.

When Miller got back from vacation and heard I'd been in the hole, he came up to me laughing and slapped me on the back, saying, "You missed me while I was gone, didn't you?"

Another guard named Long gave me an insolence charge because we all called Long "Gracie" because of the way he waddled and shuffled when he walked, plus he had these damn squeaky shoes that you heard all over the cell house with every step he took.

Kelly, Frankie Delmar and I were in the dining room talking about the waiter who would bring us coffee, wondering if he was a fag or not. I told them I thought he was, but Kelly and Delmar said they didn't think so. When I went back to my cell, I wrote the waiter a note telling him I really liked him, and if he wants to get together, just tie a red handkerchief around his left knee the next time he's in the dining room, and signed it from a fag working in the laundry. The next morning in the dining room this waiter was walking around the dining room wearing this red handkerchief around his left knee, and Kelly, Delmar and I laughed our asses off throughout the entire meal.

I remembered when a guy named DeClue stood there in the dining room and yelled at Saltwater Johnston, calling him a white-headed motherfucker. He yelled at him, saying, "Ever since I've been here you've been fucking with me and taking all my stuff." Saltwater was telling him and motioning with his hands to just keep it up, keep it up, and when DeClue walked away, we heard him telling a guard, "He's just blowing steam."

Another time Cecil Snow was arguing with Warden Johnston in the dining room, calling him a white-headed cocksucker, and Johnston screamed back at him, "You're the one with no teeth, you son-of-a-bitch, so that makes you the cocksucker, not me." Poor Cecil was always trying to make himself a set of false teeth out of wood in the model shop, but never came up with anything he could wear.

There was a black guy named Willie West that we called "Bosom" because of the massive size of his chest, that had to be at least four-feet wide and solid muscle. He came up to George and me in the movie theater and told us we'd better pull our seats back out of the way because there was going to be a rumble. We moved back a couple of rows, and when the lights went out for the movie to start, you could see a silhouette on the screen of Bosom getting up and grabbing a 200-pound guy right up out of his chair, lifting him into the air. Nobody liked the guy Bosom had the beef with because he was an asshole, so we all watched as Bosom picked him up like a rag doll and slammed him into the ground. He picked him up and slammed him down two more times before the guards came in and busted it up. Everyone in the dining room sent Bosom their dessert cake that night, thanking him for what he did to that asshole, and the cakes were piled over a foot high on his tray. The guards didn't like the asshole he beat up either and allowed Bosom to put all the cakes in a bucket and take them back to his cell.

We used to see Bosom sitting at the feet of a white guy, Odee Stevens, and he would always ask him if he could be his nigger when he got out. Odee ran a big farm using black guys as laborers, but ended up killing and burying them instead of paying them. He'd tell Bosom that he'd give him a job and a place to stay, and Bosom was delighted as hell to hear that he had somewhere to go when he got out.

The movies they let us watch were ordered by the guards for their families, so this one time they tried to show us a kid's movie called *The Song of the South*. The guys broke out in a riot when it began. They started throwing chairs at the screen, yelling and cussing, so the guards came in and just shut the movie down and got us all out of the theater area. That took care of our movie privileges for quite a while after that. Then they started passing around a list of movies for us to pick from, but hell, the entire time I was there I never saw one movie that I ever picked from the list.

There were three different departments out on the island: one was security, then administration, and then medical. They were all separate from one another, so one department couldn't tell the other what to do. There was one doctor who came to the island who had the guts to bring his dog with him every time he came. The warden didn't like it, but the doctor would just seem to do it to tell the warden to stick it in his ass.

On the island there was this wacko we called "Oshkosh," and hell, I don't know that I ever heard his real name. He was a pain in the ass with his big mouth running all the time, getting shit started between the guards and the convicts. He thought he was cocky, but the convicts just thought he was crazy, and the guards knew they had to put him in his place to shut him up. One day Meathead Miller really took care of him by running up to him and pushing him against the wall, yelling, 'Where's my knife, I'm gonna cut your fucking throat." The other guard on duty with him and in on the scheme started yelling, "Ed (Meathead), don't kill him, he's not worth it, leave your knife in your pocket, don't kill him." Meathead kept acting like he was getting a knife out of his pocket, and this went on for about two minutes, and Meathead kept telling him that if he doesn't shut his mouth he'd cut his fucking throat. It wasn't long before this guy shit in his pants, and that's when they let him go, and after that he kept his mouth shut and never started shit between the cons and guards again. Meathead knew how to handle guys like him, and we all respected him for it because he got the job done.

One time we were going to go on strike, so they took us over and locked us up in A-Block. They didn't have bars over there; it was the old flat steel slats. We were yelling and screaming and raising hell, and a guard came around and told us to shut up. Old Meathead Miller came by and yelled, "Don't stop them, hell, just let them holler. How long do you think they can keep it up?" He was right 'cause just how long could we holler? Besides, he knew us guys and had a good sense of how to handle us in there.

When we were sitting out in the yard, we could hear the tour guides on the boats taking sightseers around Alcatraz talking. They'd tell them,

"Behind those walls are the scum of the earth and dregs of society." All the guys on the yard would start booing and cussing back at them, but I doubt if they could hear them. Hell, they were right, we were.

During World War II one evening the wind was right, and we even heard music from the pier where Betty Grable was singing when she was entertaining the troops.

A Greek guy worked on making a braid out of rags all morning in the laundry and snuck up behind a guard and stuck it on his ass like a tail. It wasn't too long before another guard noticed it and told him, and the guard was so pissed he put the Greek in the hole for six days over it.

A dopehead went to the doctor and was able to get a drug for pain that he normally used on the outside to shoot into his veins. On Alcatraz there were no needles or ways to get them, so the guy cut his skin open on the inside of his arm with a razor blade and tried to put it in his veins for a high. The drug caused such a reaction to his skin and vein that he had a massive open sore on his arm for months and had to soak it several times a day, hoping that it would heal.

I used to have nightmares during which a guard had to wake me up when I was screaming. I remember one guard told me that with nightmares like I'd been having maybe I should go to see the priest and confess my sins so maybe I would feel better.

There was a guy named Gaylord Saxton from Saginaw, Michigan, who was a stunt pilot and real good at it. I remembered reading two articles that the *Saturday Evening Post* did about him two weeks in a row. He used to fly fighter planes over to England during the war, and that's how they got the planes over there for the Army instead of shipping them. Saxton got busted for flying guys into the United States from Cuba, and he beat the radar by flying three feet off the top of the water so he wouldn't be detected. He was dealing with a Croatian guy in Cuba who was his connection, but they both got busted, and Saxton got 10 years for that. He told George and me one day, they say, "You can't get anything into Alcatraz. Well," he said, "I sure got something in." He went on to tell us how he carried in one of his wife's pubic hairs, in-between his teeth.

We used to sit in the yard and watch how they got the knives into the cell blocks from the factory where they were made. The guys would go out to the yard, and they would drop them over the banister into the pile of cushions lying there. Then they'd go through the "snitch box" and go over and pick up their cushion from the pile and retrieve their knives lying there. After yard, they had to go through the snitch box again and then go put their cushions back, retrieving the knives again, and walk up the steps into the cell house.

One time I was going to get a apple raisin pie from Karpis when he was working in the kitchen, and I hoped he was sober and didn't screw it up when he made it. I just walked up to the table he put it on and put the pie down the front of my pants. I was carrying it out of the dining room, and the guard McKean stopped and asked me, "What'cha got?" I told him it was just a pie from Karpis and he let me go by with it. Another young guard stopped me and said, "You think you're smart, but I know what's going on," and we both laughed as I walked away. We were close to a lot of the old guards out there, and they were our friends.

I took the pie to my cell and put it under my pillow and left and went out to the yard. When George and I were walking back into the cell house, the guard, Bob Ord, was wiping across his lips, smacking them and saying, "Yum, yum." George asked me what the hell that was about and I didn't know, but found out soon enough when I got back to my cell. The pie was gone from under my pillow. Ord came up to us and said he had to get it out of my cell for a shakedown and had it at his desk. I told him I wanted to split it into four pieces — Kelly, Frankie Delmar, Jim Clark and myself — so he cut the pie and took the pieces to each guy.

Frankie Delmar and Clark were partners on the outside, and they worked together pressing clothes on the island, so we never saw them during the day. There were five of us that celled on the same tier and were friends — Jim Clark, Count Lustig, Kelly, Frankie Delmar and myself. Frankie was in Lansing in 1933 when they took the warden hostage and broke out of prison. He snatched a car and drove the people inside across the

Alcatraz mug shot of Frankie Delmar.

179

state line, making it a federal offense, and that's what got him sent to Alcatraz.

Another guard named Smitty knew we made coffee after they locked the cell doors and sent all the keys up front every night. He used to say to me, "Honjak" (slang word like Hunky), give me some coffee, and when he drank it, he said it was the best he'd ever tasted. I told him it should be good, it's the warden's coffee, not the crap they give to us convicts. Another young guard named Walsh caught me on the floor rolling toilet paper around my fingers in small bunches and asked me what I was doing, and I told him as soon as he got his ass out of there I was going to start a fire and make some coffee. He was learning how to be an automotive mechanic and was going to school, and the job on Alcatraz was just to get by until he graduated and went back home to New Haven, Connecticut.

Alvin "Creepy" Karpis worked in the kitchen, and he was an irrefutable drunk. As long as he was in the kitchen, the bread and rolls would come out flat as a pancake because he took all the yeast to make his booze. This one time he got burned up pretty bad by this oven in the bakery and they were taking him to the hospital on a stretcher, and the entire dining room got up and applauded to see him go. Jimmy Widner with whom I did time in Jeff City came in the bakery, and you should have seen the rolls and bread after that and how high they were. Kelly hated Karpis with a passion just because of the way he was always making his booze and not concerned about the food he was screwing up for all the other convicts.

There are very few people alive who really know how Karpis got the nickname "Creepy," and I'm one of them. He got the nickname while on Alcatraz, but I'd never disclose how because when asked about Karpis, this just wasn't something you'd discuss openly in public.

Several of us guys were sitting at this table in the laundry waiting for the machines to finish, and we'd see someone sneaking around towards the back of the washing machines where all the queers hung out. We were curious and wanted to know who was going back there to watch the fags. I went over to investigate and saw that it was Karpis and went back and told the guys. Just about every day we'd see him sneaking toward the washers to watch all the queers back there. He

Alcatraz mug shot of Alvin Karpis.

told me later that he was infatuated with this young queer kid back there and wanted him for himself and would go back there and watch him every chance he got.

So from then on when we'd see someone creeping around toward the back of the washers, we'd just remark that it was just old Karpis. Then as time went by and we'd continue to see him, we'd just say, "There goes old Creepy," and the rest, as they say, is history.

Karpis used to tell us that the story in the newspapers about Ma Barker being the mastermind behind the Karpis-Barker gang was all bullshit. The FBI had to come up with some phony story on her since they slaughtered her in that shoot-out. He said that she knew that they were all criminals, but when they traveled together it made it easier for people to think that it was a mother and her sons. Karpis laughed, then said the same thing Harvey Bailey said, "Hell, she couldn't even organize breakfast, much less any of our scores."

Karpis had his fingerprints surgically removed by having a doctor sand them off. He had to keep heavy coatings of Vaseline on all of his fingers for the entire time it took them to heal. That sure backfired on him, because whenever they took his prints and they came up completely blank, the authorities knew immediately that they belonged to Karpis.

Doc Moran was a real doctor who did the gruesome fingerprint removal operations on Fred Barker and Alvin Karpis. His downfall came when they found out that he was telling hookers about his unusual medical skills. When he vanished, Fred Barker told Karpis, "Doc and I shot the son-of-a-bitch; anybody who talks to whores is too dangerous to live."

Karpis said that he actually never expected to get arrested; he always thought that the FBI would kill him first. J. Edgar Hoover called Karpis "a dirty yellow rat," because in the 1920s he was involved with the "Purple Gang," which was a vicious group of killers out of Detroit. Karpis would always say, "I made that son-of-a-bitch," when he talked about J. Edgar Hoover.

One guy was ironing a shirt on a table with a blanket on it down in the laundry. The guard coming by to take a count just walked up to the table and knocked twice on top and got two knocks back from underneath. We knew it had to be queers under the table, so we stuck around and waited to see who came out, just to know who all the fags were in the laundry. Hell, even the guards used to ask us to go behind the washer to check and see how many queers were back there, because they were sick of seeing them hooked up together.

I was getting ready to drain the washers and went to put my rubber boots on, and I'll be dammed if some son-of-a-bitch in the laundry didn't use my boots to make their hooch in. When I pulled out my foot, it was sopping wet and raisins were stuck all over my sock.

I sat right across the dining room table from Count Victor Lustig who celled next to Eddie Bentz, the bank robber. I read all about this guy in the *Saturday Evening Post* on the outside and never imagined that I would be meeting him in Alcatraz. He was known as the king of the "Con-Men," and his cons made national news, especially for selling the Eiffel Tower twice for salvage.

The count even beat a madam named Shibal in Pittsburgh, Pennsylvania out of $50,000 and could con the best of the cons. His real name was George Miller, and he was actually from Springfield, Missouri.

He carried around a wooden box he had made out of mahogany that he told everyone could make real money by putting a quality rag in one end, turning the cranks and knobs and within a few hours eject two brand new $1,000 bills. He said he sold hundreds of them all over the country, and it was one of the best cons he used on the suckers.

Once when he was arrested in Texas he talked the local sheriff into embezzling $35,000 from the county treasury by giving it to him so there wouldn't be any heat on the sheriff. He was let go and told the sheriff to meet him in New York to split the money. The sheriff went to the lower east side of New York looking for him, but no one in the area at that time spoke English, so he didn't get anywhere or ever find the Count.

Count Victor Lustig.

They even made an old movie about this at one time, 91st Street or something was the title, and I remember going to see it.

Charlie, Ed and I were sitting in the laundry one day and saw a guy take off his shirt and another guy starting greasing his body down. Our first thought was he was going to try to take a swim in the bay to escape. Then we saw the guy tape shivs to both of his hands and knew that the grease would make blood run off his skin and wipe off easier when he cut a guy and the blood splattered on him. One guy was in the bathroom and had his shirt off bent over the sink when the other guy came up behind him and jabbed him with both shivs on each side. It wasn't until the guard was taking count that they found his body lying in the bathroom. The FBI came in to talk to a few guys about the stabbing, and all the guys wanted was to make names for themselves or get commissaries, so the FBI left with no information at all about the murder.

Two black guys were walking through the snitch box going out into the yard when the buzzer went off, and the guard standing close to them told them to stop and go back through. When they backed up to get ready to go through the snitch box again, they dropped a knife on the ground out of sight, and the guard next to them shook them down, then told them to go through again. They both backed up and one guy swooped up the knife and walked through the snitch box, setting off the buzzer again. The guard up in the tower yelled out, "I hope that you can get that damn thing fixed so it doesn't go off all the time." The guard closest to the two guys yelled back to the tower guard that he'd have the buzzer checked out and just motioned for the two guys to go ahead through and proceed to the yard.

One guy made himself a little dresser in the furniture factory and was taking it back to his cell. The guard stopped him and said, "Stop, I gotta check that thing to see if anything is hot inside of it." He pulled out the little drawers and turned it upside down to look at it inside and out and then told the guy to go ahead. Hell, the entire box was hot, but he let it go through, and the guy had it in his cell for two days before they came in and confiscated it.

There was a crazy acting guy that worked in the kitchen named Rodell that the guards hated to shake down. The guy would go through a crazy act of sitting on the floor taking all his clothes off and talking, even though the guards would tell him to stop and go on. He talked to himself and cussed the entire time, so it got where the guards saw him coming and just let him go through, and with that he became the best candidate to carry contraband around and out of the kitchen. Rodell carried a lot of cash around in his shoe that was forbidden to have on Alcatraz. They went to shake him down and told him to take off his shoes, and he sat down on the floor and went into his little crazy act, taking off all of his clothes and getting ready to pull off his shoes when the guard yelled at him to get his clothes back on and get the hell back to his cell. We all laughed about how he was able to manipulate the guards and carry contraband with his crazy act.

We were sitting in the laundry one morning and watched this guy walk up and unscrew a dummy pipe from behind a washing machine. He dropped it down inside a laundry bag, walked up behind another guy and swung the bag quickly, creasing the guy's skull and splitting it wide open as he fell to the floor. We continued to watch as he calmly walked back to the washing machine, screwed the pipe back in its place, threw the bloody laundry bag inside a washing machine and walked off. When the guards walked in for count they found the guy on the floor and he was rushed to the hospital in serious condition. They lined us all up while the guards were searching the entire laundry for the weapon without success. We found out from Karpis later it was just a lovers' quarrel amongst some queers that congregated behind the washers.

11

Gun Gallery Takeover

THURSDAY, MAY 2, 1946 is when Barney Coy, Clarence Carnes and Marvin Hubbard got the guns from the gun gallery and tried to make their break. The original plan was taking the guards' families as hostage to get off of the island after they acquired the weapons from the gun gallery.

A week before I was coming up from the basement barbershop and had to wait for the guard to let me out, and I saw Hubbard standing across from me over in B-block. He asked me, "Who's downstairs?" I told him it was guards Stewart and Ed Stucker, and he motioned an okay signal to someone above my head, and Coy dropped down right in front of me. He was on the top gallery above me bending the bars, but I never asked any further questions. He told me how they got this long piece of rope and used it to get up to the bars to spread 'em, and that he kept the rope hidden "in plain sight" in Captain Winehold's wastepaper basket.

The day it happened we knew something was going on because when we were going to work and walked down the stairs we saw the lectern on the wall that the inmates used to get a lay in at the hospital. They put your name on a card, place it in the lectern and check you in to the hospital. I told Kelly, " I guess we're going to be the only ones here in the cell house tonight because the lectern is full."

When the sirens went off on Alcatraz, all guards had to return to work immediately. Some lived 30 miles away and could still hear the sirens when they went off. People would line up on the docks across the water in San Francisco waiting and watching what was taking place on the Island.

A newspaper article mentioned all the problems they were having on Alcatraz. The warden said: "What do you think I have out here?"

Jimmy Lucas, the guy who hit Al Capone, and I were down in the laundry waiting for the clothes to wash and didn't hear the whistle blow, but we saw the Coast Guard out in the bay and the *San Francisco Chronicle's* helicopter flying overhead around and around. We knew something was going on up on the hill from the laundry in the cell house. The bell rang down at the laundry, and we had to line up for count, and the next thing we saw was all these Marines coming on the island. Then they marched us all up on the hill, and we had to stay out in the yard for three nights while the trouble was still going on inside the cell house.

At night in San Francisco it gets cold out there by the water, and we were all freezing out on the yard, so we tore down and burned the scoreboard to try to stay warm, and the ball players got mad at us over that.

The planes and helicopters were flying around and around all night long with their engines roaring. The Marines were all along the catwalk that sat on the backside of the wall approximately four feet from the top, giving them the protection of the wall. The Marines surrounding the wall still wanted to go into the cell house and kept asking, "What are we waiting for, let's go, let's go!" One of the Marines saw a guy in a window and thought it was a target and was going to shoot, but they hollered that it was only a guy in the hospital. The guys who were exposed to the outside windows in the cell house had to put their mattresses up to protect themselves from all the shells that were being fired inside.

We were out there in the yard for those three days and didn't have anything to eat, but Meathead, the deputy warden, came out and threw bread and raw potatoes down to us from up on the wall. The Marines surrounded us all around the wall, and they were dropping tailor-made cigarettes to the guys, and some of the convicts were hollering, "Throw me some of those cigarettes." They were giving the Marines away, and the Marines were doing them a favor. The Marines kept saying, "Let's go in and get these guys," but the warden wouldn't let them enter the cell house shooting.

After the third day we were all sent back into the cell house, which I never understood because Coy, Cretzer, Hubbard and those guys were still running loose in the cell house and it was full of tear gas and shrapnel. When they ran us in there, we just grabbed any cell. I was able to get into my cell, but Kelly wasn't able to get into his. They were shooting demolition grenades through the windows, so with all the shrapnel I was lucky I was on A-block because there were no windows in front of me. I could see up the hall toward the dining room and could see the shrapnel coming through the windows flying all over the place, followed by tracer bullets shattering through. The guards and Marines were just shooting at random; they didn't care where they were shooting; they just shot hoping to get those guys. I saw Johnny Johnson standing up against the wall trying to stay out of the line of fire when they were shooting; and all the shrapnel was flying around him.

We could hear jackhammers up above the cell houses and above the dining room door where they were making holes in the roof. They were dropping grenades down into the cell house through those holes, and those marks are still on the floor right in front of the dining room to this day. I don't know why they ran us all off the yard and into the cell house because it was filled with tear gas, and shells were all over the floor, plus they were still shooting wildly in there.

Some guys in there didn't give a shit, and we heard them holler when they had the place surrounded, "Bring your Goddamn guns in and kill us all." We'd holler back, "Shut up you, sons-of-bitches." Pansky was one of the guys who hollered the most, and he ended up committing suicide. We called him a "Dumb Pollock" because he got even with them by killing himself. They had him locked up in D-block, and he used a razor or something and cut under his upper arm and bled to death. He was always mouthing off all the time when he was in the dining room, and we all thought he was a nut.

They were watching us closely in the dining room because they wanted to keep an eye on any unruly guy so they could come after you one at a time and lock you in your cell.

The guards couldn't handle the takeover by themselves; they just kept shooting everywhere, so they had to bring in the Marines to calm things down and to help with the fire power.

When the Marines rushed into the main cell house, four knelt down with four standing behind them with guns at the ready. They would have shot anyone they saw, but Coy and those guys were in another part of the cell house, and Warden Johnston told them to hold their fire.

Ed Stucker was the one who put in the alarm when they took over the gun gallery.

All that shooting lasted for three days; then it finally got silent. Hell, Coy was running all around the gallery; and they were looking for him; but he was shielded from the outside windows because of A-block. He told me, "We just killed nine bulls and we got to get out of here," because he thought Cretzer killed all those guards in the cell in there.

The first day when they brought us back into the cell house, we were afraid to go into the gallery in front of any windows because we thought somebody would shoot us. Coy, Cretzer and Hubbard were still over in C-block, and that's where they found their bodies over there in the court. They were underneath the floor in C-block where they were dropping those fragment grenades down inside, and it was the concussion that killed them. Before they went in to check C-block, a rifle shot went off, and they said later that it was the rifle in Cretzer's hands, and when rigor mortis set in, his finger constricted, pulling the trigger.

When they dragged them out, they had to drag them by my cell in the direction where they took the pictures of them by the visiting room. I could see three sets of legs sticking out, but you couldn't recognize any of them; they were all blue. One already had rigor mortis set in because his arms were all stiff, but I don't remember who it was, but there is a picture somewhere that shows who it was.

Everything was planned a week before that break, but you'd have to see the way those top gallery bars were made to understand it. The bars were braced only so far up; then from the top brace there were straight pieces of iron going up five feet, then curving over at the top. That's where they were spreading the bars, but you couldn't see it unless you were on the third gallery, and no one celled on the third gallery, so no one spotted them. They used a union with reversible screws that spread the bars, and when you turned the union while each screw lay against an adjacent bar, it would widen. The guards bring everything in and shake everything down, but somehow they missed those unions and screws, and they got it through from the laundry building into the basement.

The guard Miller got killed, but Coy didn't kill him because they were good friends and I'd see them sitting together a lot of times just talking. Miller was an easygoing guy, and I think he just accidentally got killed in the crossfire, which was a shame. He used to tell us guys not to be running around in the gallery because the lieutenant was coming. We'd just tell him, "Oh, Miller, just go over there and sit down and read your paper or magazine or whatever you got over there."

There was a guard named Stites who earlier killed Red Limmerick and shot Jimmy Lucas when they tried to get away. They knew he was working in the gun gallery that day, and they just killed him outright. In fact, they said that he was a target.

Every Thursday afternoon from D-block, which is separated by a wall from C-block, there's a door that whenever a guard goes over to D-block he has to tell the guard in the gun gallery to get the key and they let it down on a string so he can proceed. Then the guy in the gun gallery calls up front to the armory telling them, and they would open the doors in D-block that were electric. What Coy and those guys didn't know was that when they went over to get the key and opened that door a red light flashed on in the armory up front. That wasn't supposed to happen, and it was a warning so the guard in the armory automatically turned the juice off.

That was a code that Coy and those guys didn't know about, and that's why the doors never opened all the way and only opened about 10 or 12 inches when they shut the juice off. Shockley was able to get out of his cell through the opening, but Whitey Franklin couldn't, and none of those other guys could because they were too big and couldn't fit through the small opening.

When Shockley got out of his cell, they thought he was in on it and he was sent to the gas chamber, but actually he didn't have anything to do with the break. He just got out of there and was running around with a gas gun. The guy had the mentality of an eight-year-old kid but was crazy and dangerous, so you had to watch him. When they had the guards locked up in a cell, Shockley walked by them with the gas gun, and when they saw him they thought he was involved, and that's how he got the death sentence.

At that time there was a small piece of glass on the door from the gun gallery into D-block. When Coy was already in the gun gallery getting ready to come out, he saw guards coming back from D-block. They couldn't see him through the glass, so when they opened the door Coy was ready and overpowered and grabbed Burch.

Then they sent the goon squad in, and when they did, Coy was dressed up in some guard's uniform. Guard Joe Burdett was walking out of the kitchen, and seeing a commotion, walked toward the front, and that's when Coy put the rifle on him right away because he was six feet four, and Coy was worried about a confrontation. Coy was dressed in Winehold's uniform, and he was built like Captain Winehold, so that's why Joe kept walking up to him. Coy put the gun on Joe and ran him back in the cell, but Joe said he wanted to go back in the kitchen, but Coy replied, "No, you son-of-a-bitch, I want to know where you are because I might want to kill you."

When they had all the guards in one cell, Joe Cretzer went and just shot wildly right into the cell. Captain Winehold told Cretzer, "You're further away from Frisco now than you'll ever be."

Three ended up dead — Coy, Hubbard and Cretzer. Then Shockley and Blackie went to the gas chamber. Miller and Stites were the two guards killed, and Miller was killed accidentally, but Stites they wanted to kill because he was a marked man.

The guard McKean just got grazed on the cheek, and afterward all of us guys would tease him, saying, "They really didn't want to kill you, they were just playing with you." McKean would come back, saying, "Bullshit, they meant to kill me and you know it."

We couldn't go down to the laundry for over a week, and we couldn't go out in the yard or anywhere for over a week. You could hardly walk in the cell house because of all the shells on the floor. Every step you took you'd roll around on top of the shells and fall on your butt.

Then they started letting a tier at a time, only 14 guys, go into the dining room, but nobody in groups any more. There were still so many shell casings on the floor you couldn't walk without rolling and slipping.

We still got three meals a day, and the guards were doing the cooking, and we were getting good meals that was all the same food for everyone and not different for the convicts.

After it simmered down for a couple of days, they sent us back to work down in the laundry, and it was so overloaded it took weeks to catch up on all the laundry we did for the Maritime and also for Fort Ord. Maritime was the United States Marines or anyone on the ships out there in the bay.

When the FBI came on the island afterward, they wanted to interrogate the prisoners about the takeover. They talked to just about four guys and ended the questioning. Nobody would talk about the takeover; all they wanted to do was gripe about conditions on the island and ask for more privileges.

They had a lot of dignitaries come out there when things settled down, but we didn't pay much attention to them. Although when J. Edgar Hoover came to Alcatraz, he got his ass chewed out, and even Meathead said he should have known better than to come out here.

Everything changed after the takeover of the guns in 1946, and all the guards had to become sterner and were not quite as friendly or close to the convicts as they once were.

The newspaper guys from San Francisco were raising hell that they wanted to come to Alcatraz to see for themselves and kept demanding, so finally they allowed the reporters in. Deputy Miller was walking the reporters down Broadway, and these convicts started hollering at him, "Hey, Jughead; hey, Meathead; hey, Miller." Deputy Miller calmly turned while pointing to us guys on the tier and told the reporters, "That's where we keep all of our stool pigeons."

Warden Johnston was a diplomat, and he was here for security and knew how to handle us guys, and we respected him for it. The fact that he was in the dining room every day at the noon meal to taste the food on the line that was to be fed to the convicts gained our good opinion of him. There was just too much publicity on Johnston after the gun gallery takeover, and things never were the same for the next 10 years.

When they transferred Johnston, they brought in Warden Swope with all his rule books, and he just wasn't the type of guy to run a place like Alcatraz. Swope used to be a warden in the state prison in New Mexico where they had barefooted Apaches and barefooted convicts back then, and us guys were out of his league.

Warden Swope had too many rules when he came to Alcatraz, which is what caused us to turn the tables over in the dining room. He never came back into the dining room and would only stand outside the locked door and look in every day during lunch. He had these little rule books that he tried to pass out to everyone on the island, but we tossed 'em in a pile and burned them the first day they came around. Then his laundry had to be sent to San Francisco because we'd send it back dirty or in pieces. The drain to each of the industry's washers was a big pipe that jutted out of the rocks into the bay, and you'd see sheets, clothing and even Warden Swope's wife's bra floating out in the bay, and the guards would have to get into boats and drag them back in with a long hook.

Then Paul Madigan came in. He was a deputy warden under Johnston, and when they made him warden, things went back to normal. You could deal with him and talk to him, and we called him "Promising Paul." When you asked him for something, he said he couldn't promise you that he'd get it, but he would try.

I remember it was Blackie McGee who was a mean son-of-a-bitch from East St. Louis who argued with Madigan in the dining room, telling him he could run the prison better than he could. Madigan said if you think you can do better and you want to wear my pants, then try it. Madigan was unzipping his pants, acting like he was going to give them to Blackie. The entire dining room watched and listened to the argument and how Madigan kept such absolute control of the conversation over Blackie. Blackie was later killed because he was such a bad-ass, unpredictable son-of-a-bitch and everyone was afraid of him, knowing he was crazy and that he'd kill you in a second with no remorse or concern.

I finally made all the guards happy when Kelly got me out of the laundry to work with him in the industries office. This was one of the top jobs in the prison, and I made $100 a month, but never spent any money because you were so limited on what you could purchase or spend it on. You could order a $1500 guitar, but couldn't purchase a nickel candy bar with any of your money. I also got five days of good time taken off of my sentence every month, which took two years off my time.

There were three of us working together in the industry office. George "Machine Gun" Kelly sat on my right, and Basil "The Owl" Banghart sat on my left, and they called us "The Gruesome Threesome." We handled all the bookkeeping for the laundry, mat factory, brush factory, clothing factory and the model shop where they reconditioned furniture.

Banghart's real name was Larry Breeze, and Kelly and I always called him Larry. We thought Larry Breeze was his right name, but

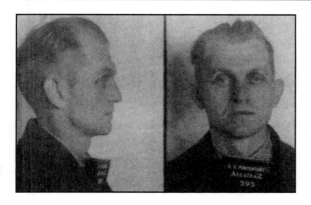

Alcatraz mug shot of Basil "The Owl" Banghart.

hell, I don't really know, he had so damn many aliases. Larry was just a burglar before he helped Frank Touhy escape from Joliet Penitentiary, making his charges federal. I say he was the leader of the Rodger Toughy gang because he was the one with the single-engine airplane. He'd fly above and along with the trains and would watch the pickups they made along the way. He'd case the trains when they'd pull into the depot and drop off the mail bags. He'd look for the bag marked in big black letters, "U.S. Treasury," and then he knew that would be the one with the money in it and their score.

Basil "The Owl" Banghart was a German out of southern Illinois, but he had the features of a Pollock with eyebrows that formed one line across his forehead if he didn't keep them trimmed. We called him Larry Breeze when we worked together in the industry office on Alcatraz. He would always talk about his young teenage daughter and frequently show us her pictures as she was growing up. Us guys, being guys, would always notice from her pictures that even at a young age she was very well-busted. When he was in Stateville penitentiary in Joliet, Illinois in 1942, he went over the wall with Roger Touhy. It was during a baseball game when he walked the warden right over to the wall; then using a ladder they had secured earlier, they made their break. Previously they bribed a guard, which gave them outside help on that escape, and when they got picked up outside the walls, they headed straight for Chicago. A short time later when Touhy and Banghart were asleep in their apartment, the FBI hit the building with powerful searchlights and loudspeakers after getting a tip on their whereabouts. Banghart wanted to shoot it out with the FBI, but Touhy talked him out of it, and they both surrendered peacefully. When Touhy and Banghart were being taken to the police car, J. Edgar Hoover, along with several agents and newspaper reporters came up and said, "Banghart, you're a trapped rat." Banghart said, "You're J. Edgar Hoover, aren't you?" When he acknowledged he was, Banghart said, "You're a lot fatter in person than you are on the radio." That's when they sent him on to Alcatraz.

I used to sit in the office and just look at the aging Banghart and Kelly and think about when they were both the top criminals in the country, Public Enemy Number One in the United States. Larry would sit there, and his head would shake all the time while he worked. I'd walk up behind him and hold his head still and ask him if he knew how bad it was trembling, and he'd answer "no" every time. When I released my hands, his head would go back to shaking up and down continuously. Kelly used to tease him that he was making us guys look bad by looking so damn old and decrepit.

Count formation on the yard at Alcatraz.

Anytime you see the picture of guys standing out in the yard in groups on Alcatraz, that was the way we had to position for count. You'll see a short line of three guys standing there, and that was "The Gruesome Threesome" from the Industry Office: Kelly, Banghart and me.

Back then the guards used to take a lot of pictures of guys out on the yard to record what guy was hanging around with who and so on.

Warden Paul Madigan would come and sit and talk to the three of us while we were working, and while he was talking we could see his right hand moving constantly in his pocket. We found out later that he was saying his rosary that he carried in his pocket all the time. The superintendent didn't like me, and it would make him madder than hell when Warden Madigan would come down to the office to sit and talk to us guys. We asked him one time why the German guy named Rodell got thrown in the hole, and he said that he called the Tower guard, Barker, a son-of-a-bitch, and Barker wrote him up. When they took him down to court, Rodell told them he didn't know that son-of-a-bitch Barker could hear him all the way up there in the tower, and Madigan cut him loose right away; he was an all right guy.

P.J. Madigan wasn't a disciplinarian; he just wanted you to do your work without any problems. He'd tell us guys about any shakedowns that were coming in case we were carrying any contraband. He idolized Jack London, the author and adventurer, and would tell us stories he read about him all the time while visiting us in the industries office.

We worked in the industry office for John Comerford, and when he came to work on Mondays he'd always be in such a good mood, but it soon changed. I had allergies and I'd rib him about where in the hell he'd been over the weekend, causing me to sneeze incessantly from the pollen he carried on his clothes. He was a graduate of Fordham University and had a M.A. degree in Physical Education and was too pleasant of a guy to be working in a place like Alcatraz with guys like us.

We would get coffee from the kitchen by pulling it up on a string we had hanging out the window, and it was the good coffee issued to the guards and not the convicts. Mr. Comerford was going to be gone on vacation, and we asked him if we could request to have his desk taken to the furniture department to have the top refinished. He agreed, but didn't know the guys in the furniture factory rigged up a dummy space by making his desk drawer shorter and putting hidden hinges on the top of the desk for easy access to the secret place we kept our contraband coffee. We would have our coffee break at 10 a.m. every day, and when Warden Madigan was around he'd tell Mr. Comerford, "Let's go up on the hill, John," getting him out of the office for us. During the day while sitting at his desk, Mr. Comerford would make the comment, "I smell coffee," and all we could do was sit there and bite our lips to keep from laughing. He was a good guy to work with, and we put him through hell with all our bullshit.

One guard, Joe Burdett, who was a 6'4" ex-highway patrolman came up to me in the office and asked if I could help Harry Wells get an increase in his wages in the brush factory. I told him, sure I could, but he'd have to sign the papers authorizing the increase, and he said do it and he'd okay it. I told him to have Wells sign the daily sheet saying that he made two more brushes than he had previously been making, and it would set him up in a higher wage category.

Once when Burdett was sitting in our office, a fight broke out in the brush factory between several big black guys, and we were all watching it through the square windowpanes from our office. Burdett called the goon squad, but remained sitting at our desk with both of his hands cupping each side of his eyes so he couldn't see into the brush factory, saying: "You're not going to get me to walk in there, just let them kill each other."

I was the one who did the payroll for all of the industries on Alcatraz. I figured out all the piecework and the hourly pay for everyone. I was the guy who billed all of the guards for doing their laundry on the island and never once charged Mannery for his laundry because he was such a good guard. He's the one who would tell us there was going to be a shakedown, so don't carry anything on you, and you had to respect the man for sharing that kind of information with us.

When we worked in the office, there was a lieutenant who was a tough guard and really strict about rules who worked in the brush factory, but the guy liked the three of us and would even bring us local newspapers and lay them on the desk for us to read every day, which was a total restriction. We found some extra pipe fittings down in the model shop, and we asked him if we could rig up a shower outside the brush factory just for the three of us. He let us do it, and we took showers any time we wanted to in privacy. When I'd go out the door to run down to the shower, I'd yell to Harry Winegar, the guard who worked in the tower, "Hey, Harry, would you jigger for me?" He'd just laugh and tell me to go ahead. The old guards were good guys and our friends and they treated us right and we respected them for it, but the younger ones remained cold and inaccessible in becoming friends, especially after the gun gallery takeover.

I used to order bird books and magazines for Robert "Birdman" Stroud because he had no money on the books since he was locked up in a cell in the hospital and was not allowed to work around other prisoners.

Stroud was in the hospital on Alcatraz when Kelly and I went up there, and I felt sorry for him, and I think I was the only friend he had who would talk to him. We all knew he was a fag, and a lot of guys teased him with stories about a young boy moving into the cell next to him. He'd get all excited in expectation of a possibility of getting close to him. Every day when they'd let him out of his room to carry his shit bucket down the hospital corridor to empty it, he'd be looking from side to side for this young kid in the cell that the guys told him about.

Bob was raped as a kid up in Alaska and was a male prostitute at the age of 21 and hung out in the local saloons to survive. There were very few women in that part of the country back in those days. He killed the bartender who had been his lover and was convicted of manslaughter and sent to McNeil Island, where he became incorrigible and was later brought to Leavenworth Penitentiary by horse and buggy in 1911.

He was nothing but a queer who would try to solicit every guy he came in contact with, making it impractical to keep him out in the general population. He progressively sustained and increased his violence, murdering a guard, which caused him to be locked down permanently. He received a death sentence for which his mother pleaded to President Woodrow Wilson, who later commuted his sentence to life without parole.

He then became known as the "Birdman," but still caused problems with authorities, so they decided to ship him out to the West Coast. He arrived on Alcatraz in 1942, and the administration felt safe to keep him locked up in the hospital by himself to avoid adverse contact with other prisoners.

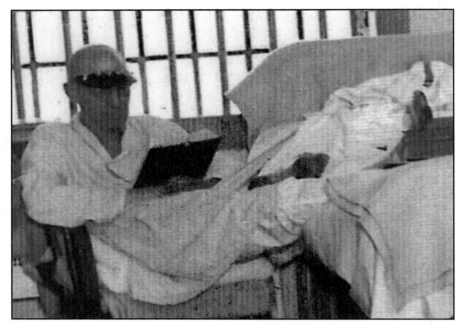

Robert Stroud sitting by his bed.

He had a beautiful Spencerian handwriting that is an ornate style of writing using rounded letters all slanted to the right. Bob attempted to write a book once, and he asked Kelly and me to look at it when we were up in the hospital. Kelly saw one excerpt where it stated: "I was speaking to a well-known bank robber the other day, and I asked him, 'George, what do you think of homosexuals?' " Kelly got so mad, saying that son-of-a-bitch referred to him in his damn book, and tore out five pages. I laughed at Kelly, saying, "What's a' matter, Kelly, you afraid it will hurt your reputation to be in Bob's book?" The government must still have those two journals that Stroud wrote on Alcatraz, and I wish I'd kept those five pages Kelly tore out just for the Spencerian penmanship.

Bob had been locked up so many years that when he talked to you, even though you were both standing next to the bars facing each other, he'd shout so loud you had to tell him to lower his voice.

Bob was 6'4" tall, and when he stood up his knees would shake uncontrollably because his body was so weak from lack of exercise. I would send him magazines to read, and if he wanted anything else, I would try to get it for him. He always wore a sun visor cap, and you could see where his chest was caved in and how bad his legs were when he stood up. Stroud would get to go out on the yard after we all went to work and the kitchen help went out and came back in. He was so feeble I don't know how he made it up and down the steep steps that went to the yard.

Although the prison captain and other officers thought of Stroud as a psychopath or psychotic, I felt that he was a very intelligent, well-read man who had been locked up in a small cell since 1911 and certainly developed a severe mental condition from the experience.

We had to laugh one time when the hospital was full and Karpis' partner, Freddy Hunter, had surgery. They had to put him in the same room with the Birdman to recover. Freddy got better all right and Birdman was happy doing him over and over again while the poor guy was lying there on the cot knocked out from the anesthetics.

During the entire seven years that I did on Alcatraz, I received only one piece of mail from anyone in my family. My brother, Frank, was stationed in France during World War II, and he sent me a card. I wrote him back, and Frank told me later all his buddies wanted to know who he knew on Alcatraz.

Later I was told my cousin, Joe Clements, was on leave in San Francisco from the Navy during World War II and stood on the pier pointing and telling all his buddies that he had a first cousin out there on Alcatraz.

You read about what a bad place Alcatraz was, but in all the time I did over the years Alcatraz was the best place I ever did it. You knew you were there for security, so you accepted it and all the restrictions. Just having the privacy of your own cell was something I'd never experienced in the past at other prisons, and that was a bonus. You had the warden and the guards who were your friends who you were on a first-name basis with, having normal conversations where they never showed any vindictive authority.

Then when you walked out in the yard, you saw the most striking panorama of pristine blue water of the bay, the Golden Gate Bridge and the skyline of San Francisco. So what other joint ever had a view as striking as that one?

Of all the years that I spent on Alcatraz, not one time was it ever referred to as "The Rock." That name came up later from the movies and articles written about the place, but us guys never heard of it on the island back then.

12

Leavenworth Federal Penitentiary
April 1952

WHEN WE WERE getting short, they decided to transfer some of us guys to Leavenworth Federal Prison, "The Big Top," to do the remainder of our time until our release date. A 40-foot wall that was also 40 feet below ground and four feet thick surrounded the 16 acres of the prison.

Kelly was transferred first in 1951 and sent word back to me that things were a lot different and not good and that I wouldn't like it there. George said it was rough trying to keep away from all the guys who wanted to meet him and talk to him on the yard, plus they had these rule books.

I was transferred August 20, 1952, and found out what he was talking about right away, but luckily things changed after I got there.

They brought some of the guards from Alcatraz to be with us old guys, and we ended up all on one tier together.

One guy named Joe Nance would always come around to talk to me about escape. He knew I would always try to break out no matter where I was if I got a chance. I had already gotten the word he was a snitch, so I didn't say much to him and just listened and let him talk. Then a guard who was a

Leavenworth mug shot of Willie — August 23, 1952.

Leavenworth mug shot of George R. Kelly — 1951.

pretty good guy who I had become friends with came over to me one day and told me that whatever I was planning, it would be a snitch that got me caught. I got the hint right away and knew he was telling me that it was Joe Nance and he was waiting for me to go along with his escape plans so he could snitch me off.

There was a guard named Larkin who I met in Leavenworth, and he was also in St. Vincent's Orphanage right after I was. We often talked about how we were both adopted out to foster homes and how we both took separate paths after we left the orphanage, his being a path of righteousness and mine a road to disaster.

I was in the dining room one night when they had steak on the menu. One guy picked up his tray and was walking away toward his table when he collapsed into an epileptic fit and was lying on the floor jerking and shaking. A big black guy ran up and grabbed the steak off his tray and said, "That son-of-a-bitch ain't going to eat this." Nobody would even help the guy on the floor; they just ran up and stole all the food off his tray and walked away. Guards finally came up with a stretcher and took the poor guy away to the hospital.

There was another good guard named Stanley McKean who was not only a friendly guy, but also sensible. He'd let us old Alcatraz guys roam around the cell house to visit each other. We all went down to Count Victor Lustig's cell once, and he asked us if we wanted something to eat and pulled out some old bread and sprinkled sugar on it for us.

McKean called me down to talk to me and told me to go tell the guys that were shooting craps in B-cell house that they are in a place where the lieutenant could walk by and see them, so tell them to move. McKean was a guard who was on Alcatraz, but transferred to Leavenworth to be with us old guys.

When Basil "The Owl" Banghart, or Larry as we called him, finally got out of Alcatraz late in 1954, he went to live with his daughter in Los Angeles. His wife wrote to me in Leavenworth, and we kept in contact with each other for years, and I was deeply grateful because when I was out on parole I was able to go see Larry before he died.

Without Larry in Leavenworth, we had Frankie Delmar transferred to work in the office with us guys. Frankie never walked around with us on the yard until we got to Leavenworth. He talked in a low muffle sound that George wasn't able to hear, and one time when Frankie was talking, George busted out laughing. Frankie said, "What I said wasn't funny, so why in the hell are you laughing?" George told him he couldn't hear or understand a damn thing he said the entire time he was talking, and it just hit him as being funny as hell.

I was working in the office of the industries along with Kelly and Delmar. It was the best paying job in the place, and they paid you 20 days a month good time. Warden Willingham was the one who offered Kelly, Delmar and me the chance to go out to the farm, but we all turned it down because I'd lose the job that gave me all the good time. I was sentenced to 25 years plus 10 years, adding up to 35, and only did 12 years with all the good time that was taken off.

When my stepfather, Steve Tomasegovich, died, the Warden even let me go home for his funeral. When others asked for similar requests for home visits, he refused them, saying, "I'm very particular who I let go out of here."

Working in the furniture department in Leavenworth, I found out most of the furniture made went to governor's offices and high-ranking officials, generals, majors, colonels and on down the line. A lot of the furniture even went to the White House, and one piece in particular was this 20-foot table that was made in the furniture factory. They had to bring a special flat-bed train car inside the walls to take the table to its final destination. I've caught glimpses of the table on the news and in other films taken inside the White House.

I was very organized while working in the office, and they used to make comments about it. Someone would come in asking for the files of such and such, an order taken years and years ago, and I'd check my notes, then tell them that all the information they want is in box number four down in storage. There were only so many file cabinets in our office, and lots of the real old orders had to be filed away somewhere in boxes.

I remember a nice officer named Williams who came to me saying they wanted us to look up some real old records that dated way back. Williams went on to say that he was spending most of his time staying busy just trying to get all these old records. I told Williams what we should do was tell them that we had all the old records packed up in a box and that someone accidentally threw them away, and it worked. Then when someone would ask for extremely old records from another building, we'd just say, "Oh, hell, that was in that old box that they accidentally threw away."

The television show, *America's Most Wanted,* did a story on three guys who were supposed to have escaped from Alcatraz, and the Gold and Blue Fleet offered a million-dollar reward for their capture. Those guys were too dumb to make an escape and clean getaway. When they were in Leavenworth, they wanted to go out in a trash truck and were going to try it that day until I told them it was a stupid idea. I told them the trash truck sits out in the Sally Port all night, and before it even leaves the prison grounds it's inspected, and they wouldn't have a chance.

I knew another guy named Kenny Palmer who worked in the prison hospital. He was getting out on parole in a few days, but didn't have any place in particular to go. I felt sorry for him because I knew he didn't have any family, friends or money on the books for a fresh start. I told him to go down to my mother's house, and she knew from me to give him $200 so he could get a good start and a chance of staying out of prison. The son-of-a-bitch got the money from my mother, then went out and got drunk on the money and got picked up by the cops that night, and they brought him back to the prison the next day on parole violation. He couldn't stand up and was still half-drunk passing out when they tried to talk to him. I could have gotten into a lot of trouble over that one, and here all I was trying to do was to help the guy out.

A guard in Leavenworth showed me a picture once of himself in a National Guard armory with all the weapons that they kept there. I said to myself, "Hell, that's the place to go to get your firepower."

Lieutenant Noah Stucker and Warden Madigan, both from Alcatraz, came to visit George, Delmar and me while we were in Leavenworth. Warden Wilkerson told us later that when Warden Madigan came to visit he spoke well of us guys.

Now that Meathead Miller, I think he died of a broken heart when he left Alcatraz because he didn't have us guys to argue with any more. I remember him arguing with Blackie McGee in the dining room. They were both yelling and banging on the tables and eventually ended up getting along after that. Blackie had a younger brother who I did time with in Hutch, and they were just a couple of Hoosiers. They kidnapped and raped a girl named Mary McElroy and were given the death sentence. The girl pleaded with the court to commute their death sentences to life because she couldn't live with the thought of them being executed.

The auditor for all of the federal prisons in the United States was named Lawless. He'd hang around and talk to me, George and Banghart on Alcatraz whenever he came in for the audit and really enjoyed shooting the shit with us guys. Later on when we were transferred to Leavenworth, Lawless came for an audit and requested to the warden that he wanted to visit his old friends, George, Delmar and me.

Remember me telling you about Cecil Snow, the guy with the cackle laugh who I celled next to when I first got to Alcatraz? He finally got out and went down to Arkansas and got caught again and was sent to an Arkansas joint to do time. He eventually came back to Leavenworth and told Red and us guys that they whipped his ass down there, they whipped him bad. We all knew that they whipped you down there in those days because we heard all the horrific stories. Cecil was happy to be back in Leavenworth with us old guys because they didn't beat you in the federal joints like they did in all the state joints back then.

Gino Genovese was in the hospital while he was in Leavenworth. He was a big Mafioso and lived and was treated like a king while he was in there.

Years ago on the outside a guy named Ray Stevenson talked to me about robbing an abortion clinic, and I told him that there wouldn't be any money there and I wasn't interested. I told Ray to stay away from John Walden, the guy setting him up on these jobs, because he wasn't any good and neither were the scores. He came and told me later that they robbed that abortion clinic and only got $59. Then I read in the newspapers both Ray and John went to rob a loan office west of Chicago and came out empty-handed. While they were driving away on a road west near the DesPlaines River, they ran into a roadblock and got busted. Ray did a lot of time in Illinois, and then later they sent him to Alcatraz. When Alcatraz closed down, Ray was sent to Leavenworth Penitentiary and tried to escape. He was washing windows one day and tried to make his break and inadvertently fell from the window down into the snow. He broke his leg and lay there for a long time until they finally discovered he was gone from his job and went looking for him, and the guy almost froze to death before they found him.

Benny Binion, the guy who owned the Horseshoe Casino in Las Vegas, used to walk around the yard with Kelly and me and told us that after 11 p.m. when the customers in the casino would be drinking and drunk that they'd tighten up on the wheels of every slot machine in the joint. Benny also told us, "When they hang a charge on you, you gotta wear it." Benny was a small guy who had a comical little walk like he was pigeon-toed with real short steps and a funny shuffle, but a nice smile and easy to get along with.

Benny weighed about 200 pounds, and on the farm he owned in Montana he raised cattle and would tell us he must have eaten the whole herd. He had been wanted for a murder rap in Texas that was self-defense, and that's why he moved out to Nevada and opened the casino. Benny came to Leavenworth on a tax evasion charge during the 1950s.

Binion and a guy named Tom Banks lived in the firehouse station at Leavenworth. They had it a lot easier than living inside the walls, and how often would you have a fire in Leavenworth? The walls are four feet thick, and even during a tornado they just warned you to move away from any glass and didn't send you to any place special.

Even 20-some years later I continued to tease George about still having a crush on that silent movie star, Fi-Fi Dor'se. He said he didn't give a shit 'cause she had some nice-looking legs, and he thought about them a lot over the years.

Kelly and I would reminisce about the good old times when we met back in Kansas City at a dive down on James Street in the 1920s when he was a booze runner and going with a big blonde named Bess Williams from Wichita. We always ended the conversation in astonishment, concluding that we never thought we'd meet again and become such great friends.

Kelly and I were together all the time, and I knew everything there ever was to know about that guy. I knew all about the Herschel kidnapping and who got the money and how it was spread around. Gus Winkler, who's dead now, even got some of the money. When Tom Banks from Minneapolis came to prison on income tax evasion, he and Benny Binion even got in on it.

Benny walked up to us and said, "George, Tom wants to see you, so I'm gonna be standing there, and when you come out I'm gonna bring you over and introduce you to Tom. When Benny took George over to meet Tom, George asked him, "How much money are you still holding for me?" Tom replied: "$45,000." George told him he wanted to take $10,000 of that money and give it to Willie so he could take it to his lawyer to get Kathryn out of prison. George got the name of a lawyer from a guy doing time inside Leavenworth because he was desperate and it's hard to get a lawyer you could trust from the inside. He was going to have me give the guy $10,000 to get Kathryn out of prison because he got the word that she was really doing hard time and getting beat up frequently because of her bad mouth.

Tom Banks said he gave some money to Kid Cann, whose real name was Isaac Bloomberg, a mobster out of Minneapolis. I met him later when he came to Leavenworth on tax evasion. He controlled a lot of crime up there in Minneapolis, and he even got a split of the kidnapping money.

I had nine months to go to get out on parole when Kelly died. Kelly had high blood pressure and took nitro pills, and a lot of times when he took them he had to stop for a while until he could get going again. I'll never forget that Friday and how he loved those baked beans. George would say, "I don't know why, but I love those baked beans." They had some real good cooks in there, and the food was excellent. The steward in the kitchen was a good guy, and he'd even let some of the convicts cook. There was a Dago guy who could cook lasagna and make sauce better than you could buy anywhere on the outside, and he made all the Italian food. The steward would even let some Mexican guys cook, and we'd get the best Mexican food north of the border.

The food there was delicious, and one night they had those baked beans and George ate quite a bit, then went back to his cell. I asked him if he wanted to go out on the yard with me, and he said no, that he wanted to stay in his drum — that's what he called his cell — and that his pump was acting up and he didn't feel too good and wanted to lie down. When I got back from the yard, the guard came up and told me that they found George on the floor and rushed him to the hospital and that it was his heart. It was around midnight when the guards came and told me that George had died and asked me if I wanted to go to the hospital to see him. I told them no, that I wanted to remember him like I saw him last. George died at midnight on his 59th birthday and was just months away from a full parole.

But after George died, I told Benny that conversation never took place out on the yard, so just forget all about it. Those guys were billionaires, and they would just get you out of the way without any hesitation if they even had a hint of a reason. I knew even before I was going to go in and get that $10,000 that I would send a "Mule" in to get it. I wasn't that crazy to just go in and get it all by myself.

I had a phone number that you called in Montana, and that was the way to get in touch with Benny Binion, who later got in touch with Banks. Tom Banks lived on Drew Avenue in Minneapolis, and when I got out I went up there to visit him and just cased his house and all the houses around his place. He even had a whole floor in an office building, and I cased all of that because I wasn't taking any chances and watched my back.

After George died in Leavenworth, Benny came up to me and said that I could still get the money that Tom was holding. I told him, "Benny, that money ain't no good any more now that George is dead. Banks got $45,000 of that ransom money, and he told us he would send $10,000 to that lawyer in Chicago for Kathryn."

Gus Winkler told me he got $25,000 of the ransom money. Gus also told me where he had $10,000 buried with a machine gun down in Texas, but I never went down to get it.

That machine gun would've been worth some money today, and now I regret not picking it up. He told me he just bought them right out of hardware stores for $250 during the 1930s in Texas somewhere, and you could get them with clips or drums.

George had other charges and detainers on him, and when he finished his time in Leavenworth, we figured they were just going to transfer him to another jail. Whatever jail they were going to take George to, we were going to break him out. We figured that they'd take him down to Oklahoma and hold him there on those detainers just for the publicity. Gaylord Saxton, the guy out of Saginaw, Michigan, was going to back me and help Kelly escape from jail. We'd talk and make plans on how Saxton was going to fly us in, and we were going to bust George out, but when George died in Leavenworth, that ended that plan.

He was my friend and I would have done anything to have him experience freedom, if even for a short time, so he could get that young blonde he always talked about. It truly saddened me that he was never able to taste freedom after all those years of being locked up. Kelly always talked about that young blonde, and I wish that he'd have lived to enjoy his dreams, plus all the attention he would have gotten from being in the movies with Brynie Foy. Brynie Foy, one of the original Seven Little Foys, was a movie producer, and he wanted both George and me to come to his studio when we got out.

After George died, Frankie and I continued to walk around the yard together, but then when Frankie died, I just walked by myself. Others asked if they could walk with me, and I told them I'd rather just walk alone. Once in a while one of the old guards who were my friends from Alcatraz would walk around the yard with me.

Frankie Delmar was like George. When he got sick, he wouldn't go to the doctors, and then when it was too late they had to carry him on a stretcher to the hospital, and that's where he died. They came to me and asked if I wanted to go up to the hospital to see him before he died, and I did. The poor guy didn't know who I was or what was going on, and foam was coming from his mouth, and I wish I'd never gone

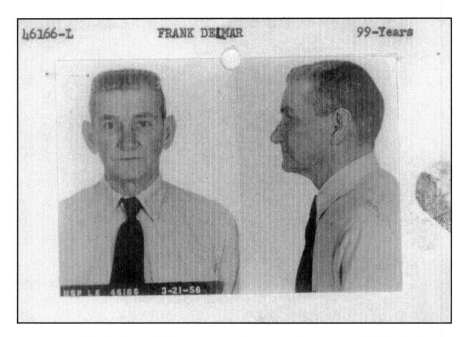

Frankie Delmar's Leavenworth mug shot, March 21, 1958.

up there to see him like that.

Frankie Delmar had no family or friends except Kelly and me. He was very quiet, soft-spoken and never talked about having any family. He came from Armourdale in Kansas City, Kansas. He had over $6,000 in his account when he died in Leavenworth, and I often wondered what happened to it.

I never did count the years or days when I did time like a lot of the other guys. I just did my time until they let me out because it was a lot easier for me to do the sentence that way.

13

Out On Parole — 1954

I GOT OUT on parole in 1954 and went back to Kansas City, Kansas, but most of my old partners were either dead or doing time, so I decided to leave.

While I was in Leavenworth, I sent money home to my mother to put into savings bonds monthly. When I got out, I went to the Federal Reserve Bank and tried to cash the bonds, but they refused at first, saying I didn't have the proper identification. I said, "Hell, I just got out of prison and the only identification that I have is my parole papers." After a few phone calls they were satisfied and gladly cashed all the bonds for me.

When I got out, I used to take my mom to St. John's Church every morning to the six o'clock mass. I always did this when I was in town because she was proud to have me finally with her after all these years away. When I'd walk in the church, my old classmates would comment the roof was going to fall in because I walked in there. Then when it came time for holy communion, I'd walk my aging mother up to the communion rail and kneel down beside her. My old friend who was now Monsignor John Horvat would bless my mother and place the holy communion wafer on her tongue. Then he'd move in front of me, bless me, and then hit me on the nose with his finger, proceeding on to the next person.

There was a big politician out of Chicago named Jim Murray who was out on Alcatraz, and we became good friends. He liked me and he'd always want to talk to me, pounding on my chest with his finger, saying, "Hey, kid, hey, kid." He owned two big apartment buildings in Chicago and was a powerful man and always told me to look him up when I got out. Well, I looked him up when I got out, and he took me into his apartment, and I had to laugh when I saw it. He didn't have just an ordinary size refrigerator; he had one as big as a butcher store would have and the big freezer sitting right next to it with all the doors on it. He didn't have a normal-size dining room table either; he had one where at least 30 people could sit and eat. He was a powerful man, and he used to walk around the yard with Kelly and me all the time and say, "Now, kid, now, kid."

I ended up getting my parole transferred to Chicago, and Jim was able to set me up with a job. When I got there and wherever he took me all over Chicago and introduced me, everyone would tell me that any friend of Jim Murray's was a friend of theirs. He was a big politician and owned all the honky-tonks down on Madison Avenue. They were nothing but dives, but they were money-makers, and the biggest joint he had was up on Touhy Avenue.

Jim introduced me to this guy who ran the boilermakers, and with them all you needed was your parole papers as a resumé to get a job. This guy would tell me, "I'm the granddaddy to all youse guys, and I take care of every part of the business for you." I didn't even have to show up for work when I was with the boilermakers. A foreman named Bill Ruby told me: "Bill, we know all about you, and we're going to let you go with these other X-con's, and you won't have do any work, just draw a weekly paycheck. I went along with two other Croatian guys who were also drawing a paycheck there. There was a young kid named Willie Resack, and he would talk about the guy named "Meatball." I asked him, "Did you do time in the Illinois State Prison?" and he said, "Yeah." I knew that he did because that was the nickname for the warden, Joe Regan. I used to hear Basil "The Owl" Banghart talk about Meatball.

Anyway, there were the gasholders, the nickname for the great big tanks that had narrow catwalks all around the top of them. We'd go up on the empty tanks and tie ourselves to the rail so we wouldn't fall off and take naps. The rail was so narrow my feet would dangle off the edge when I was lying down, but hell, everybody was sleeping up there and no one ever came around looking for us.

This superintendent named Tony would go around and make chalk marks to show how far we worked for that day, and we'd go right behind him rubbing the chalk marks off.

Then Bill Ruby, our pusher, came over and said that he'd seen us talking to this guy and he wanted to know if that guy was trying to tell us what to do. I told him no and he said, "No son-of-a-bitch has any business telling you what to do but me."

So me and Willie Resack, the Croatian kid, were laying out in the back and the pusher, Bill Ruby, came up and asked us, "Who put that iron over there?" He was pointing to a little piece of iron about a foot long lying there on the ground. I told him, "I don't know, why?" He said, "No son-of-a-bitch has the right to move any iron around here but the boilermakers." I started laughing because to me it was funny him raising hell over that little piece of iron lying on the ground. I asked him if I could move it and just toss it out of the way, and he said no, that another crew had to come in to do it.

We were coming to work one day, and a guy said to us, "Where you going?" I told him that we were on our way to work, and as we walked past him he turned to the guy next to him and said, "Those two guys look mighty strange to me, do they to you?"

Jim Murray got us this job, and he was a hell of a politician so the company man couldn't say anything or they'd all walk off the job. He had a contract to fill to get the job done in so many days for the pay, so he had to go along with it.

While I was working in the field with the Boilermakers Union, the guys we worked with noticed that someone was stealing their sandwiches out of their lunch boxes. To get even, they just made ham sandwiches with "Croton Oil" on the bread and packed them in all their lunch boxes. That stuff will make you crap for four days straight, so they just looked for the guy who was shitting all the time, and that's the way they caught the son-of-a-bitch stealing and eating their sandwiches.

We'd clock in and they'd tell us to get lost until four o'clock when we clocked out, and we'd get paid good money for doing nothing.

A guy doing time in Leavenworth told me where some diamonds was hidden in a field on the East Coast. I followed the directions he gave me and climbed a high mountain, not a hill, and walked five miles to a farmhouse. I was digging and digging; then I realized that I was digging in shit. I gave up after not finding anything and stepped back to one side to rest for a while. It was then I was able to see a short cut back to exactly where I started that was only a one-mile trip instead of the five miles I just walked. I saw this guy later, and we talked about those diamonds, and he told me that his old girlfriend got her new boyfriend to dig up the diamonds and he never saw or heard from her since.

I also went to visit a guy named John who lived in East St. Louis that I knew from Leavenworth Penitentiary. While I was with him, he said that he had to go out and check on all his whores. One whore wasn't working, and she told him she was sick. He told her, "Goddamn, you can't be sick. This isn't your day to be sick." He really raised hell with her and eventually got her back out there to work. He said that you gotta stay on their ass or they won't work, and you gotta talk to these gals all the time to keep them on the job. Then he'd go around to all the shacks that looked like little doghouses and collect his money from them. So in back of the bar he worked out of, you'd see the little shacks that the gals would take guys to. You'd see all the workers walking down this hill with hard hats on and filthy dirty from working all day heading for a shack with some broad. He took good care of all those broads because of all the business they brought in, especially on paydays. I told John that I sure would've liked to have the life of a pimp, but shit, I was what all the whores liked to have come around.

I went out to try to visit Bruce Barnes, Kelly's son in Los Angeles, because Kelly asked me to check on him and see if he was doing okay. I don't remember exactly what happened, but it was a crummy-looking apartment and he was never home, so I gave up after about three tries. I went to see the movie that Bruce Barnes was in. George told me about it, saying he played a police dispatch operator in the background of this scene and was only on screen for a few seconds.

I hooked up with some guys I did time with to case some places to score later. We cased a restaurant in Detroit for a couple of weeks, and when we went in the grab the guys, we found out that they changed the date when they took the money to the bank and came up empty on that one.

It was my day off, so I'm sitting at a bus stop waiting for the streetcar to come by, but just a bus keeps coming by, then another bus and another one. One of the drivers stopped and asked me what I was waiting on. I told him the streetcar, and then he told me that they didn't run on Sundays. I would just ride around casing places to rob on my days off and remembered the racetrack at 111th and Bell that was a big horse track, and they had lots of cash over there. The guy who ran the place was named Tiponelle, and I walked right into his garage in back of the place and saw him standing by his race car. Two guys and I had plans to grab him and hold him until we got all the money. See, at the racetracks there they never used the same money they got in to pay any money out. That way they knew exactly how much money went out and exactly how much money came in. They never mixed the two piles together, and it was better bookkeeping that way.

I was down at the racetrack one morning when an armored car pulled up to the curb. There was a long sidewalk from the armored car to the building, and the gun guards were carrying the cash inside big iron boxes that took two guards to carry. I watched them for an hour as they carried three of the heavy boxes of money inside just waiting for us to take.

There was a jewelry store in Aurora, Illinois that we cased for weeks. I just about lived with the guy. I followed him everywhere and knew his routine. He would always come back to the jewelry store at 6 o'clock at night and take all the good stuff out of the window and put it in the vault.

He would go down to the YMCA every night and go into the chapel and pray. I was right in there with him every night to see what was going on. Then he would eat right there at the YMCA, and I would be in there eating in the cafeteria right along with him. He'd leave and catch a bus to go home, and we knew that he and his wife never came home together or even around the same time. After we broke into his house, we just sat around waiting for them to come home as they did every night. I knew that when he came home he always turned on the light in the upstairs bedroom, so we had the light on when she came in the front door. She said: "Hello, are you there?" When we grabbed her, she fought us, so we had to hold her mouth to muffle the screaming while we got her all tied up. The whole time we're holding her, she's saying, "Our Father who art in Heaven and so on." She's praying and praying non-stop, so we put tape on her mouth and she's still praying, so we put more tape on her mouth, and we can still hear her praying and we put more tape on her mouth. Then we decided to push her in the closet and wait for him to come home. We thought that we might have a lot of trouble out of him, but when he came through that door, he came in saying, "Hello, are you there?" Then when he saw me coming after him, he fell on the floor right in front of me. I pounced on him and we were able to get him under control right away. We threw him in the closet with his wife for a while.

The inside of his house was something to see, and just any burglar would have had a good score if he came in there. In the dining room there were boxes and boxes and more boxes of sterling silverware stacked from the floor to the ceiling all over everywhere you looked. There were dirty dishes everywhere, and the only rooms that were clean were the bathroom and the bedroom where they slept. We took this place on a Saturday night, and Sunday morning we were still in the house. I told my partner, John Alkes, I was going down to his jewelry store and get into his safe since this guy carried the combination to his safe around in his wallet.

I got into the car and drove down to the Fodor Jewelry Store at 54 Main Street in Aurora, Illinois, and parked a few doors away as not to draw suspicion. I unlocked the front door with the big circular key that looked like a tube and went inside. I knew I had to turn off the alarm from nighttime to daytime right away, so that's the first thing I did. I crawled on the floor so no one could see me through the window and got to the safe in the back room and opened it up. I got all the money that was in his safe, and it was all in bundles of $1,000 bills, plus all the loose jewelry in the drawers.

When we got away from the place, we decided to pull over and get a pop at a gas station, and I told the guys that we should stop and eat and wait a while. I'm glad that we did because all the cops were running up and down the highways with their sirens on. We found out later in the newspaper that the guy wasn't tied up that well and got loose and ran into the street screaming for help. After we saw the newspaper, we didn't have to mail the letter to the cops telling them that man and woman were tied up inside of the house and to go cut them lose.

We took the diamonds to downtown Chicago to a building that deals in nothing but diamonds and was some kind of Diamond Mart. The guy told me to just leave the stones and he'd give me the money on the side and away from his office later that day. When I went to pick up the cash for the diamonds at the jewelry store, the guy told me to pick something out from the jewelry case in front of me. I picked out a $1,800 Longine man's diamond watch for myself' and when he pulled it from the case' he wrapped it with the cash from the stones. We only got $6,500 or 10% for all those stones, but the cash from the safe added up to $45,000.

Later I read in the newspaper that the FBI investigated the jewelry store owner we held hostage. He told the cops that one of the stones that we stole was a $10,000 diamond, but he couldn't come up with proof that he owned such a diamond or that he purchased it from the Diamond Mart there in Chicago.

He was just beating income tax having all that cash in his safe and all that silver in his house. The FBI came in to investigate the case because they thought the diamonds had crossed the state line.

There was a movie made called *Desperate Hours,* and I think it was Humphrey Bogart who starred in the original film. They even made a remake of the movie just a few years ago starring Mickey Rourke. This movie was made about this partner of mine, John Alkes. They escaped out of Lewisburg Penitentiary in Pennsylvania and grabbed a family hostage and held on to them all night long. They had one big clumsy guy with them who they made more of a comedian out of in that movie, but he really was a crazy son-of-a-bitch, dangerous and nothing to laugh at.

I used to ride the train back home to Kansas City periodically to visit my mother and brother. My mom told me that John Uziel Sr., my X-brother-in-law, had opened a café named Jean & Pat's down on Central Avenue. I stopped in for a visit, and my nephew, Johnny Jr. and his sisters, Jean and Pat, were there having lunch. I pulled out a couple of $1,000 bills from my billfold to show the kids and remember Patty sitting there counting all the zeros after the one over and over again.

When I got back to Chicago, I bought two brand new 1954 Pontiac Star Chief automobiles. I paid cash for them and took them to a guy I did time with, and he fixed me up by welding a couple of hidden boxes right into the front seats to stash our guns. The boxes were completely undetectable to anybody, and when I got busted and lost the cars, our guns were still hidden inside those boxes.

We decided to go to Detroit, Michigan to case and hit a few places, and when we got up there, John Alkes went to pick up a prostitute that we all knew from times before. She said she wasn't working any more because she caught something from a John and showed us her chest covered with open sores that were also all over her body. She said she needed some money and asked if she could work with us to be able to go to a doctor. We decided to let her drive the getaway car, and she was good because while she was sitting there waiting for us a cop car drove by and she didn't make a move. We had other guys who would drive for us who would have shit their pants and taken off when they saw a police car drive by. When we left town, we all gave her a few thousand dollars plus her cut, so she could go to a doctor and have her problem taken care of.

Our intention before we went in to rob the bank in Flint, Michigan was to hit a National Guard Armory in Wisconsin somewhere to get our firepower.

I should have known when Lopez chickened out that he was no good. He said, "What do you want to go in there for?" I said: "For firepower, you stupid son-of-a-bitch, firepower." I went up there and was casing the place, and there was only one guy in there all by himself. The way I knew this was a good place to get your firepower was when I was in Leavenworth Penitentiary my office manager, Williams, let me in on it. He was in the National Guard, and he had the keys to the vault to all the machine guns at the National Armory. He showed me pictures and told me all about the weapons that they had in there. That's when it hit me if you want to get fire power, just get this guy who has the keys to the vault at the National Guard Armory and have him open it. Anyway, we knew that they had choppers in there with drums and clips, but I don't like drums because they can jam; I like clips better.

We didn't go in that one in Wisconsin because of that chicken shit Lopez being scared and not wanting to go in. All he wanted do was get drunk because he was nothing but a bar room fighter. He ended up getting into a fight and hitting a cop in a bar, putting heat on all of us so we had to split and get away from him. I had a cute little prostitute that I was seeing, and she let me stay at her place until the heat was off and I could safely get out of Chicago. Lopez would get drunk and want to whip everybody in the bar, but when you want him to do something that took guts, he'd shit in his pants and wouldn't do it. I told him we needed the firepower for protection, but the chicken shit wouldn't go in with us, so we had to blow that score.

When I was back in Leavenworth, I saw a picture of a cop from Morris, Illinois in the newspaper. He had a shotgun in his hand, and plenty of other weapons were on the wall behind him in the picture. The picture showed off the inside of the police station, so that's where we were going to get our firepower. I started casing the police station and even walked inside when I saw there was only one woman by herself at the desk with all those machine guns hanging on the wall behind her. I talked to her for 30 minutes about her job and got the general information I needed to know, then left. We got ready to go in and hit the place a couple of days later without Lopez, and I parked our car right in front. When I got out of our car, I looked over into the back seat of the police car parked next to us and saw that it was full of weapons. I told the guys we didn't have to go inside and hit the place because all the artillery we needed was in that car. We got machine guns with clips, rifles, handguns and all the shells we wanted and left. I read in the newspaper later that the police station was hit, without any mention of any guns being taken from the back seat of a police car parked out in front.

When we robbed the Citizens Commercial and Savings Bank in Flint, Michigan, we went in with heavier arsenal than the police. The police only had 10-gauge shotguns and we had machine guns, handguns and high-powered rifles. We bullet-proofed the car by loading the trunk up with piles of blankets so the bullets couldn't come through.

When I walked into a bank to rob them, I didn't go in shooting or get loud like some guys did. I found out that just subtle intimidation was good enough to get the job done and not scare the employees too much since they were usually young women. We were in and out of the place in just about five minutes with all the money.

I never went out to the West Coast to rob banks back then because it wasn't populated like the East Coast, where you could rob a bank, drive around the corner and hide out in a crowd. It was a lot like Florida where you only had one main road in and out for your getaway.

We lived in an apartment building one time that was right on top of a bank. We stole a car, robbed the bank, drove around the corner, parked the hot car, then just walked up the back entrance to our apartment and laid low until all the heat was off.

Now my partner, John Alkes, was the son-of-a-bitch who snitched on me in Flint, Michigan. We hit a bank for $62,000 and went to hide out at Alkes' father's house. I was going to go rent a house, but he said no, that we could stay at his dad's place in the garage and give his dad the money instead. We were staying in the garage, and a woman saw Alkes walking in and out of the house all the time, and the son-of-a-bitch was wanted for burglary in that town and I didn't know it. Here we were supposed to be hiding and he's walking around the yard all the time. The neighbor woman saw him and called the cops and told them he was over there. George Ballin was watching out the window and saw the cops pull up and yelled to us, "Cops, cops, cops." I got out of there and was running down the street with $62,000 stuffed down the front of my shirt. I was yelling at George, who was running right alongside of me, to go across the street and get away from me and run by himself. The son-of-a-bitch panicked and didn't know what to do, so I got pitched off and we ran back to the garage we just came from for cover. George laid low in the front seat and I was in the back seat under a blanket when two cops came inside the garage and yelled, "Stick 'em up!" I jumped up and said, "You stick 'em up yourself, you son-of-a-bitch!" I wasn't going without a fight, and I figured he was a family man, and I don't have nobody so I didn't have anything to lose. I popped a few shots in the air, and they both turned and ran out of the garage, yelling to all the other cops that "they were shooting in there." Hell, you could hear all the damn shots, but they ran out to tell them we were shooting. When they ran out, I followed them firing the machine gun, and when they dove for cover, I was able to slip away in the opposite direction.

When I was heading to steal a car to get out of there, I was hiding in the bushes and all the cops were walking by going from house to house searching for me. I just stayed in the bushes until they went through the whole block and then made my run. They walked right by me a couple of times and didn't see me, and if they'd had dogs, they would have caught me for sure.

George Ballin and John Alkes got caught right there, but I got away.

I ran down the street to a house that had steps going down into a basement. The door had just a hook latch on it, and when I opened it up and got inside, I took something like a screwdriver or something, put it through the crack and locked the door by hooking the latch behind me just like it was. That's what saved me because when they came in that basement looking for me I was hiding in the corner under a sewing machine that had a cloth covering it. They were right in that basement just a few feet from me, and if they had dogs they would have found me for sure. The cop said, "Do you keep this door locked like this all the time?" The guy said, "Yeah," and that's when they turned around and went back out the basement door. Later on, I could hear the guy upstairs talking, and he was telling someone that the police were looking for some guy. I said to myself, "You son-of-a-bitch, I'm right down here in your basement." The guy had cases of hot soda pop in that basement, so I had plenty to drink while I was down there and, man, was I thirsty!

Now later in Flint, Michigan I was tired and hungry and wanted to get something to eat. I wanted to find a house, but first I went into a garage, and damn if it wasn't some guy's smokehouse. There were sausages and meat hanging around all over in there, and I ate till my belly was full and stuffed my pockets, then left.

Later on that evening, I broke into a house because I wanted to get into a safer place to hide. When I got in, I saw this picture of a woman and kid on the wall and said, "Oh, no, if they come home, I'll have to grab them." There was a little dog, a Chihuahua that was yapping and yapping and barking making all this noise, so I grabbed the little son-of-a-bitch and shoved him in the refrigerator. I was getting ready to leave the house a few hours later and almost forgot about the dog, and when I opened up the refrigerator door he was shaking uncontrollably and his nose and body were all white from the cold. I stood him on the floor and he could hardly walk he was so stiff, but I could see he was headed for a little bed he had on the kitchen floor. I picked him up and put him in the bed and took the blanket lying there and covered him up real good and got out of there.

When I was ready to leave the city a couple of nights later, I went down to a parking garage and got in where all the keys to the cars were hanging on a board. I was already wanted for jumping bond in Flint, Michigan, and the keys to my car were back in the house we were staying in. I knew it was too hot to go back and get them, so I picked me up an Oldsmobile and left and went down to Kalamazoo where I parked the car and caught the train that took me to Chicago. Arlene was working there on Chicago Avenue at a car agency, and Sharon Stone had nothing on this gal — she was a knockout blonde and sincere. I walked in, and she saw me and froze, saying, "Oh, my God!" She was married to my partner, John Alkes, and originally from Joplin, Missouri, and over the months we got pretty close and started seeing each other on the sly. I told her to stay there in Chicago and not to leave that job because you never know if there is going to be any heat on her because of us guys. We found out later that they were watching her and it was a wise move for her to stay put.

Would you believe that there was a mud street in Chicago? Arlene's mother lived down on the south side of Chicago on a muddy street with a Croatian guy, and Arlene wanted me to go down there and stay, but I said no and went back to my apartment. I should have stayed with her like she wanted me to, but I didn't. I went back to my apartment, and that's where they nabbed me.

I found out later that Alkes told the cops everything, even where the apartment was in Chicago, so when I walked into the apartment at 3822 W. 62nd Street, the cops were inside waiting for me. When I opened the door and saw the cops standing there, I backed up and headed for the window in the hallway, knowing it was only a one-story drop. I smashed through the window and hit my heel on a ledge coming down, and when I got up I couldn't run and that's how they were able to nab me just a block away. I couldn't get away fast enough and found out later I broke my heel bone and that's what slowed me down. The Bureau agents said that although I didn't offer any resistance, I was extremely uncooperative by refusing to be handcuffed and they had to carry me to their car, then out of the car into their office.

In the newspaper article where they said they had to carry me to the car and into the building, believe me, I clearly remember why. There was one great big FBI agent who knew his business when he grabbed me and jerked my suit coat down off my shoulders, restraining my arms, and beat the shit out of me. He even threw my hat on the ground and stomped on it three or four times because he was so mad, and I'm just glad my head wasn't in that hat at the time. I knew I was no match against that big guy and didn't have a chance, so I just lay still waiting for him to stop. I didn't want to move to give him a reason to start back in again, so they had to carry me to and from the car and on into the jail.

Arlene was married to Alkes, but started spending time with me. When I was locked up, she came to visit and asked me if I trusted Alkes. She was giving me the best tip to watch my back with this guy, and I didn't take it that seriously. She was what they called a "Twenty-Six Girl." She would sit on this stool by the crap table and lift her skirt up and cross her legs, getting the guys' attention just like Sharon Stone did in the movie *Basic Instinct,* while they fixed the dice. Some dice had a B-B inside of them and they had to tap them on the table so when the heavy side hit you'd crap out. Some places had magnets in the dice and would turn on a switch and the magnets would make sure you would crap out. They even filed off the corners, but whatever they did you can bet you could never make your point.

Arlene told us that in one joint she worked at, the magnets on the craps table were so strong that when they turned them on a metal waste-paper basket, it moved across the floor towards the craps table. Guys hustling with phony dice caught a lot of men at bus stops in the mornings on their way to work.

Arlene would have done anything for me; she even wanted to get a gun into the courtroom for me. You don't go in at court time when they are checking everyone for guns. You go in early in the morning when no one was around and tape the gun to the underside of the tables. She even wanted to bring me a hacksaw blade in jail, but I told her to forget about me, that I'd be gone for a long time. Throughout the years I've often thought about her and wondered what happened to her and where she was.

When we got busted and were sitting in jail in Michigan, what we didn't know was that John Alkes was throwing notes out of the cell where we couldn't see them to the cops snitching on all of us to save his neck.

When we were locked up in jail, I had a friend of mine from Jeff City tell me he couldn't give me the record, but when he mimeographed it one could fall on the floor for me to read. I picked it up off the floor, and it said how Alkes snitched to the FBI, telling them every job we ever did together to try to cut his time. The sheet was passed down to all the guys at our table in the dining room, and they passed it around for everyone else to read.

Every place we were transferred, we put the word out that he was a snitch. We found out later they had to transfer him four or five times from prison to prison because the word preceded him, and snitches didn't last long in jails and prisons back then with the solid cons.

The Flint, Michigan bank robbery made the front page of the *Chicago Tribune.* I remember reading the headline when I was heading to Chicago to see Arlene.

I also saw the front page of *The Kansas City Star,* and it read that they had indicted me for motor vehicle theft in regard to a bunch of hot cars I had at a guy's garage. The FBI told me later they put that bogus story in the paper so I'd think the heat was off since they claimed they caught me and I'd show up in Kansas City.

The other partner with us when we robbed the bank in Flint, Michigan was George Ballin. I told him before the score, "When you go with me, George, I don't know that I can promise that you'll come back." He ended up being another guy who made the statement to the FBI and the cops telling them all about the Flint bank robbery. He told me that they told him it was all off the record and that's why he talked. I showed him the typed statement and said: "Hell, it's right here in front of me in black and white, you silly son-of-a-bitch."

When I was in the courtroom in Flint, Michigan for the bank robbery, I was standing up with my suit coat hanging over the belt and manacles they had on me. There was a plain-clothes detective near by in a disheveled old suit and hat sitting in front of the door. The prosecutor came up behind me and commented, "Should you have him sitting so close to that door?" I turned around, and you should have seen the expression on his face when he spotted my shackles and manacles. He thought that the disheveled detective was the bank robber and I was the detective standing there in my stylish attire.

14

Return to Leavenworth — April 1956

HELL, I WAS only out a couple of years and now I'm back in for another 30.

After I'd been back a year or so, both palms of my hands were becoming heavily calloused from working out on the parallel bars daily just to stay in shape. The authorities became concerned and started watching me closely, and I got the word that they were all worried that I was getting in shape to make a break.

In 1959 Bob "Birdman" Stroud was being transferred to the Federal Medical Center in Springfield, Missouri from Alcatraz. They brought him into the hospital in Leavenworth

Leavenworth mug shot of Willie —July 2, 1956.

penitentiary before going on to Springfield. They let me go to the hospital and visit him while he was there. I took him cigars, magazines and books to read, and he was grateful. I felt sorry for the guy because he didn't have a friend in this world or anyone who could stand to be around him very long. Bob always thought that he'd make the front page of all the newspapers when he died, but the day he died John Kennedy was assassinated in Dallas, and all Bob got was a short paragraph somewhere on a back page.

To pass the time I taught myself to paint using oils, acrylics and even watercolor. I painted everything from landscapes to bullfighters and even portraits to keep busy and sent them home to my mother to give to family and friends. They even had them hanging up for sale at Casa De Tacos Restaurant at 19th and Central Avenue in Kansas City, Kansas to help me out.

My mother had to depend on transportation from a friend whenever she came to visit me. Rose, the woman next door, had a daughter, Louise Standish, who lived about four houses south of my mother. Louise and her sister, Rose, began to drive my mother to the prison for our monthly visits. Over the months the relationship between Louise, her sister Rose and I became an amiable one.

There was a guy on Alcatraz named Clyde Johnson 864AZ who was public enemy number one for bank robbery. He was a very nervous guy who would get volatile and excitable all of the time. He couldn't stand to be around a phony guy, and when one would come around, he'd go off the handle every time. When the guards in Leavenworth told me about how much of a problem they were having with him getting along with other guys, I told them to bring him down to work in the office with me because we got along real well when we worked together back on Alcatraz. They brought him around, and he starting working with me in the business managers office.

I had to laugh at him and how upset he would become because he had to send invoices out to all of these post offices all over the country. Then he'd say, "Why can't they just have one address instead of all these separate ones?" He was a good typist and fit right in the office with us guys, and it helped to calm him down.

I knew Clyde even before the joint. I knew he was from Tennessee and hung around with a kid I went to school with. Later on, the two of them got busted, and both ended up doing time in San Quentin. I didn't know much about his personal life; he didn't mention if he had any family, and I didn't ask.

Clyde Johnson.

Leavenworth mug shot of
Willie — April 5, 1966.

Leavenworth mug shot of Willie
— November 4, 1969.

They always took pictures of you periodically when you were in the joint, so in case you escaped they'd have a recent photo of you.

Old Karpis was paroled to Montreal, Canada in 1969 after serving a little over 25 years on Alcatraz. I knew he was afraid to stay in the United States because he rolled over on two bad-ass brothers out of Minnesota. He knew that the brothers had a contract out on him and wanted him eliminated, so that's why he left the States and went on to Spain. When they found him dead, they said it was possibly a suicide or maybe natural causes. We always thought that it was foul play, but since there was no autopsy that conclusion was never confirmed.

Louise notified me in a letter that my mother had a stroke, her health was failing, and she had to have special care. Louise hired one of the nuns to come in daily from the convent next to Bishop Ward High School that offered hospice care called the Sister's Servants of Mary. Louise continued to visit my mother daily to make sure they had something to eat and take care of her and my elderly brother, Joe.

My day out was actually not until March, but my boss, Bernie, went up and got me a couple of extra months good time that made me eligible to go home before Christmas. All the guards knew about it when I was called to the warden's office, but didn't say anything to me. They were all smiling and congratulating me when I got back, saying they all knew but held back from saying anything to me so I'd be surprised. Then that day when I walked out of the prison, I looked back and saw all the old guards up in the windows waving good-bye to me.

15

Out for Good — 1969

I WAS PAROLED about a week before Christmas in 1969 to my mother's home in Kansas City, Kansas. I was able to get a job working for the city's water department at first, then transferred to the Shawnee Mission School District. I even started painting houses on the side for additional income.

By this time Louise Standish and I had become pretty close because I came to depend on her for the care she had given my mother and elderly brother, Joe. We decided to move in together and got an apartment just two doors from my mother and next door to her mother at 515 North 5th street.

After we'd been living together for three months, I told Louise that we had to sit down and have a serious talk. I told her I didn't feel right living with her, which to me was disrespectful, and if she didn't agree to marry me, we'd have to separate and go our own ways. She agreed to be my wife, and for the first time in my life I was looking forward to being a one-woman man.

When I was released on parole, Louise began di-

Willie and Louise — Christmas 1969.

vorce actions from her husband to be with me. She acquired a little house in Prescott, Kansas from the proceedings. Prescott was a small country town 75 miles south of the city that had a population of about 180. We were married in Linn County on September 4, 1970. We would drive out of the city on my days off and spend time at our little shack in the country.

My mother's health began to deteriorate, and she ended up in the hospital with no recourse to improve. Louise was at her bedside when she passed away in 1971.

An old partner of mine named John Coutz had a son who became a big union man up in Chicago. John told me that his son was the top man, and if I came up there I would have it made. I would have had a good go up there, but Louise didn't want to move to Chicago. John even told me to make the date and he'd get the plane ticket to Chicago and he'd get me a job with the Local #41.

I know now that Louise knew me better than I knew myself, and mixing me up with guys I knew in the past wasn't a good move because I always fell back into my old ways.

Louise also knew how I was about my clothes and never said a thing when I continued to buy my tailor-made suits at Jack Henry's on the Country Club Plaza, along with silk underwear to match. When we went out, I wanted to wear the best, but never could convince her to buy herself the posh tailored outfits for ladies to go with mine.

When we completed our move to the country in 1971, I continued to work in the city, but eventually the commute became too much. Louise told me to quit the jobs in the city and get one down in the vicinity of Prescott. I was worried that I couldn't get a job because of my past record and the fact I hadn't worked that much over the years. Jobs weren't that easy to find out in the rural areas, but I landed a good one with Prairie View High School in Linn County as a janitor.

I bought a motorcycle, thinking it would be more economical to ride back and forth to work instead of driving my truck. Coming home one night, I was going too fast when I made a turn onto a gravel road, and when I hit the gravel I lost control and went into a skid that sent me right into the ditch. When I got home later that night with the dented bike and a few cuts and scratches, Louise immediately got a hammer and went out and busted the spark plug off in the motor and busted the key off in the ignition. That was her way of convincing me decisively to stop riding that bike.

I continued to move up the ranks within my job over the years and eventually became the janitorial supervisor for five high schools.

When I was the janitorial supervisor, I never used to just show up at one of the schools to check up on the guys. I would always call ahead and let them know I was coming because I never wanted to be sneaky to any of the guys working for me, and I sure didn't want them to run from me.

Years later after I retired with 11 years in at the school, I'd go back occasionally to visit my boss. He told me, "We knew all about you and still promoted you, and the floors haven't been cleaned in the corners since you left."

Over the years I'd kept in touch with Harvey Bailey's nephew and knew where he lived when he was paroled to Joplin, Missouri. Louise and I would drive down to Joplin to visit Tom and his wife Mary. I took Bailey up to visit Louise's cousin, Fred George, who had a private club named "Outlaw" in Kansas City, Kansas. In the picture Fred took of us at the bar, Bailey had a black eye where he had slipped and fallen on some ice and broke his glasses. Louise, Tom, Mary and I would get together and go visit his son, Voss Bailey, who worked on assembling cars in Leeds, Missouri. When Tom was paroled to Joplin, he got a job and worked as a cabinetmaker. He married an old girlfriend, and they

Harvey Bailey and Willie, December 1973.

moved into their own little home. Bailey, like all of us old guys back then, agreed that if you were a partner of ours you never talked to or told your wives, girlfriends or whores anything about your business. Tom never liked Kathryn Kelly hanging around and made sure George never brought her when they were talking business.

Bailey told me that he went to Ward Parkway and made $200 signing autographs on his book, and that was the most degrading thing he'd ever done in his life and would never repeat it.

His book is *Robbing Banks Was My Business,* a biography by J. Evetts Haley.

Another true story of bank robberies in the 1930s is *Run the Cat Roads,* by L.L. Edge.

Later on, a reporter did another story on me for *The Kansas City Star* that showed one of my paintings on the page. In another article by Jean Haley, Louise told her that I talked like a broken record, was stir crazy, and she just didn't pay any mind to me.

A few days after the article came out, I got a phone call and the caller said, "You son-of-a-bitch." I said, "Who is this?" The caller said, "You know who this is, you son-of-a-bitch. You ought to know who in the hell this is." I said, "Who in the hell are you?" Then he said, "You son-of-a-bitch, it's Bud!" This was one of my old partners, Harry O'Dell, who we called Bud. He said he was living in Foster, Missouri, which was only 15 minutes away from Prescott. He said to come on over, and Louise and I hurried over to visit him. When I got there, he said, "Let's go down and meet somebody." I couldn't believe it because we met up with Alfie Kanton, another one of my partners, and he lived only eight miles from Prescott. They had no idea I was even alive, much less in the area, until they read the stories in the newspaper and couldn't believe it. Alfie said he went to the grocery store one day and just saw Bud shopping around in the store. We couldn't believe that after all the years that had passed and everything that had gone down that all three of us would be married and meet down here in the country just a few miles from one another.

We'd get all dressed up, and we three couples would go out to eat and to movies and just talk about old times every weekend. We'd talk about the last time we were together and how we had to shoot our way

From the **KANSAS CITY TIMES,** *December 14, 1973:*

CONTENT WITH LIFE ON OUTSIDE

By Jean Haley, a member of the staff

A sweet little wife, enough work to keep him busy, good friends and good whiskey are about all Harvey Bailey wants out of life.

At 86, Bailey, one of the Midwest's most notorious bank robbers who spent more than 30 years in state and federal penitentiaries before being paroled in 1965, has two dreams, to visit Hawaii and to obtain a pardon for his conviction in the 1933 kidnaping of Charles F. Urschel, Oklahoma millionaire.

"I'm going to try for that in the near future," Bailey said yesterday, noting it would be mostly a formality. "I'm living happy. I'm free to go wherever I want to.

"I had nothing to do with that whatsoever," Bailey continued, his eyes wandering around a room full of friends at a downtown motel. "I did 30 years for a crime that I did not commit. I didn't even know they had Urschel kidnaped. I read about it in the papers."

Bailey does not deny he was a bank robber. He says the truth about his career is in "Robbing Banks Was My Business," a recently published biography by J. Evetts Haley. Bailey will be autographing copies from 3 p.m. to 6 p.m. today at the B. Dalton Bookseller bookstore at Ward Parkway Shopping Center.

Neatly dressed in a warm brown suit brightened with a gold on blue mod tie, he relaxed with friends, some of whom he had been in that business with him. But Bailey wouldn't talk about it.

"Oh, they're just friends I met here years ago," Bailey said evasively, his eyes twinkling as they did most of the time. "I used to play golf; they knew some people I played golf with. I used to play golf with the vice-president of the Missouri-Pacific. No, he didn't know what business I was in. Only I knew that."

William Radkay, 62, a painter who will be spending his fifth Christmas here after 14 years in the federal penitentiary in Leavenworth, met Bailey in Alcatraz. Radkay, too, used to be in the business of robbing banks.

"Tom — everybody always called him Tom, I don't know why — was always close-mouthed," Radkay observed. "He's a man of principle and character. He's honest. You could give him money — I don't care how much you gave him — come back 20 years later, he'd have it for you.

"He was respected among the convicts," he added, "and the officials felt they didn't have to worry about him as far as violations of rules were concerned, as long as he didn't go over the wall."

Bailey did that, too, in a dramatic escape with several other convicts from the Kansas State Penitentiary at Lansing on Memorial Day, 1933. Bailey was credited with saving the life of the warden who was taken hostage.

Bailey spent a lot of time from 1927 to 1930 in Kansas City, living in the Plaza area "making plans, casing the banks, learning the times they

(Continued next page)

were making their steps." He was first captured in 1932 on the Old Mission Golf Course in what is now Roeland Park.

He stole with some of the well-known criminals of the 1930s such as Pretty Boy Floyd, Machine Gun Kelly, Alvin Karpis. He remembers Floyd best.

"Pretty Boy Floyd and I were awful close friends," Bailey said. "He did more to help the poor people than he used for himself of what he took out of banks. In the driest season (in the early 1920s) down in the hills of east central Oklahoma, he and I had a Ford truck, a Model T. We used to go around and kick down grocery stores and just load that thing full of groceries and take them up to them poor Indian people in the hills. They were starving to death."

After he was paroled in 1963 Bailey went to Joplin. He married in 1966 and worked at a woodmill there until he retired in May.

"Now I work around the house, me and my sweet little wife Mary," he said. "I'm through with banks. I can make a living and that's all I want now, and my sweet young wife. She's 81 years old but that's young to me."

His energy and enthusiasm amazes and sometimes frightens his associates here, like his proposal to get up at 2 a.m. tomorrow to drive to Leavenworth on business. Bailey said his doctor made him retire "because he said my legs might give out and I'd fall into one of those saws."

The white-haired man gave his opinion on keeping young. "It's living a good clean life," Bailey said, his eyes twinkling again, "a little scotch — not getting drunk, that's something I haven't done for 60 years — but I have my highballs every day, me and Mary."

Bailey said he had little difficulty adjusting to life in society after spending so many years in prison because he "settled down" years before his release and because of more than two years of "almost freedom" in prison at Seagoville, Tex., before he was transferred back to Kansas.

Friends and neighbors in Joplin apparently have forgiven Bailey's past, Radkay said. He told about his first visit to the Bailey home there.

"I forgot the envelope with the address on it, but I remembered it was 823 or 826 St. Louis," Radkay recalled. "We got on the 800 block of St. Louis, stopped, knocked on a door. I asked the man if he knew where Mr. Bailey lived. He just waved his arm and said 'right over there.' "

out of Niagara Falls and shoot our way into Buffalo, New York.

We thought it was about 1940, and we'd just robbed this gambling joint up there East of Niagara Falls. There was one highway with the Hudson Bay on one side and Erie Canal on the other side, and all the gambling joints were all over up there and the town was wide open. To hell with the banks; those gambling houses had more money than any one of them. We didn't think these sons-a-bitch would call in and re-

From **THE KANSAS CITY STAR,** *October 27, 1977:*

Salad Days Over for Ex-Con

Willie Radkay, who discovered his artistic talents late in life, displays his painting, "Looking North on Main Street, Kansas City, 1911."
(Photo and story by Greg Edwards)

Prescott, Kan. — The lucrative days of big cigars and motor cars are over for Willie Radkay, a former hoodlum now in retirement.

During the 1930s, '40s and '50s, when he wasn't in jail, Radkay was cruising the Kansas City area in shiny new cars with the latest extras. He wore $300 silk suits and during World War II bought all the gasoline and coffee he wanted. They were rationed luxuries for everyone else.

But now Radkay, an alumnus of the FBI's 10 most wanted list and his wife, Louise, and their five dogs live in this small Kansas community on a monthly Social Security check. The modest bungalow where the couple has lived since 1972 is at the end of one of the town's two main streets. Radkay drives an economy pickup and has trouble remembering the last time he put on a suit.

But he isn't complaining. Radkay

is an accepted member of the community and even something of a local celebrity.

"You want to know how I'm living? I'm living good. This hunky is the only person in my life who gave me a home." Radkay said affectionately, shooting a smile toward the woman of Croatian ancestry he married after his parole in 1969. Both Radkay and his wife grew up in the slavic section of Kansas City, Kansas, known as Strawberry Hill.

"I pick up all kinds of strays — dogs, cats and birds like Willie," Mrs. Radkay teased.

Sitting in the kitchen of their home about 70 miles south of Kansas City, the Radkays tossed many a good-natured barb across their kitchen table and shared some laughs recently while reminiscing about Radkay's escapades in and out of prison....

port the robbery to the police because they were illegal, but they did, and that's how we got all the heat on us. We had to go through the toll gate at Niagara Falls, and we were on a road with the water on both sides and saw the black-and-white come flying by us. I could see in the rear view mirror that he hit his brakes because I could see his tail lights, but there was nothing else we could do but go straight ahead. We drove to Buffalo, New York to Delaware Park, and they were sitting there waiting for us. One black-and-white police car was on each side of the road with two parked in the middle. We were sitting there waiting for the light to change and noticed one of the black-and-whites turn its wheels inward to try to block us. I said, "Let's go," and we headed right for them at top speed. We broke through the roadblock, but now they were all on our ass coming after us. They turned their sirens on when they were coming after us, and that was in our favor because all the traffic was pulling over to the side, and it was wide open for me to drive straight down the highway. I banged a curb along the way and thought I had a flat, but I kept driving as fast as I could to get away. We finally got out of sight of the black-and-whites and decided we were going to abandon the car. I wanted to take off the plates and ditch them, so Alfie and I got out and took off our suit coats, then handed them to Bud. When we got done, I said, "All right, give me my coat." Bud said that he threw them over the fence, and we knew then we couldn't stick around and waste time to go get them. I said, "What the hell did you throw them away for?" Before he could answer, we could hear the sirens getting closer, and here I was out on bond at the time and knew we had to get the hell out of there.

That's how they got us connected with that robbery. We always wore the most expensive clothes we could buy, and when they found the abandoned car, they saw those jackets on the other side of this fence and looked inside and saw on the tags that they were a limited edition from Jack Henry's on the Country Club Plaza that could be traced back to us. Alfie and I took off running in the same direction and saw two girls that were just walking down the street. We walked up alongside of them and asked, "Do you ladies know how far it is to Gazer's place?" We calmly kept walking along with them, and one of the ladies said, "Gosh, there sure are a lot of police out here; I wonder who they are looking for," and we acted like we didn't know.

The cops just went driving back and forth and didn't pay any attention to two guys walking with two girls. When we came to a railroad overpass, I said to Alfie, "George, this is a short cut to where we work." We left the girls and walked down to the railroad tracks and walked and walked until we came to a terminal. We went in one at a time and called a cab and got back to the apartment we had down there, and Harry O'Dell was already there. We all met back at the apartment, but we knew we had to get out of town because it was too hot there, and they were all over trying to find us.

Harry said that he'd just go back home and make up an alibi and lay low. I told him to forget about it because we were all too hot now. What screwed that up were the jackets with numbers in them that they linked to Alfie and me. Harry called his girlfriend in Kansas City and told her he was coming, and the cops knew all about it because they had her phone lines tapped.

The FBI guy said in his report that he must have just gotten a lay from his girlfriend because when they stormed in the room she was lying there on the bed with her legs open. His girl was a waitress at the Hotel Muehlebach in Kansas City and a good-looking babe, but had this big ugly, burly brother who thought he was a bad-ass. The FBI stayed with Harry for quite a while at that apartment, thinking that I would be coming, but I never did. Then Sam got caught by calling a cab, as all of the cabs back then had police radios in them, and it was the cab driver who turned him in when he heard the dispatch on us.

In the late 1970s the Prescott State Bank was robbed, and the FBI came down to investigate. They stopped at my house and asked me if I knew about it, and I said no. They caught the guy almost immediately because he just drove down the main highway instead of taking all the back roads to make his getaway. The guy was even wearing house slippers when he was robbing the bank.

At that time, the FBI invited me to Kansas City, Kansas to their main headquarters located in the Commerce Bank building at Sixth and Minnesota Avenue. I went up there, and they showed me the cell where they held me in when I was captured back in 1943. This was after the Cincinnati jailbreak when I made my way back to Kansas

City, Missouri and was walking back to the hotel that they had surrounded. Red kept calling his girlfriend, and they had the lines tapped and traced it back to the hotel, and they swarmed in and only caught me. They held me in a bank vault, using it as a cell that you had to walk through vault doors to enter inside the room. They didn't want anyone to know that they had me in custody until they caught the other two guys, and that's why they kept me there. They told me that the FBI still talked about me after all these years as quite a challenge to them back in those early days. Even the old city hall and police station at Sixth and Ann Avenue in Kansas City, Kansas had my mug shot and wanted poster hanging up on the wall for years until they moved into the new police station up on Seventh Street. I topped the FBI's 10 most wanted list for serial bank robberies.

When we escaped from the Hamilton County Jail in Cincinnati and got back to Kansas City and were holed up in that hotel, we discussed getting out of town with the help of a truck driver we knew. He would put us in the back of his truck and put a "seal" on the back of the door. If they stopped and wanted to search the truck, they would see the seal was unbroken and assume that no one had illegally made an entry into the truck and let it go. This never materialized because of the FBI swarm and my capture.

Tom was working with a lawyer trying to prove he didn't have anything to do with the Herschel kidnapping, and I was going to be his witness. When I was going to go to court to testify, Kelly told me that Tom didn't have anything to do with it at all. All this was getting set up, but Tom died in 1976 before we could get to court and get his name cleared.

He's the bank robber who was asked, "Why did you rob banks?" He said, "Because they were there." Anyway, I went down to visit him, and a reporter named Lloyd Edge from *The Kansas City Star* did a story on us.

Now that I was working closer to home, I began remodeling our little house after work and on my days off. I bought those how-to books on electrical wiring, plumbing and carpentry, plus all the power tools. I lowered the high ceilings and completely renovated the entire place by myself, turning it into a seven-room house.

Every spring we'd put in a big garden, and Louise would can enough fruits and vegetables to last throughout the entire winter, plus pass along to friends and relatives. Louise had a green thumb, and I always said that she could grow strawberries on a barbed wire fence.

Louise had two children, a son and a daughter from an earlier marriage, and as a result when I married her I gained a family. Her son, Jim 'Butch' Bousman, was close to his mother and visited often, and we became good friends and have remained that way over the years. Her daughter, Rosemary, wasn't around as much, and their relationship was a once in a while occasion.

When Jim and his wife, Mary Ann, would bring the grandkids by, I felt something I never thought I'd ever pull off with the life I led, and that was to be a grandfather with grandkids. Although we didn't spend as much time with Debbie, Wayne and Kim, the two boys who were Grandma's favorites were, Jim Jr. and Robert, nicknamed Jimbo and Bob-a-lou. I ended up having nine grandkids and somewhere around 19 great grandkids.

Jimbo and Bob-a-lou spent an entire summer with us, and we treasured every moment of it. They were typical boys, but overall good kids who loved their grandmother. Louise would fix a pot of chili, and they'd tell her they didn't want to eat chili, so she'd dump it and tell them then you won't eat. They learned the hard way to eat whatever Grandma fixed. Later on when they'd tell Grandma they wanted pizza for supper, I knew I had to eat pizza whether I liked it or not. In Grandma's eyes, those boys could do no wrong and became her favorites. I'd come home from work and see all these holes dug up in the yard everywhere you looked. It was just Bob-a-lou digging worms for Grandma so she'd take them fishing, and I'd have to be the guy who patched up all those holes. I even put up a spot for them to hold all the turtles they found so they could feed and take care of them while they were there.

Those two boys were the apples of our eyes, and we were always so thankful for that short time they stayed with us.

I was 59 when I got out and I'd been locked up 35 years, more than half my life. When I got married, things got better and better and better, and I said that I wouldn't take any chances on losing what I have.

I had someone during an interview ask if prisons reform you. I told them none of those prisons reform you; you just grow old and out of steam and can't whip the police any more, so you don't take the chances. You finally grow up.

My wife was a great cook and had all my meals prepared when I got home from work. On holidays she would cook enough food for an army with different kinds of meat, along with several kinds of desserts. We used to drive around and take food to several of the old folks in town that we knew were alone.

On weekends we'd go out to eat breakfast or lunch at all the small towns around us. We'd start out by driving down all the back roads, enjoying the scenery and looking at the old farmhouses and barns that were now empty and deteriorating with age.

Louise always had dogs, so they all came along with us down to the country. Her favorite dog was named Teenybopper, and she would follow Louise around wherever she went. Louise could put a piece of food between her teeth, and Teenybopper would gently remove it and eat it. One night Louise was sitting at the kitchen table when Teenybopper came up and lay down by her feet, let out a cry and died right there. She was human; she wasn't a dog.

We had dogs of all sizes and even had 12 at one time. I brought a small black puppy home one night that I found on the riverbank in the city while working for the water department. We called him River, and he grew to be a huge dog that was so protective of Louise I had to watch how I threw my arms around her because he would even growl at me. No one ever came into our house who wasn't afraid of River.

I came home from work one night and was headed for bed, and Louise told me that I had to sleep on the couch because Teenybopper decided to have puppies in the middle of our bed. We didn't plan that to happen because Louise made a special bed for her to have her puppies in, but she decided she wanted to have them in our bed. I didn't care because she was a good dog and could have them anywhere she wanted to.

Over the next few years both of my partners, Alfie and Bud, got sick and died, and Louise and I attended their services. I was just thankful for the time we were together in our old age talking about all the things we'd done when we were young.

Louise's son, Jim, took the two of us, along with his wife, to visit San Francisco and tour Alcatraz back in 1988. I enjoyed going back to the old place for the memories, but best of all, I enjoyed being able to leave.

Then my life hit rock bottom when Louise, the love of my life, was diagnosed with cancer. Her son and I both agree that over the time that she suffered it wasn't the cancer that killed her; it was the overdose of chemotherapy they gave her.

Louise passed away in 1991, and I was left alone in our house with just our dogs. Family and friends would call and come by to console me, but it never fills the void left inside you once they are gone.

Louise was my hands and eyes and watched over me and took care of me. When I'd come home, I'd throw my shirt and coat on the backs of the chairs and throw my hat in the seat. The next morning I would retrieve my shirt, jacket and hat in the closet where they were supposed to be. Now when I put them on the backs of the chairs, they just stay there, and it makes me miss her so much for the little things that she did for me. If there was anything I was looking for in that house, all I'd have to do is ask and she knew right where it was every time. I always knew exactly where everything was in my little cell, but would not remember in this big house.

After she died, I decided one morning to go to the store, but couldn't find my billfold. I tore the house up looking for it, and after about four hours went in the front room, looked up at her picture hanging on the wall and said, "Louise, honey, please help me find my billfold," collapsing with exhaustion on the couch. When my butt hit the couch, my eyes went directly to the floor below the coffee table, and there was my billfold just lying there.

Louise was the one who always saved money, and even I was surprised to see how much was in our savings account after she passed away. I started taking all the money out of the bank and spending it. They always say you can't take it with you, and I always say, "You don't see a luggage rack on a hearse, do you?"

I ended up buying myself a brand new cherry red Thunderbird and spent most of my time driving around in that car listening to music.

After Louise died, I had a dog named Muffin, and she became a diabetic and I was giving her insulin. I'd have to watch her closely and would have to give her sugar when she'd go into a diabetic seizure. She eventually got worse and had to be put to sleep, and I cried like a baby. I went up to Animal Haven in Shawnee, Kansas, and was looking around for another dog. I remember someone saying that when you lose a dog you'll always find another one just like it. I walked around looking in all the pens, and I heard a dog cry from behind me, and when I turned around I saw this dog that looked just like Muffin, same size and same color. I got emotional over seeing her and told them that I wanted that dog. They told me that I couldn't have her for six days in case her owner came looking to claim her.

I would call up there every day to see if anyone claimed her yet. They told me, "Mr. Radkay, nobody is going to get that dog but you." I think they were getting tired of me bugging the shit out of them. I got up early in the morning to go get her, and when I put her in the car, she was so happy she looked out the window and wagged her tail all the way home. I would pet her and tell her, "Honey, you're going to have a good home now." She had a tag around her neck that said "Shawnee stray," so that's why I named her Shauna for Shawnee. She's old now and going blind with cataracts, but I'll never get rid of her. She is the matriarch around here, and you can tell because she doesn't take shit from any of the other dogs.

One morning after I got up, I went out to get the paper as I always did and got a nice surprise. When I opened up the door, there was a little puppy that looked like a fuzzy bear with raccoon eyes. I brought him in and kept him hidden from the neighbors, thinking it might belong to one of them. I would carry him inside my coat up to the post office every day and show everybody what I had. I named him Caesar, and he looked like a German Shepherd Chow mix. I figured anyone who'd let a little puppy run the streets didn't take care of him anyway and didn't deserve to have him.

That dog became a big part of my life and helped me through the loneliness of being without Louise. I got my dog Caesar five years after my wife Louise died on October 1st. When I got him, he was a little runt of a puppy, but he grew up to be a pretty good-size dog. When he was full-grown, I went down to the newspaper office in Fort Scott and wanted to put an ad in the paper saying, "Good-looking boy looking for a bitch in heat." They wouldn't let me say bitch in the

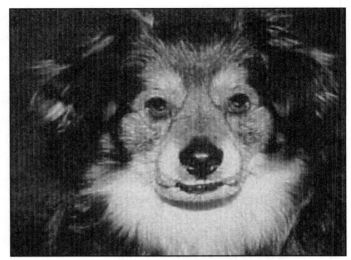

Willie's dog, Caesar (a.k.a. "Bubba").

paper, so I didn't get the ad in. Then a guy at the Prescott Post Office told me that he had a female dog in heat and he'd bring her down to meet Caesar. He brought his female down, and my Caesar got his first piece and was a man after that.

Then another little black and white puppy would start coming to my house all the time. So one day when she was on the porch I let her in the door, called her Appy, and she's stayed here ever since.

When I go to the bathroom, Caesar even follows me in there, and he lies down and waits for me to get through and then walks out with me. I sure love that guy, but I get mad at him for following me around all the time and yell at him to go lie down. Then I see him staring at me, and I know that he just loves me, so I can't get mad at him, and I call him back. He's so happy and gets so excited, and that makes me happy, plus I was so happy to get him after Louise died; he sure keeps me company.

I saw a stray cat on my porch one day and put some food out for it and ended up feeding seven or eight cats from the neighborhood. They had some kittens under my porch, and then I was feeding eight cats and seven kittens. I was going to get all the females spayed, but got lucky when I found out there was only one female in the litter.

I go out on the porch and call all the cats by their names, and they come from all directions knowing it's time to eat. When I walked up to the post office, most of the cats would follow me up there and back home again.

I do a lot of reading and spend a lot of time in the library when I'm down at Fort Scott buying dog and cat food. I do a lot of walking for exercise, and I won't even park my new cherry Red T-bird close to the door because I would rather walk. I even got me a bicycle to ride around town to keep in shape.

I'll always recall reading the stories in the papers in the late 1930s of how Admiral Byrd went to explore the Antarctic and ate a lot of chocolate to keep warm. That's always been my excuse every winter for eating lots of chocolate.

I was contacted to go out to Alcatraz to be in several documentaries that were being done about the place and gladly went. The documentaries that I was in are:
- *The Rock,* 1994, an A La Carte Production.
- *Return to Alcatraz,* 1994.
- *Super Max Prisons,* which was made for the Learning Channel.
- *Behind Bars-Alcatraz,* 2000, by the BBC.
- *Return to Alcatraz,* 2002, by my great-nephew,

Willie and cats coming from the post office.

Steve Davis Productions.

• *Alcatraz Reunion,* by John Paget, 2004. (He sent my niece and me, along with two girls from the nursing home, to Alcatraz for a piece in his documentary, but it hasn't been finished yet.)

The four documentaries that I was in have been shown on the History Channel, Discovery Channel, Learning Channel and A&E.

It was Chris Buchanan, the associate producer from the BBC (British Broadcasting Company), who contacted me to be in a documentary about Alcatraz. He flew me to San Francisco and set me up at the Hilton Hotel at Fisherman's Wharf, all expenses paid. I was able to view Alcatraz out in the bay from the window of my room. I even had a limousine to drive me anywhere I wanted to go, even if it was just across the street. On another trip out there to be in a documentary, I even stayed at the Top of The Mark and enjoyed every minute of it.

I would attend as many of the reunions as I could on Alcatraz just to experience again the memories I had of the place. The first time I went, it hit me the hardest when it came time to leave because it made

Back row (L to R): Chris Buchanan, CEO BBC-TV, producer; camera tech; interviewer. Front row (L to R) Phil Bergen, ex-Captain of the Guards; Willie Radkay, Ex-666AZ.

Willie standing by Cell 140 in 2000.

me realize all my friends from back in those days were all dead.

My favorite two nieces, Susan and Patty, and I went to spend time with my brother, Frank, and his family in Sacramento, California, during one of our visits to the Alcatraz reunion. We also stayed at my

Willie sitting in his old cell, 2002.

247

Willie sitting at his old seat in the dining room, 2002.

great-nephew Steve's house with his girlfriend Mary and spent time with his sisters Eileen and Lisa.

BBC came to my house again in March 2001 to do another documentary on prohibition years. When the producer had the camera set on me, he asked me, "How many bank robberies did you do?" I remember answering with a laugh, saying, "The only ones that I'll admit to are the ones I got caught at." I don't know if I ever made the cut in that film since I haven't heard from them about it.

Dave Ward from the University of Minnesota department of sociology called, and we met to discuss my criminal background. He was writing a book and said that I didn't need to write one since he would write all about me. Every time we met, he would turn on a tape re-

Willie sitting at his spot out on the yard, 2002.

BBC interviews Linn County resident

Local claims fame as last surviving inmate of the first group on Alcatraz

♦ Jeremy Bray
Linn County News reporter

What do Al Capone, Machine Gun Kelly, Pretty Boy Floyd and Prescott resident William "Willie" Radkay have in common? Time spent together on "The Rock," Alcatraz.

Radkay, now 89, is a source of history for his path to and eventual stay at the Alcatraz Federal Penitentiary. He has been sought for interviews about his internment at Alcatraz by the Learning Channel, the BBC and for the book, "Six Against the Rock". The most recent interview by the BBC pertained to his activities during the time of prohibition.

During the short-lived days of prohibition Radkay was making his money by hijacking bootleggers and sticking up gambling houses. "They had no right to operate, so we would rob them," said Radkay. After hijacking a load of whiskey in Kansas City, Radkay and his accomplices found no problem selling it to students in Lawrence, Kan.

But, when prohibition ended, so did his income.

Still leading a life of crime Radkay resorted to robbing banks and jewelry stores. The day after robbing a jewelry store, Radkay was walking down the street when police confronted him. Upon fleeing down an alley he was shot in the back five times. Radkay managed to get away in a stolen car from a nearby auto agency. Wounded, Radkay crossed over to Missouri where a bootlegger's dad who was a veterinarian would care for him. Eventually Radkay was apprehended for the jewelry store heist and incarcerated in Missouri for 10 years.

After serving his time for the jewelry store heist, he was apprehended for a bank robbery and placed in an Atlanta, Ga. prison. While in segregation he and other inmates took the guards hostage and gained control of the guard shack for five days.

"I thought they wanted to go over the wall, but all they wanted was some commissary and newspapers," said a disappointed Radkay. After this the government considered Radkay uncontrollable and sent him to the only place guaranteed to hold him, Alcatraz."

Upon entering Alcatraz in 1945, he was given the inmate number 666 and a cell next to a bootlegger he briefly met on good terms in Kansas City, Machine Gun Kelly. While spending

William Radkay shares his experiences of Alcatraz.

his seven years in Alcatraz, he met many famous criminals, "The cream of the crop," said Radkay. Radkay is considered a great source of history for Alcatraz because he is the last surviving inmate of the first group on Alcatraz.

Pretty Boy Floyd, Al Capone, The Birdman of Alcatraz, have all passed away.

Radkay remembers it like yesterday and told his late wife Louise, "I made the best friends of my life here (Alcatraz)."

---

corder to record our entire conversation. He may have written about me, but it didn't put anything in my pockets like it did in his.

Dave also has *The Kansas City Star* Extra Edition that says we were one of the toughest gangs in the United Sates and had our mug shots on the bottom. *The Kansas City Star* took credit for catching us with that extra, coming out the night before the story in the *Kansas City Times*.

I still would like to get those three pictures that Dave Ward has of us three guys out on the yard. I had on a baseball cap, and George had his hat off lying back on the steps getting a suntan, while Larry Basil Banghart was sitting below us in front. Larry and I used to tease George about getting a tan and looking good for the silent movie star, Fi-Fi Dor'se.

ounty

OSAWATOMIE
Graphic

Wednesday, April 25, 2001 / 1-B

ALCATRAZ

Linn County man served time with celebrity crooks

By MICK GALL
Osawatomie Graphic

MICK GALL/GRAPHIC

Willie Radkay

Willie Radkay remembers a nun at the orphanage where he was reared asking him why she had to read about him in the papers when she remembered him being such a good boy.

But read about him she did.

Life as a bank robber made Radkay a front-page news item. A headline from a 1943 Kansas City Star article read in bold-faced type, "William Radkay, Leader of Desperate Criminal Band, and Samuel Ricketts Captured Here without any Gunplay or Resistance."

Life as a bank robber also placed Radkay, now 89, on the FBI's 10 Most-Wanted list and in the most notorious prison in the United States — Alcatraz. While serving his sentence, he did time with incorrigibles whose personalities have become larger than life — Al Capone, George "Machine Gun" Kelly and the famed Birdman of Alcatraz.

"I was so full of larceny, you couldn't do anything with me," Radkay said.

Radkay's career started during prohibition in the 1920s.

"Whiskey was gold in my day," Radkay said. "They was gamblin' in those days, which made 'em easy targets."

Prohibition ended, and Radkay moved on to more lucrative targets: jewelry stores and banks. He got shot after one run-in with authorities, and still has pieces of shot in his back.

But of all those hits, it was robbing a Cincinnati bank which led him to Alcatraz.

From 1945 to 1952, Radkay was inmate No. 666, and was in a cell next to George "Machine Gun" Kelly, a friend and acquaintance. Radkay's bed was bolted to the same wall as Kelly's. Whenever an inmate snored too loudly, Radkay said, Kelly would reach over and hit him on the head with a magazine; never mind if it was some other inmate snoring.

Alcatraz was a different place than others Willie had been in, including Leavenworth.

"I'd rather be there than in any other joint. It was easy to do time there. You were treated like a man," Radkay said. "The guys out there were just a different breed."

But even Alcatraz could be dangerous for an inmate.

"The first guy that'll kill ya is the guy that's scared of ya. It's not the big tough guy," Radkay said. He said he decided early on to keep his mouth shut.

Even keeping his mouth shut, Radkay couldn't keep out of trouble that exploded on the island. In May, 1946, several inmates surprised a few guards, killing them and taking their guns. The prison immediately went into lockdown mode, preventing the inmates' escape. Radkay was in the prison's laundry room at the time, but he eventually made his way out to the prison yard. From there he watched units from several military branches come to the island to contain the riot. For days, Radkay and other inmates stayed in the yard while the standoff became more tense. They ate raw potatoes and bread thrown to them by guards. Desperate to stay warm, they broke down the baseball scoreboard and burned it. Eventually, the potential escapees were all killed, and the remaining inmates went back to their routine.

While in, Radkay passed his time painting and watching San Francisco. The Rock was becoming a tourist attraction. He met Cary Grant once, who took a private tour of the prison. But the boats that would pass by the island, announced for all to hear — including the inmates — that Alcatraz was home of "America's most-dangerous criminals, dregs of society, scum of the earth."

After Alcatraz, Radkay went back to his old ways. He and two friends knocked over a bank in Flint, Mich., making off with more than $60,000. That night, while hiding out and on the run, Willie slept with a bag stuffed full of cash as a pillow. He was caught in Chicago, and sent to prison again.

When asked how many banks he robbed in his career, he says, grinning, "You mean 'how many did I get caught for?' Two."

He was 59 when he got out of Leavenworth, after a total of 35 years in jail.

"I just took it easy when I got out," Radkay said. "I got to workin' and things just got better and better. And I says 'Don't take no chances now. You got more to lose than you do to gain.'"

He stayed straight, he said, by getting married, getting a job and just growing up. He served as a janitor and janitor superintendent at Prairie View.

As a former felon, Radkay has spent his retirement years doing documentaries. Cable network series on The History Channel, The Learning Channel, and even England's BBC, have tapped Radkay for his memories and experiences of life on The Rock.

For now, he enjoys the mild amount of local fame his checkered past brings him. He has solid credit at the local bank; a fact which still amazes him. He's in good health for an 89-year-old, despite being shot once and his penchant for cigars.

"My doctor, he just shakes his head at me," Radkay said chuckling.

His wife died several years ago, but he's since filled the house with three dogs and nearly a dozen cats . . . .

I visited Dave Ward and his wife out in Mill Valley, California, and saw all the folders he had gotten from Alcatraz that were records of all the inmates. Those folders were in a closet that reached from the floor to the ceiling, and those three pictures were in there. Norman Carlson, the prison director, was a friend of Dave Ward, and he's the guy who gave him all the records from Alcatraz.

Dave Ward sent me a letter in 2003 telling me about a May 1951 Alcatraz "Special Report" they had written about me:

"Radkay, well-oriented, intelligent, very criminally sophisticated ... seems to personify the axiom, 'a man who knows where he is going' ... his determination and self-planning have been successful ... he restricts his friends to a few of the more mature prisoners ... Kelly, #117, is a close associate. [He was transferred to Alcatraz] as a serious custodial risk and a menace to effective discipline at the Atlanta institution. More intelligent and literate than many of his fellow prisoners, he aided mutineers in the preparation of written complaints to newspapermen at the time of a rebellion in that penitentiary's special treatment unit ... his previous experience in fleeing from custody marked him as a potential leader among escape-conscious inmates."

After I got out, I found out they had transferred Clyde Johnson to the federal medical unit in Springfield, Missouri, because he had cancer. I wrote to visit him at Dave Ward's request. Dave was instrumental for the authorization for those visits. I used the letterhead of my position as custodial supervisor of five schools to impress them. I went to Springfield, and Johnson was so surprised and happy to see an old familiar friend. He pleaded with me to help him commit suicide in some way when I visited him. I was able to write regularly to Johnson's nurse to keep up on how he was at all times and let him know I was out there concerned about him. I would visit as long as he was rational, but after he got worse his nurse and I kept in constant communication by mail or phone right up until the time Clyde died. Dave Ward even called to tell me that the warden in Springfield, Missouri knew who I was because he had seen me on TV in the documentaries that I was in about Alcatraz.

Years after I was released, I went up to visit the furniture factory in Leavenworth penitentiary, and I asked my old boss, Bernie, if he had a good crew working in the office now, and he said, "I only had one good clerk the whole time I've been here, and that was you."

My sister was put in a nursing home out in Yorba Linda, California, and had to get rid of her two Dachshunds, so I had her send them here. Winky was 15 years old, and he died after three months, and I think he died of a broken heart from leaving my sister. The youngest one named Jay-R gets along fine with my other dogs, and I call him "Shortdick." He knows his name and runs to me when called. I tell them at night, "All right, kids, time for bed." Little Appy gets under the covers and goes down to the foot of the bed. The old lady, Shauna, gets up on my extra pillow, and Caesar lies besides me. Shortdick has to be helped up on the bed, and he lies on my other side. I love all my animals.

This picture was taken one week before I fell and broke my hip the first time.

Even though I am now an old broke dick in a nursing home, John Paget, a young filmmaker from Olympia, Washington came to Fort Scott to do an interview with me. He also sent me out in San Francisco for the 70th reunion of the opening of Alcatraz. While we were on the island, John wanted to do some filming of me in an area of Alcatraz

Willie and his beloved dogs.

Willie with Tresa and Julie on the way to Alcatraz, 2004.

that was closed off to the public because it led down to the dungeons. While we were waiting for a national park ranger to come with a key to open the iron gate, John asked me, "Hey, Willie, do you know how to pick a lock?" I said, "Yeah, with a sledgehammer."

I made that trip in a wheelchair with the help of Tresa and Julie from the nursing home, along with my niece. We stayed in Sacramento with my great-nephew, Steve, his girlfriend, Mary and his son, Darrell. I also spent time with my great-nieces, Lisa, Eileen and their families. My brother, Frank, went with me to the Alcatraz reunion, and I enjoyed having him visit the place they kept me for seven years.

Four national park rangers had to carry me in the wheelchair up the steep flight of steps to the old hospital several times that day for the snack and lunch they provided.

One young man knelt down beside my wheelchair and shook my hand, asking if he could take a picture with me while handing me a 250-dollar Dinar with Saddam Hussein's picture on it. He said that he just came back from Iraq a week ago and would trade the money for an autograph.

Willie and National Park Ranger John Cantwell, 2004.

Park Ranger John Cantwell was kneeling down beside my wheelchair talking to me on Broadway, the main floor of the cell house, with a crowd of at least 40 people standing by listening. When he finished talking, he stood up and said to the crowd, while placing his hand on my shoulder, **"This is the most famous 'Rock Star' you'll ever meet."**

From the **SAN FRANCISCO CHRONICLE,** *August 12, 2002:*

REUNION ON THE ROCK: Time has blurred lines that once separated the bulls from the cons. Ex-bank robber Willie Radkay, 91, of Prescott, Kansas, snaps a photo of the main administration building of the prison where he was jailed from 1945 to 1952. "I want to know where I was. I want to follow my own footsteps."
— (Photo by Michael Maloney.)

From **THE EXAMINER,** *San Francisco Hometown Newspaper,*
July 12, 2002:

GOOD OL' ALCATRAZ
67th anniversary as federal prison
By Nina Wu of The Examiner Staff

Prisoner No. 666, a professional bank robber from Kansas who had been caught a second time after escaping from a low-security prison, faced seven years of isolation as he lumbered in chains up the hill at Alcatraz.

He knew what his transfer to Alcatraz meant: no escape. The dazzling city he saw only a mile across the Bay seemed forever out of his reach.

Fifty-six years later, that man, Willie Radkay, walked back onto the island not just as a free man, but as a veritable celebrity. Radkay joined other ex-convicts and former prison guards Sunday to retrace memories for the island's 67th anniversary as a federal prison.

The ex-convicts were trailed by a flock of tourists who asked for autographs and wanted to hear a firsthand account of life in the once escape-proof prison that is now one of The City's most popular tourist spots.

"You'd get along here," said Radkay, who donned a fedora and plaid suit to tour the place where he once called cell B240 his home. "We were on a first-name basis with the guards."

Former Capt. Phil Bergen, now 96, says he loved his job and tolerated most of his charges.

"They were the outsiders and the rebels," he said. "Our job was to calm them down and straighten them out."

Not all of them could be straightened out, he said, but it was worth trying. The job had its dangers. Bergen took his share of punches and kicks, and risked being stabbed with a sharp piece of porcelain.

"I was in a position where I could help people," he said. "I could order people

Halls of memory — Former Alcatraz inmate Willie Radkay walks the halls of the prison Sunday morning, remembering the time he spent on "The Rock" during the 67th anniversary of the U.S. penitentiary, which was open from 1934-1963.

around when I thought they should be doing something. It was very gratifying."

His rules: never start a fight. At the reunion, he shook hands with former inmates. After all, the former prisoners and guards now share the same nostalgia for the past.

Bergen remembered Radkay and said he was "no angel," but was smart enough to behave himself in Alcatraz.

"He was an asset to the prison," Bergen said.

Radkay said he wouldn't recommend the experience to anyone.

From the **SAN FRANCISCO EXAMINER**, *August 13, 2001:*

BACK ON THE ROCK: Former Alcatraz inmate Willie Radkay stands in the jailhouse and tells stories about his time spent on Alcatraz Island in the cell next to his friend George "Machine Gun" Kelly. Radkay was one of the former convicts making an appearance during the 67th anniversary of the opening of the penitentiary.

— Photo by Dave Kennedy / Examiner

From the **SAN FRANCISCO CHRONICLE,** *August 15, 2004:*

70th Reunion of the Opening
of Alcatraz— 2004.
Willie Radkay, prisoner No. 666, with his
old cell #240 visible just above his hat,
was a convicted bank robber.
— Photo by Mark Costantini

CONCLUSION

EVEN THOUGH MY uncle now resides in a nursing home in Fort Scott, Kansas, he will never walk again, and the hopes of returning home with his dogs is not likely, but that's all he thinks about. He is 93 years old and gets confused easily and recently asked me: "Patty, am I doing time down here? What's it going to take to get my lawyer to get me back in my own home with my dogs where I belong?"

I have been caring for his dogs, and my wish is to have him back in his own home with them soon.

I told him that I finished the book I wrote about him and was going to have it published. He said, "You can't publish that book." I asked: "Why not?" and he said, "I told you some things that the cops never knew, and I'm worried that I might end up getting 'pinched.' "

I asked my Uncle Willie a few questions while he sat in his wheelchair at the nursing home:

1. **How do you feel about living in a nursing home?**
   This place is more convenient than a hospital, with lots of service. I like all the people around me, and they take good care of me and do things for me without me even having to ask. It's a good place to be until I can go home and be with my dogs.

2. **Do you wish you had lived a different life?**
   Not really, I just became accustomed to all the changes in the life I led.

3. **How did all those years in prison affect you?**
   They dulled me up a hell of a lot and made me answer to a bell.

4. What's the most important thing you regret about your life?
Being accused of a murder I didn't do, but having it on my record for years, giving the authorities a reason to keep me in prison longer.

5. What was the happiest part?
The happiest part was walking out of the penitentiary.

6. Would you like to say anything to the people who have read this book?
These footsteps are not for anyone to follow.

Unk and me at the annual Alcatraz reunion, San Francisco 2004.
Attendees include former inmates, prison guards, and their families.
The former prison island is now part of the National Park Service.

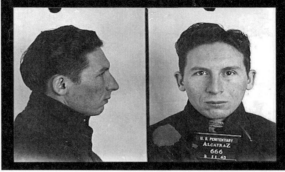